From Village Commons to Public Goods

DISLOCATIONS

General Editors: August Carbonella, *Memorial University of Newfoundland*; Don Kalb, *University of Utrecht & Central European University*; Linda Green, *University of Arizona*

The immense dislocations and suffering caused by neoliberal globalization, the retreat of the welfare state in the last decades of the twentieth century, and the heightened military imperialism at the turn of the twenty-first century have raised urgent questions about the temporal and spatial dimensions of power. Through stimulating critical perspectives and new and cross-disciplinary frameworks that reflect recent innovations in the social and human sciences, this series provides a forum for politically engaged and theoretically imaginative responses to these important issues of late modernity.

Recent volumes:

Volume 34
From Village Commons to Public Goods: Graduated Provision in Urbanizing China
Anne-Christine Trémon

Volume 33
Corporate Social Responsibility and the Paradoxes of State Capitalism: Ethnographies of Norwegian Energy and Extraction Businesses Abroad
Edited by Ståle Knudsen

Volume 32
Glimpses of Hope: The Rise of Industrial Labor at the Urban Margins of Nepal
Michael Hoffmann

Volume 31
Bulldozer Capitalism: Accumulation, Ruination, and Dispossession in Northeastern Turkey
Erdem Evren

Volume 30
Facing the Crisis: Ethnographies of Work in Italian Industrial Capitalism
Edited by Fulvia D'Aloisio and Simone Ghezzi

Volume 29
Big Capital in an Unequal World: The Micropolitics of Wealth in Pakistan
Rosita Armytage

Volume 28
Fifty Years of Peasant Wars in Latin America
Edited by Leigh Binford, Lesley Gill, and Steve Striffler

Volume 27
Brazilian Steel Town: Machines, Land, Money and Commoning in the Making of the Working Class
Massimiliano Mollona

Volume 26
Claiming Homes: Confronting Domicide in Rural China
Charlotte Bruckermann

Volume 25
Democracy Struggles: NGOs and the Politics of Aid in Serbia
Theodora Vetta

For a full volume listing, please see the series page on our website:
https://www.berghahnbooks.com/series/dislocations

From Village Commons to Public Goods

Graduated Provision in Urbanizing China

Anne-Christine Trémon

Published in 2023 by
Berghahn Books
www.berghahnbooks.com

© 2023, 2026 Anne-Christine Trémon
First paperback edition published in 2026

All rights reserved. Except for the quotation of short passages
for the purposes of criticism and review, no part of this book
may be reproduced in any form or by any means, electronic or
mechanical, including photocopying, recording, or any information
storage and retrieval system now known or to be invented,
without written permission of the publisher.

Library of Congress Cataloging-in-Publication Data

Names: Trémon, Anne-Christine.
Title: From Village Commons to Public Goods: Graduated Provision in
 Urbanizing China / Anne-Christine Trémon.
Description: New York: Berghahn, 2023. | Series: Dislocations; Volume 34 |
 Includes bibliographical references and index.
Identifiers: LCCN 2023004662 (print) | LCCN 2023004663 (ebook) |
 ISBN 9781800739000 (hardback) | ISBN 9781800739987 (open access ebook)
Subjects: LCSH: Urbanization—China. | Villages—China. | Human services—
 China. | Public goods. | China—Social conditions—2000–
Classification: LCC HT384.C6 T746 2023 (print) | LCC HT384.C6 (ebook) |
 DDC 307.760951—dc23/eng/20230330
LC record available at https://lccn.loc.gov/2023004662
LC ebook record available at https://lccn.loc.gov/2023004663

British Library Cataloguing in Publication Data
A catalogue record for this book is available from the British Library

EU GPSR Authorized Representative
LOGOS EUROPE, 9 rue Nicolas Poussin, 17000, LA ROCHELLE, France
Email: Contact@logoseurope.eu

ISBN 978-1-80073-900-0 hardback
ISBN 978-1-83695-118-6 paperback
ISBN 978-1-80073-901-7 epub
ISBN 978-1-80073-998-7 web pdf

https://doi.org/10.3167/9781800739000

The electronic open access publication of *From Village Commons to Public Goods: Graduated Provision in Urbanizing China* has been made possible through the generous financial support of the Swiss National Science Foundation.

This work is published subject to a Creative
Commons Attribution Noncommercial No
Derivatives 4.0 License. The terms of the license
can be found at http://creativecommons.org/
licenses/by-nc-nd/4.0/. For uses beyond those
covered in the license contact Berghahn Books.

CONTENTS

List of Illustrations vi
Acknowledgments vii
Note on Anonymization viii
Glossary ix

Introduction Graduated Provisioning in China's
             Urbanized Villages   1

Chapter 1   Three Villages-in-the-City   31

Chapter 2   From Village Commons to Urban Public Goods   72

Chapter 3   Creating Visual and Public Order   106

Chapter 4   Building Moral Communities   139

Chapter 5   Segregated Public Space and the Right to the
             City   173

Conclusion   Exclusion and Rivalry, Lasting Inequalities, and
             Neoliberal Provision   208

References   223
Index   247

Illustrations

Figures

2.1	Mausoleum in Pine Mansion, Shenzhen. © Anne-Christine Trémon.	79
2.2	Minibuses in River Hamlet, Xi'an. © Wang Bo.	86
3.1	The new residential towers, Pine Mansion, Shenzhen. © Anne-Christine Trémon.	117
3.2	Street cleaners, Pine Mansion, Shenzhen. © Anne-Christine Trémon.	119
4.1	Beneficence Day in Pine Mansion, Shenzhen. © Anne-Christine Trémon.	145
4.2	North Gate's community center and canteen, Chengdu. © Jessica Wilczak.	158
5.1	Public square in Pine Mansion urban village, Shenzhen. © Anne-Christine Trémon.	179
5.2	Children playing basketball in Pine Mansion. © Anne-Christine Trémon.	188

Maps

1.1	People's Republic of China. © Bureau Relief.	34
1.2	Shenzhen districts. © Bureau Relief.	37
1.3	Chengdu's districts and counties. © Bureau Relief.	41
1.4	Xi'an's districts and counties. © Bureau Relief.	43
1.5	Pine Mansion, Shenzhen. © Bureau Relief.	47
1.6	South Gate, Chengdu. © Bureau Relief.	51
1.7	River Hamlet, Xi'an. © Bureau Relief.	54

Tables

1.1	Village and *shequ* economic and administrative organization, 1950s–today.	45
1.2	Summary of the main characteristics of the three case-study villages-in-the-city.	68

Acknowledgments

The empirical research on which this book is based was funded by the Swiss National Research Foundation from October 2017 to December 2020. My heartfelt gratitude goes to the Public Goods in Urbanizing China project team members, postdoctoral researchers Wang Bo and Jessica Wilczak, for spending three years collaborating on this research with me in a respectful and friendly atmosphere, and for the intellectual stimulus their participation gave me. I also thank all the research participants and students who helped us with the surveys and interview transcriptions. The manuscript had the good fortune of benefiting from Sally Sutton's sharp editing and tireless spotting of any lack of clarity. I also thank Don Kalb, the coeditor of Berghahn's Dislocations series, for his support and enthusiasm for this project, the three anonymous readers for their constructive comments on the manuscript, and Winnie Lem for her valuable comments.

Wang Bo and Jessica Wilczak gave several presentations at the bimonthly research seminar I led in Lausanne from September 2019 to October 2020, as well as at the EASA Conference panel on urban public goods that I co-organized with Rive Jaffe of the University of Amsterdam in the summer of 2020. These all took place online during the Covid pandemic. Although I had initially planned to coauthor this book with Wang Bo and Jessica, in the current unwelcoming academic context both withdrew from the project to pursue nonacademic careers shortly after their contracts ended. Almost all of the empirical material on Chengdu and Xi'an cited in this book, with the exception of some additional online research that I did on policy documents and scholarly publications, is theirs, and is referenced accordingly. As it was I who devised the book's structure and selected the material cited, I am responsible for any shortcomings.

Note on Anonymization

Pine Mansion, South Gate, and River Hamlet are pseudonyms for the urban villages described and compared in this book. They are not necessarily close to the actual Chinese names. Each researcher chose the name for the village she worked in; in the case of Pine Mansion, I reused the name I had already given the village in previous publications.

Because of the material's complexity and diversity, I chose to anonymize the people mentioned in this book by referring to them only by a family name—that is, not to invent an alternative first name (in Chinese, a personal name). None are composite characters; all are real people with whom we had casual conversations, formal interviews, or both. All of the family names I used for anonymization are widespread in China. In some rare cases I kept the real name, but in most instances I used a range of common names in ways that would avoid confusion between persons bearing the same name but belonging to different cases (living in different villages). The only exception is the Pine Mansion Chens, with whom I have worked in Shenzhen. I anonymized their former village's name, but not the Chen surname, for reasons linked to my previous research on this former emigrant village—so that people in the diaspora reading my book would recognize their kin—and because almost all native inhabitants of this village bear the same name as it was a single-lineage village prior to urbanization. Naming people "Mr. Chen" or "Mrs. Wang" sounds even more formal in Chinese than in English, and therefore in many instances, after introducing them in this polite way on the first occurrence, I drop the title and refer to them simply as "Chen" or "Wang."

Glossary

Chengguan (in full *Chengshi guanli zonghe xingzheng zhifa ju*)	City Urban Management and Law Enforcement Bureau	城管 (城市管理综合行政执法局)
cunweihui	village committee	村委会
jiedao	subdistrict (street level)	街道
juweihui (in full *shequ jumin weiyuanhui*)	resident's committee	居委会 (社区居民委员会)
qu	district	区
shengchan dadui	production brigade	生产大队
shengchandui	production team	生产队
shequ	urban community	社区
xingzheng cun	administrative village	行政村
ziran cun	natural village	自然村
shequ zhongxing (in full *shequ dangqun fuwu zhongxin*)	community center (party service center for the masses)	社区中心 (社区党群服务中心)
wangge (in full *wangge guanli zhongxin*)	grid governance center	网格 (网格管理中心)

Introduction

Graduated Provisioning in China's Urbanized Villages

In 2014, China's central government unveiled its National Urbanization Plan, presenting it as "people-centered." The plan is part of Xi Jinping's "new era," which began in 2013 and hails the ideal of a "peaceful and prosperous society" hinging on a more equal distribution of wealth. Socioeconomic inequalities became acute in China's first three decades of reform (1978–2006), which, though not as exacting as Eastern European shock therapy, saw the end of the delivery of free social goods such as housing as well as general state retrenchment on the distribution of welfare and social services (Selden and You 1997; Wong 2006; Zhang and Ong 2008; Duckett 2011; Ong and Zhang 2015).

Proclamations about the need for a more egalitarian development path can be traced back to Hu Jintao's presidency (2003–12). In 2004, the Chinese state pledged to create a "harmonious society" by rebalancing the economy, improving public services, reducing regional inequalities, and promoting fairness. Two years later, "urban-rural integration," intended to bring urban and rural development into the same framework, became a national directive after decades of a sustained drive aimed at urban and industrial development.[1] Although it continues these efforts, for the first time in Chinese history the National Urbanization Plan acknowledged the importance of urbanization and the need to remedy the inequalities generated by the urbanization process itself.[2] The plan, promoting a "new type of urbanization," was a response to the challenges of mass environmental damage, social unrest, as well as the generation and reproduction of inequalities created by the speed of China's urbanization.

The main drivers of China's widening inequalities and their reproduction over time have been uneven development favoring large coastal cities and the differences in access to education and welfare for urban citizens and migrants from the countryside resulting from the institutional, social, and economic separation of urban and rural areas (Kwong 2004; Liang and Chen 2007; Goodburn 2009, 2015; Liu et al. 2009; Solinger 2018). China's urban population grew from 172 million in 1978 to 691 million in 2011, when it exceeded the number of rural residents, and reached 902 million in 2021. In 1980, at the outset of the country's market-oriented economic reforms, the urban population comprised 19.36 percent of the total population. This grew to 63.88 percent in 2020; however, the share of the *registered urban population* in the total population is far less: in 2020 only 45.4 percent of the total population were registered as residents of the city in which they lived (National Bureau of Statistics 2021).[3] The remaining 18.48 percent consists of the so-called floating population: people living for more than six months in an urban place other than where they are registered, i.e., to which their *hukou* is attached.[4]

Hukou is a form of local citizenship, which entitles people to certain rights, notably rights to welfare and education, based on people's place of origin, not work or residence. The *hukou* registration system has enabled several decades of export-oriented economic growth based on both a low-waged labor force and low-cost socialized reproduction, in what has variously been termed China's "temporary urbanization" (Sklair 1991) or "semi-urbanization" (Chan 2021).[5] Until very recently, the temporary residence status of migrant workers has excluded them from the social services and welfare entitlements provided in the urban localities—mainly urban villages—where they live, and city infrastructure planning and resource allocation have paid little attention to migrants' needs, taking into account only the population with *de jure* urban registered residency, i.e., the *hukou*-holding population.

China's recent reforms aim to eliminate the unequal entitlement to social protection that rigidly divided urban and rural residents according to the conventional household registration system. One of the goals of the National Urbanization Plan, which unfolded from 2014 to 2020, was to grant urban *hukou* to approximately 100 million people. Even more noticeable was the policy paper issued by the State Council announcing the abolition of the classification of *hukou* as rural or urban as they had been since 1958: Chinese citizens will universally register simply as "residents" (*jumin*).[6]

This book's primary focus is on the intertwined processes of creating urban neighborhoods (the transformation of rural villages hosting large sections of migrant workers into urban communities) and of making public goods (among others pensions and health insurance, public parks, education, and senior care) equally accessible to all living in these recently urbanized communities.[7] Public goods are a major political issue in countries whose constitutions profess an ideology of equality that is belied by high-speed capitalist urbanization. Despite political proclamations and increased state redistribution, equality is not the only principle taken into consideration by the Chinese authorities: it is kept in check by their commitment to "trickle-down" ideology, creating a "moderately well-off society" (*xiaokang shehui*), and by the capitalist logics of uneven development. The burden of solving the dilemmas resulting from these contradictory commitments falls on the governments of fast-growing cities facing scalar reorganization, which has created fiscal pressure, and intercity competition to attract capital and talent.

Examining the making of new urban neighborhoods in China through the lens of public goods provisioning offers a way of analyzing the shaping of Chinese cities according to a variety of processes, of which neoliberalization is one key aspect, as both a sociospatial function of "socialism with Chinese characteristics" (Lim 2014b: 223) on the national scale and a tool of local governance in conditions of budgetary scarcity. The reforms adopted under the National Urbanization Plan aim at facilitating migrants' access to urban public goods, but do so in highly graduated ways, and discrimination remains high. The book explores the way in which municipal governments have sought to extend rights such as education benefits, employment assistance, housing, eldercare, social welfare, and social assistance to newcomers. Local governments bear the brunt of the financial responsibility of meeting the central government's directives for equalization and better service provision without burdening their budgets.

In so doing, they are comforted by the central government's call to "gradually achieving equality" (State Council 2014). "Gradual" is an omnipresent qualifier when it comes to equalizing access to public goods, which local governments interpret both literally, to legitimize their slow progress toward equalization based on their budgetary resources, and more figuratively by interpreting "gradual" as "in graduated measures": policies that differentiate and select those most worthy of access to public goods.

The processes by which they increase their intervention in the provision of urban public goods are multifaceted and uneven. This book takes a pragmatic and historicized approach to public goods. A historicized approach retraces changing provisioning paths and shows that although provision is no longer based on the classification of Chinese citizens as either rural or urban, enduring legacies of this old dichotomy are still apparent in the inequalities and tensions that surface in China's urban villages. A pragmatic approach avoids some of the dead ends of the debate about whether neoliberalism is predominant in China, which is mainly about ideology and discourse instead of practice; this book looks at actual practices of provisioning in Chinese urbanized villages. The concept of graduated provision highlights the contradictions between the authorities' economic and social policies.

I first introduce China's villages-in-the-city (*chengzhongcun*), or urban villages, which are ideal sites for observing the immense challenges facing the Chinese authorities in terms of managing rapid urban growth, reducing inequalities, and ensuring social stability, and which have come to stand for many of these problems. The urbanization of these formerly rural villages raises particular challenges in terms of the provision of public goods, and the social division between natives and migrants poses issues of inequality in access to public goods. Next, I present the ways economists have initially defined public goods according to inherent characteristics distinguishing them from other types of goods—private goods, club goods, and common-pool resources. This has been shown to be highly problematic; I therefore advocate a political economy approach that defines public goods as the result of political decisions to provide them. A focus on public goods allows consideration of both the state's importance as a provider and its shortcomings in providing public goods. The recent literature's preoccupation with commons tends to neglect these issues or even to construe public goods as antithetical to commons (see discussion in later sections). However, they are not: both are social goods.

Instead of romanticizing the commons by opposing them to public goods, as in much of the current literature, we should be looking at practices that change the status of goods. The third section shows how Elinor Ostrom takes a different approach that has resulted in her well-known work on commons, which result from *practices* of management and distribution at the local community level. This leads me to distinguish between the logics of clubbing and of commoning practices. Although they differ in that one is based on market logics and the other is not, both delineate the contours of a community of users, and both are deployed as neoliberal practice, in spite of Chinese leaders' ideological proclamations about neoliberalism's absence in China.

The Chinese state continues to use a developmental narrative of progress and civilization as marked by urbanization, and it embraces modernist ideals of universal service access. I argue that this teleological vision of urbanization, in combination with the goal of "gradually equalizing access," accounts for the set of practices encapsulated in this book by the concept of "graduated provision." This book's comparative approach and ethnographic focus on the actual provisioning of and access to public goods in urban villages reveals how provision is graduated both temporally and spatially. In temporal terms, graduated provision reflects the evolutionary view of urbanization that prevails in China. Spatially, the concept and its practices provide different public goods to different communities based on their social composition, and to different categories of population within the same communities.

China's Urban Villages

Chinese urban villages are particularly interesting sites for observing how the authorities endeavor to reduce the extreme socioeconomic inequality that has emerged since the adoption of state capitalism. The book compares three urban villages, located in the cities of Shenzhen, Chengdu, and Xi'an. These three sites, anonymized as Pine Mansion, South Gate, and River Hamlet respectively, have experienced similar demographic explosions, with tenfold increases in population within the same time frame. This growth has brought dramatic changes to their landscapes, the livelihoods of their native inhabitants, and the power structures governing residents. All three were rural until the 1990s, when peasant incomes no longer primarily derived from the cultivation of land, and Pine Mansion, South Gate, and River Hamlet were legally urbanized—became administratively urban—in 2004.

The literature published on urban villages is so extensive that it is impossible to cite all of the works. Most available studies focus on only one village or create a composite portrait of a typical village based on a few cases studied in-depth (Li 2004, 2020). Monographs often retrace a village's evolution over time, drawing on classic sociological functionalism (Zhe 1997; Zhe and Chen 1997; Zhou and Gao

2001). This is especially the case when they deal with the "problem" of urban villages through the lens of Wirth's (1938) notion of urbanism.[8] The most influential research in this regard is that of Li Peilin (2002, 2004), who describes the psychocultural resilience of rural identity and the endurance of rural traditions among native urban villagers and migrant workers (see also Lan 2001, 2005; Wang and Zhang 2008; Wang 2015). Others are concerned with the sociospatial functions and planning problems of urban villages (Tang and Chung 2002; Song, Zenou, and Ding 2008; Tian 2008; Wang, Wang, and Wu 2009; Liu et al. 2010; Chung 2010, 2013). Most recently, a political economy approach has been adopted to focus on urban village redevelopment, making policy recommendations for progressive steps that protect the interests of local inhabitants, both native and migrant (Li and Liu 2018; Zhan 2018, 2021; Li 2020; Zhang 2021).

None of these studies focus on issues of public goods provision, although these are intrinsically related to the formation of urban villages in China, and their social characteristics in turn make public goods a central issue. Urban villages, or "villages-in-the-city," which can be found in all Chinese cities, differ from the definition that Western urban planners have lent the term when designing new types of "village-like" neighborhood, notably in the UK (Chung 2010: 423). Moreover, they differ from squatter settlements and even from "migrant enclaves," although they usually host large sections of the migrant population.[9] While they can be very loosely defined as distinct spaces within the city, there is broad agreement among both Chinese and Western scholars that the term refers to a more precise phenomenon: it designates formerly rural villages, built by their native peasant inhabitants in the absence of planning, that have been engulfed by urbanization (Li 2002, 2004, 2020; Chung 2010; Wang 2017).

They are the product of China's rapid urbanization, the political origin of which lies in the reshuffling of state power (Lin et al. 2015: 1964). The recentralization of fiscal resources in 1997 reduced local governments' share of China's growing fiscal revenue while increasing that of the central government,[10] the fiscal pressure heightened by the decentralization of responsibilities along with increasing pressure on local governments to provide public goods such as compulsory education as part of the "harmonious society" project (Oi and Zhao 2007; Wong 2010; Jia, Guo, and Zhang 2014). This rearrangement of central-local power relations concerning responsibilities and tax collection since the mid-1990s is a state-led instance of the rescaling processes that have given increased importance to the subnational scale, with local strategies for attracting investment and rationalizing the management of welfare in many countries (Brenner 2004; Kennedy 2017).

As a result, municipal governments face substantial budget deficits that drive them to seek extrabudgetary resources, mainly by promoting land conversion on the city's rural fringes. Only after collective agricultural land has been converted to state-owned urban land can its use rights be traded on the market, generating conveyancing fees and land-leasing income to strengthen municipal budgets (Wu Weiping 1999, 2010; Lin 2007; Wu, Xu, and Yeh 2008; Lin and Yi 2011; Lin et al. 2015; He, Zhou, and Huang 2016). Chinese municipal governments' massive conversion of land from rural to urban use, often within the extensive boundaries of urban jurisdictions, has played a crucial part in the urbanization of capital and the expansion of the built-up urban area.[11]

The dramatic increase in China's urban population is the result of changes to the classification of the urban population and urban settlements and to the administrative boundaries of many cities (Zhou and Ma 2003; Chan 2014) following the recategorization of tens of thousands of previously rural villages.[12] In the sixteen years from 1985 to 2001, the number of Chinese villages dropped from 940,617 to 709,257. In 2001 alone, an average of seventy villages vanished from China's map every day (Li Peilin 2020: 23). These villages have undergone a process of legal urbanization involving their administrative conversion to urban communities under which their residents, formerly categorized as rural, become urban citizens. While the 1980s and 1990s were marked by a process of rural urbanization (Guldin 1992, 1997), by the early 2000s rural villages on the outskirts of expanding cities had been partially or entirely overrun by rapid urban sprawl, spurring this administrative change.

When a village is urbanized, the power of the original village leaders is eroded, and urban public goods replace the village commons. Indeed, while rural villages are autonomous organizations and village collectives legally own their rural land, urban communities are under direct state control, and the urban land they occupy is owned by the state. This principle was instituted under Mao and reasserted in the revised Constitution of 1982 (Zhao 2009: 97).[13] As a consequence of this rural-urban dichotomy, a dual regime of public goods prevailed. The local state was responsible for the provisioning of urban areas, the basic provider under the urban public goods regime being the *danwei*, the local work unit. Rural collectives were largely responsible for their own welfare, infrastructure, public security, and sanitation (Han and Huang 2019). In the 1980s, the state severely cut its already very small amount of direct aid for rural collectives (Howard 1986; Wong 1988), and many village communities had to largely finance their own infrastructure and other public services even as they started to urbanize their infrastructure and their populations expanded (Jiang 2005; Po 2012; Cheng 2014).

With administrative urbanization, villages (*cun*) become urban communities (*shequ*) under the jurisdiction of the municipality—that is, the local state—and, at least in theory, their land is transferred to the state along with responsibility for the provision of public goods. The ultimate goal of China's policies is to entirely rid these former villages of their rural characteristics, based on an ideology that values the urban as the hallmark of modernity (Xie 2005; O'Donnell, Wong, and Bach 2017). Urban villages are still called *chenzhongcun*, villages-in-the-city, despite having been officially urbanized. The reason for this labeling, which carries a negative connotation, is that such neighborhoods are physically marked by their former rural status. Urbanized villages are conglomerations of highly diverse types of buildings and housing complexes constructed at different moments in time, many built informally by villagers in the absence of state planning, generally prior to the administrative urbanization. Moreover, their social characteristics starkly distinguish urbanized villages from other urban neighborhoods. They retain close-knit native villager communities that coexist with large sections of the floating population that the authorities view as a potential source of social instability (Xiang 2005; Zhang 2006), playing a functional role in providing inexpensive housing for the growing urban population (Tang and Chung 2002; Song, Zenou, and Ding 2008; Liu et al. 2010; Zhang 2011; Wu, Zhang, and Webster 2013; Wang, Du, and Li 2014; Cheng 2014; Zhan 2018).

Indeed, urban villages are the main recipients of the massive inflow of migrants from China's towns and countryside. Statistics show that while migrant workers account for 20 to 50 percent of the population in some of China's major cities, they often account for 80 percent or more of the total population of villages-in-the-city (Zhao et al. 2003; Li 2006; Chung 2010). They outnumber the native villagers by up to ten to one but are denied permanent residency rights and many of the associated social benefits that the native villagers, now urbanites, enjoy.

This book compares three villages-in-the-city, which were legally urbanized in 2004, through the lens of public goods. The change in the status of social goods from village commons to public goods in urbanizing villages illuminates the complex processes of China's uneven urbanization. In principle, administrative urbanization should result in the local state (municipal government) taking over village land and assuming responsibility for the provision of urban public goods; however, because land requisition involves the payment of compensation and entails additional infrastructure and service costs for the government (Po 2012), and because urbanized villages have large immigrant populations, this transition can lag behind the official declaration of a village as an urban community and is a highly conditional and fragmented process. The urbanization of rural villages thus generates tensions in the provision of social goods.

Public Goods and Club Goods

Public goods are one type of social good. Social goods are those essential to social reproduction, such as housing, roads, and electricity, including services such as education, healthcare, and welfare. Public goods are goods whose provision is regulated by a public entity, usually the state, although their actual delivery can be delegated to village-level public collectives and private actors. In Chinese economics, public goods are called *gonggong wupin,* but people more frequently refer to *gonggong sheshi* (public facilities or services) and *fuli* (welfare benefits). Reflecting these grassroots understandings, this book adopts a broader and more flexible approach to public goods than that used by economists.

Economists usually distinguish between four types of goods: public, private, club, and common-pool-resources. Public goods were invented in the period running from the late 1930s to the early 1950s, i.e., in the post–Great Depression context of the expanding interventionist state, by the economists Robert Musgrave (1939) and Paul Samuelson (1956). They defined them as neither rivalrous nor excludable owing to their natural characteristics. Nonrivalrousness, or nonsubtractability, means that one person consuming the good does not diminish another person's consumption of it. Nonexcludability describes the impossibility of preventing someone's access to a good when they wish to consume it.[14] According to Samuelson (1956), in both these respects public goods—the typical example he gave being a lighthouse guiding all boats navigating in the area—stand opposed to bread, the quintessential private good. The premise that the features of public goods encourage free-riding (benefiting from a collective good without paying for it) and discourage private companies from profiting through their provision has laid the foundation for arguments supporting their provisioning by governments.

However, many public-sector economists have come to recognize that few goods are inherently nonrivalrous or nonexcludable (see Trémon 2022). Locally delivered urban public goods in particular do not exist per se; rather, they are social and political constructs (Ellickson 1973; Goldin 1977; Malkin and Wildavski 1991; Stiglitz 2000; Kaul 2006). For instance, bread—the prototypical "private good" in Samuelson's polar model—can become a matter of public concern in times of shortage, and the government can take over its distribution (Colm 1956). In the context of a pandemic, vaccines can become a "global public good" if states lift intellectual property rights allowing exclusion.

As Mary Douglas points out, absolutely anything can be a public good; it all depends on decisions regarding whether healthcare, schools, and parks should be public goods (1989: 43). If there are no inherent features that help to distinguish between private and public goods, and if the boundaries stem from social and political decisions, there is no way of justifying governmental intervention (and the imposition of taxes) on the basis of the nature of goods. "Economic theory can tell us about the efficiency of that choice. But it cannot make the choice for us," write Malkin and Wildavsky (1991: 365). The subject matter, they conclude, has to be taken away from economics and put squarely back into political economy (1991: 373).

Public goods are goods essential to social reproduction; their modalities of distribution conform to more abstract visions of the common good, and therefore their provisioning is often a government monopoly. The "provisioning path" (Narotzky 2012) ties together the production and the consumption of public goods and raises questions about the politics of distribution (who is entitled to and who has access to public goods) and about the politics of responsibility (who provides them). The anthropologists Laura Bear and Nayanika Mathur, in a special issue on bureaucracy (2015: 19–20, 22, 26), refer to a new range of public goods that includes "the public good of fiscal austerity" and "the public good of transparency." However, this stretches the definition of public goods far beyond provisioning. To be sure, they bear a close relationship to the public good in the singular. The Chinese term *gongyi*, a contraction of *gonggong liyi*, translates as "the common good," "the public interest," "general welfare"—a political horizon or utopia used to justify policies and reforms (Madsen 1984; Zhao 2009). In grassroots understandings *gongyi* sometimes takes an adjectival form with the addition of the suffix "de" (*gongyide*), designating goods and services that conform to this vision of "what is good for all." This book primarily focuses on public goods in the plural, but the question of what the state should be providing relates to visions of the public good in the singular.

One branch of economics, public choice theory, departs from the Musgrave/Samuelson public goods theories by emphasizing governmental action rather than the goods' natural characteristics. According to its founder, James Buchanan, governments can decide to adjust the number of consumers to the quantity of goods they can offer depending on their available budget, and search for an optimal number of consumers for the goods according to the costs of producing them. Thus, to deliver public goods efficiently is to *make them excludable.* The result is what Buchanan (1965, 1999) calls "club goods": public goods available only to members of restricted groups. One solution he supports is restricting entry to certain groups via zoning mechanisms, especially in large cities (see Harvey's 1973 discussion).

Municipal governments make urban public goods available to city dwellers. Roads, schools, and public parks are generally distributed locally, and in China this also includes welfare provision. Since they are usually provided through some locational mechanism, they spatially exclude all those who live too far away to use them: they are accessible only within certain territorial limits, and to this extent some classify them as club goods.[15] However, I prefer to use the term "local goods," restricting the definition of club goods to instances where access ("membership" of the club) is deliberately determined by the ability to pay: that is, by a clubbing logic.

Before providing examples of such clubbing logics in China, the next section introduces commons and the context of their emergence in relation to public and club goods. The club goods theory has an advantage over the Musgrave-Samuelson public goods theory in that the technical properties of the goods do not play a role: Rather than starting from the premise that certain goods are intrinsically accessible to all, what is important is governmental action (Buchanan 1999). This approach influenced Ostrom's research on common-pool resources.

Commons

Public goods have been largely neglected, if not outright rejected, by the anti-capitalist literature, which has made "commons," "the common," and "commoning" central to its critique.[16] The commons serves both as an alternative language and as a descriptor of struggles against market- and state-backed capitalism. The language of the commons is a way of recognizing the collectively produced nature of many resources and goods that should be freely available to all members of society (Klein 2001; Bollier 2002; Harvey 2005; Gibson-Graham 2006; Nonini 2006, 2017; Hardt and Negri 2009; Gidwani and Baviskar 2011; Susser and Tonnelat 2013; Dardot and Laval 2014; Stavrides 2014; Borch and Kornberger 2015; Kip et al. 2015; Amin and Howell 2016; Blaser and de la Cadena 2017; Huron 2017; Holston 2019; Chatterton and Pusey 2020). The anthropological literature on commons overlooks state provision for two sets of reasons. One has to do with the privileging of small-scale communities and economic anthropology's traditional focus on reciprocal exchange rather than vertical transactions (among which are tax payments and state provision). The other is the influence of post-Marxist literature on commons and "the common," which not only ignores but also largely rejects the state's role as a potential provider, for reasons in sympathy with immanentist philosophies of power (Hardt and Negri 2009) and Proudhonian anarchism (Dardot and Laval 2014).

This new line of scholarship has drawn attention away from commons in nonurbanized settings toward urban commons. Hardt and Negri (2009) see the city as the very place where cognitive (knowledge-intensive and tech-driven) capitalism becomes prominent, allowing new modes of organization to be tried out. Movements for the reclamation of common wealth take place in the more diffuse locus of the city rather than the factory workplace. Dardot and Laval (2014) argue, against Hardt and Negri, that foregrounding cognitive capitalism overlooks the fact that the workplace, whether factory or corporation, largely remains organized according to the logics of capitalist exploitation (see also Kalb 2017: 164).[17] They maintain an understanding of the commons as institutions for managing resources along the lines of Ostrom's definition. However, as Ostrom's work shows, there is no a priori reason why a self-governed commons should be more egalitarian and less exclusionary than a state-provided public good.

Pierre Dardot and Christian Laval (2014) note that the commons are too often defined "by default" as a defensive reaction to the logics of capitalism rather than given content, and they emphasize the added value of Ostrom's approach in this respect. Because it was awarded the Bank of Sweden Prize in 2009, her work is the most famous among a vast body of studies by economists and anthropologists who have highlighted processes of communal self-organization and self-governance for the managing of resources (Ciriacy-Wantrup and Bishop 1975; McCay and Acheson 1987; Feeny et al. 1990; Bromley and Feeny 1992; Baden and Noonan 1998; Gudeman 2001).

Elinor and Vincent Ostrom (1977) started by looking at common-property resources, which Elinor Ostrom later renamed common-pool resources (CPR), contrasting them with private and public goods. CPR can be natural or human-made resources, for instance pastoral or forest land, that are available to a group of users (2015: 30). Commons are not resources but institutions for managing CPR. For Ostrom, CPR share the attributes of rivalry with private goods and nonexcludability with public goods (2015: 31). Commons overcome the challenges that these CPR properties pose. Drawing on empirical cases, Ostrom shows that individuals engage in institution building when they perceive the benefits of creating rules and monitoring their application. Ostrom's work is extremely valuable with respect to her inquiry into the *practice* of rulemaking, independently of the intrinsic nature of the goods in question.

Her work—at this point influenced by club goods theories—shows that although resources such as fisheries may be intrinsically vulnerable because they are open-access, i.e., nonexcludable, they are *made* excludable by the drawing of boundaries. Likewise, although they are naturally rivalrous and therefore depletable, setting rules about their usage renders them less depletable. Commons prevent both market and state failures by restricting their use to the members of a community and regulating access according to locally determined rules of use. Ostrom cites several cases that failed when governmental intervention opened up a CPR to outsiders, resulting in its depletion.

The freedom and legitimacy to make local arrangements is one of the commons' "design principles" (Ostrom 2015: 203). The other design principles are cooperative arrangements that rely on neither the market nor the state but are facilitated by mutual trust and shared information in small communities. Ostrom's professed preference for the small-scale community and focus on sustainability renders her less aware of the social and power relations shaping such communities (Harribey 2013: 397; Dardot and Laval 2014: 157). This is due to her main preoccupation with resource conservation rather than with issues of inequity and domination: for instance, she notes that in a Swiss mountain village, access to pastoral land is defined by a proportional allocation rule, depending (among other factors) on the amount of meadowland that farmers own (Ostrom 2015: 64), and thus on unequal property relationships. In her view, commons are institutions that protect these resources and ensure their long-term sustainability.

Not only this absence of attention to social justice but also Ostrom's insistence on the possibility of changing the properties of CPR or other goods are lost in the literature on "new commons," such as cultural, neighborhood, infrastructure, knowledge, medical, health, market, and global commons. Apart from some recent attempts to clarify the concept (Kip et al. 2015; Huron 2017), much of this literature makes only fuzzy references to the intrinsic properties of CPR, drawing a broad analogy about how they can be vulnerable to private appropriation and depletion.[18] For instance, Charlotte Hess maintains a distinction between "neighborhood commons" and public goods based on the idea that a commons "is a resource shared by a group where the resource is vulnerable to enclosure, overuse and social dilemmas. Unlike a public good, it requires management and protection in order to sustain it" (2008: 37).

This reasoning is puzzling: it means that a public good such as a public park can be relabeled a commons when there is a threat of it being sold to a private developer. This book departs from the confusing notion that vulnerability to enclosure is an intrinsic feature of commons. The same applies to the debate around the intrinsic rivalry or nonrivalry of urban commons, which I do not discuss here as issues of rivalry emerge only in chapter 5: it is fundamentally misleading. Although the idea of vulnerability to enclosure has inspired a vast strand of valuable research on how urban commons may be subtracted from capitalist logics, it also supports a false opposition between commons and public goods. There is no difference in nature between a park labeled a commons and one labeled a public good. When it is managed by a community outside of state and market logics, a park is a commons; when managed by an urban government, it is a public good.

In China's urbanized villages, when the state sells former common land that it has expropriated for development by a private real estate company, this operation is indeed an enclosure aimed at fostering capitalist accumulation. Many situations encountered in this book follow this pattern. However, some former-village commons such as burial land or a village-funded school become urban public goods when the state takes them over from former village collectives. Local communities react in various ways to the transformation of village commons into (or the substitution of village public goods by) urban public goods. With urbanization, some commons that were essential to the functioning of small rural communities may lose their appeal, with the necessity for new public goods and services, such as care for the elderly and parking spaces, recognized instead.

Rather than starting from predefined notions of public goods as accessible (i.e., nonexcludable) and available to all (i.e., nonrivalrous), a more fruitful point of departure is to use the criteria of nonexcludability and nonrivalry not as intrinsic qualities but as issues that render public goods fragile. In the concluding chapter I argue for a pragmatic approach that treats criteria such as excludability and rivalry as indicators of larger social and political issues rather than as goods' natural properties.

Public goods and commons are not antithetical: both are social goods as opposed to private goods. As stressed by the French alternative economist Jean-Marie Harribey, both commons and public goods are provisioned as a result of a political decision; only the scale at which the decision is made and the good is provided differs (2013: 400). Commons are more local and exclusive than public goods. Their differing status as commons, public goods, or club goods results from management and distribution practices that *make* them different: commoning and clubbing.[19]

Neoliberal Commoning and Clubbing

Public goods are not essentially different from commons, in that both are crucial to people's daily social reproduction and are free to all; the main difference resides in their mode of provision and scope of access. This calls for a pragmatic approach using verbs rather than nouns. Several scholars have therefore drawn attention away from *commons* to *commoning* as a verb, referring to collective practices of sustaining and managing common assets (Linebaugh 2009; Harvey 2012; Kalb 2017). Linebaugh's frequently quoted recommendation that the word "commons" should be kept as a verb rather than a noun is followed by, "But this too is a trap. Capitalists and the World Bank would like us to employ commoning as a means to socialize poverty and hence to privatize wealth" (2009: 279). Several scholars have also pointed out that the self-governing ideal of the commons is perfectly attuned to neoliberalism's endorsement of communal self-management, seen as a way of cutting public spending and offloading the costs of social reproduction (Lazzarato 2009; McShane 2010; Pithouse 2014; Enright and Rossi 2018).

Public goods provisioning is neoliberal when the state espouses commoning and clubbing logics. Both delineate the contours of a community of users whose members have access to schools, parks, social care, and welfare. Whereas clubbing practices are adopted by the state and grounded in market logics, giving access to social goods on the basis of ability to pay for them, commoning practices are encouraged by the state and are based on nonmarket logics, drawing on ethical commitment to care for others.

Although they profess principles of equality, the mechanisms that local governments have adopted for provisioning social goods are uneven and conditional as they embrace clubbing practices that amount to the de facto restriction of access to those goods. China's larger city governments practice clubbing—i.e., the creation of clubs, in Buchanan's sense—on the city scale when they cap the number of urban dwellers granted urban citizenship each year, selecting applicants on the basis of their contribution to the municipal budget to match the quantity of public goods they are able (and willing) to provide them with (chapters 1 and 5). Membership of the club of *hukou* holders, who have access to local public goods, is thus largely dictated by ability to pay. Such clubbing also occurs on the local neighborhood scale. China's urbanization since the 1990s conforms to a club goods model of allocation in which private developers are incentivized to provide public goods to those who have purchased property in new residential complexes (Lee and Webster 2006). This widespread model results from the tendency for local city governments to increase their revenue by encouraging real estate redevelopment projects, a telling sign of the neoliberal entrepreneurialization of the governance of Chinese cities.[20] Moreover, what appears to be a public good can turn out to be a club good when it is, although nominally free, useful or even profitable for a particular class (Gioielli 2011; Loughran 2014), for instance when a new public school or a public park raises the value of property owned by those living in the vicinity (see chapter 2).

James M. Buchanan, the "inventor" of club goods, was, along with George Stigler and Milton Friedman at the Chicago School of Economics, one of the main exponents of American neoliberalism. Buchanan's work on fiscal transfers (see Collier 2011) and on club goods demonstrates that neoliberalism is a strand of thought that differs from nineteenth-century economic liberalism in that, emerging at a time when the social state was firmly in place, it sought market-based solutions for more efficient public goods provisioning. Conventional accounts of neoliberalism as an ideology that professes the state's *laisser-faire* approach and withdrawal from any intervention in redistribution need revision. Such accounts are used by the Chinese party-state to cast itself as anti-neoliberal. Point 4 of the leaked *Communiqué* issued by the Central Committee in 2013 presents neoliberalism as an ideology that "opposes any kind of interference or regulation by the state" and which foreign powers seek to impose on China.[21]

Commoning practices are increasingly encouraged by the state as part of its neoliberal mode of provisioning. Although a clubbing logic is at work in the three case studies presented in chapters 1, 2, and 3, public goods provisioning in urbanized villages is not reducible to it. Lee and Webster (2006), predicting a generalization of market mechanisms in China, did not anticipate the return of the state with a strengthened commitment to addressing inequalities and creating a sense of community at the urban community (*shequ*) scale. Until recently, local Chinese officials' careers were determined primarily by a performance-based assessment system that focused heavily on promoting local economic growth and less on social welfare provision (Edin 2003; Li and Zhou 2005).[22] Under Hu Jintao and then Xi Jinping, reforms of the evaluation system have introduced other criteria besides GDP (Zuo 2015). The new model that has emerged in Xi Jinping's era is that of the "livable" community (*yiju shequ*), which continues and enhances the community-building policy (*shequ jianshe*) instituted in the 1990s (chapters 3, 4, and 5). The livable community is shaped by an image of the good life, where the "good" pursued is not only wealth and growth but also culture, leisure, and a sense of community solidarity.

Commoning may at first sight seem incompatible with state interference. It consists of protecting community members' collective rights of use from privatization and subordination to market and state logics. Community members are successful in creating a commons when they succeed in "fencing" and "patrolling" its boundaries "to ensure that no outsider appropriates"—i.e., can use—the CPR (Ostrom 2015: 203). Harvey offers the ironic observation that rich property owners can create a commons that excludes poorer city dwellers: "the ultra-rich, after all, are just as fiercely protective of their residential commons as anyone" (2012: 74).[23] Commoning generally requires restricting use rights to the members of a community, meaning that a commons can exclude outsiders such as poor newcomers, for instance migrant workers in urbanized Chinese villages where natives hold use rights to their common land and distribute the welfare benefits drawn from real estate income among themselves. In such cases, state intervention can equalize access to essential social goods. However, graduated governance practices (see next section) tend to be extremely selective in the way they open up access, notably to schooling.

This book identifies various and not always successful commoning logics where communities of native villagers attempt to defend their village's public goods against encroachment by outsiders, whether migrants or the state. For instance, the cemeteries central to formerly rural communities' collective life retain their importance and become the object of commoning practices in the face of state encroachment (chapter 2). However, as Ostrom highlights by including this among her design principles, in a country with a strong state such as China, commoning logics are successful only when there is some degree of state encouragement of local initiatives and/or tolerance of self-organization.

Furthermore, the state encourages forms of commoning through a range of activities, such as charity work and volunteering at the urban community scale. Because the offloading of responsibilities burdens public collectivities' budgets (Harvey 2012: 62–68; Xue and Wu 2015), communities are required to rely on their own resources and to compete for complementary, project-based funding from urban governments (chapter 4). Such community-based governance displays contradictions that focusing on public goods brings to the fore. On the one hand, the Chinese state authorities seem intent on overriding categorial divisions between native villagers and migrants by making commonality central while simultaneously deploying tools of governance that are radically different according to the categories of population that they target within the same community (chapter 3); on the other, the means for fostering self-governance—encouraging the urban community to generate and manage its own sources of income—and the tools used to foster a sense of community (e.g., volunteering and charity events)—are often selectively directed only at certain elements of the population, reproducing socioeconomic inequality (chapters 4 and 5).

Neoliberal provisioning includes but is not reducible to clubbing; state-encouraged commoning is also a cost-effective, neoliberal method for ensuring that state redistribution remains compatible with urbanization-driven capitalist accumulation, and in this respect it involves subject-shaping governmentality. While I reconceptualize these practices and logics more precisely as graduated provision (see next section), they can be subsumed under the broad conceptual heading of neoliberalism. Rather than relinquishing neoliberalism altogether as an analytical optic (Laidlaw 2015; Dunn 2017), a long-called-for reconciliation of political-economic and governmentality approaches is needed (Barnett 2005: 10; Clarke 2008: 145). In this book, my approach builds on and revises the insights of the governmentality school by placing the emphasis on the ways in which techniques and technologies of governance shape the political-economic process of the provision of public goods while being shaped themselves by capital accumulation and circulation. These practices obey logics whose dominant features share many traits with neoliberalism as it is understood both political-economically as a process of economic liberalization backed by the state and from a governmentality point of view as a subject-shaping moralized mode of governance.

Bringing public goods back into the equation without eschewing the state's role involves documenting and critiquing actual problems and tensions around the delivery of basic goods and services to city dwellers. Their lack of accessibility and availability may result from accidental governmental failure, but it is more generally related to deliberate graduated provision.

Graduated Provision

The three case studies presented in this book are located at different stages of a process that is explicitly framed as evolutionary in the sanctioned Chinese discourse, which is not merely rhetorical but translates into action by officials in different echelons and can be called "graduated governance."[24] All three of the urban villages presented in this book were legally urbanized, although differently, in 2004, in a nationwide wave of legal urbanization for which Shenzhen, which claims to have become the very first Chinese city without rural villages, set the model. However, contrary to what could be expected from the habitual narratives about Shenzhen's pioneering reforms, the conversion from a rural to an urban public goods regime occurred much faster in Chengdu's South Gate than in Shenzhen's Pine Mansion, with River Hamlet, in Xi'an, the slowest. South Gate comes closest to the ideal pursued by the Chinese authorities: a vision of cities populated by well-educated, property-owning, and self-governing (including when it comes to public goods) citizens (Tomba 2004, 2014; Zhang 2010). River Hamlet is at the other end of the spectrum, with Pine Mansion between the two. The differences are due to specific combinations of regional and local histories and social configurations that either accelerate or slow down what we found across our field sites to be a coherent ideological discourse with performative effects and a largely top-down planned process. However, state decentralization produces considerable disparities in policy implementation depending on each local government's fiscal means

(Smart and Smart 2001; Ngok and Huang 2014; Carrillo, Hood, and Kadetz 2017), while also leaving space for local experimentation.

Students of China's political system have shown how an experimental approach derived from the adaptive governance instituted in the Mao era prevails, in which local innovations are first piloted in a few localities, with only those proven to produce desired outcomes then diffused to more localities and potentially eventually becoming national policy (Heilmann 2008a, 2008b; Heilmann and Perry, 2011; Cai 2016). Among the best-known forms of this approach are the special economic zones that have by now spread all over China under new names (cf. Naughton 1995; Ong 2004), but the approach also includes experimental regulation in selected areas or sectors (Heilmann 2008b). The experimentation process is neither completely top-down nor completely bottom-up, involving an interplay between local initiative and central sponsorship. Pilot projects often involve temporary extralegal policies that can be legalized a posteriori.

Graduated governance does not refer to incremental change but rather to the way the grand teleological narrative of urbanization is taken into consideration by local officials and civil society actors. It involves attunement to the state of maturity and the stage reached in this evolutionary framework in a given locality (here, urbanized villages) when deciding on the next steps to be taken and the goods to be provided. Although the Chinese state is committed to reducing inequalities, actual practices in the provisioning of public goods show that not only principles of equality are considered in urbanization policies: in practice the model communities who come closest to the authorities' expectations in terms of their degree of urbanization receive the most resources. Local officials create showcases and designate model urban villages for the prioritization of subsidies and budgetary allocation.

What also counts as part of graduated governance is a propensity to govern by differentiating between categories of the population. Egalitarian values are balanced, and often checked, by principles of territorial entitlement, that is, access to public goods based on *hukou*, and increasingly by evaluations of worthiness. The household registration system "helps maintain and produces social and spatial hierarchies no longer through exclusion, but through differential inclusion" (Zhang 2018: 863). Despite the recent reforms, urban governments are reluctant to grant full residence rights, i.e., local *hukou*, to migrants due to budgetary scarcity. They tend to grant the rights to the city using selective points systems for those who are able to contribute financially to the costs of the urban public goods regime.

Graduated provision is the variegated, selective, and conditional delivery of public goods informed by the teleological ideology of urbanization and by neoliberalism, understood as the generalization of capitalist market logics and their shaping of governing techniques, including clubbing and commoning. As mentioned above, fiscal recentralization and the transfer of responsibilities for public goods to the lower echelons of the state (Wong 2010) have put a strain on local governments and encouraged them to engage in the pursuit of economic growth, with public goods often used as an instrument for attracting private investors and buyers.

In China's urban villages, the state's financing of public goods is often conditional upon villagers relinquishing all or part of their land-use rights to the state. The provision of public goods and infrastructure is a strategy to attract private developers and drive up future income-generating land-leasing fees. Even when local state representatives are committed not only to generating growth but also to the well-being of urban dwellers, the logics of public goods provision in many urbanizing villages favor the tendency to use them to enhance the wealth and income of particular social groups—the native villagers, and more generally, the propertied middle class. It is also the case that even without the state having to finance new public goods, the use value of what were formerly village public goods is extracted to generate exchange values in redevelopment programs, turning them too into sources of public revenue for the state.

In contrast to the nationwide political campaigns of the Mao era, local officials are encouraged to take local circumstances into account and attune to them in a process of "community building" to which I return in later chapters. But they do this while also having to keep an eye on the national objectives of urbanization. Thus, while it may look as if I am "reducing cases to instances of a general law" (Burawoy 2009: 49–50), I am rather looking at how a teleological framework—the law of inevitable urbanization-cum-modernization—matters in practice in the course of the distinct paths followed by the three cases.

Evolutionary logic is central to local cadres and other key actors' understanding and actions: they select the urban villages they consider most advanced along this evolutionary path and turn them into model communities. In nonmodel villages, while officials may leave things as they are for long transitional periods, sudden crackdowns may be used to discourage "less advanced" behavior. Indeed, while they may have some latitude in applying top-down directives, local officials have no choice but to follow nation- or citywide campaigns decided from above. South Gate and Pine Mansion have been put forward as models by the Chengdu and Shenzhen municipal authorities, while the Xi'an authorities explicitly devalue River Hamlet as a countermodel. These temporalities of governance intersect with local history to produce stark contrasts among the case studies.

Comparing Three Urban Villages

Although I designed the research project that led to this book, the outcome is the result of team collaboration. Having worked since 2011 in a Shenzhen urban village where I initially focused on the relationship between the native inhabitants and their diaspora, I came to realize the importance of public goods not just in that relationship but also in the process of transitioning from a rural locale to an urban community. Based on this finding, I produced a comparative research plan aiming at expanding the focus to China's urbanization process: away from the specifics of the former emigrant village, which has become an immigrant urban neighborhood, toward an understanding of how public goods matter in the transformation of rural villages into components of China's megacities.

With funding for this project from the Swiss National Research Foundation, I recruited two postdoctoral researchers, Wang Bo and Jessica Wilczak, who proposed researching urban villages in the cities they know well—Xi'an, from where Wang Bo originates, and Chengdu, where Jessica conducted her doctoral research—for comparison with Pine Mansion in Shenzhen. Although the main goals of the project were predefined, both brought their own sensibilities, expertise, and disciplinary backgrounds in anthropology and geography respectively. I was fortunate enough to receive generous funding that allowed for time in the field—while I (Anne-Christine) made my sixth and seventh research visits to Pine Mansion in 2017 and 2018, Wang Bo and Jessica arrived in Xi'an and Chengdu in April 2018 and, after spending several weeks selecting their field sites, stayed there almost uninterruptedly for a year. As mentioned in the acknowledgments, having decided not to pursue academic careers, they entrusted me with the writing of this book. For this reason I use "I" throughout the chapters when referring to my analyses and my own fieldwork and refer to Wang Bo and Jessica by name when describing their fieldwork—and to the villages they worked in by the pseudonyms they chose for them. In this section, however, I use the plural pronoun to describe the methods we agreed on collectively.

Wang Bo and Jessica's arrival in Lausanne in the early autumn of 2017 was followed by a phase of intensive familiarization with the interdisciplinary literature on public goods, with an emphasis on political-economic anthropology, and then with a preparatory period during which we collectively designed the canvas for the survey and interview questions, creating a common methodological framework that left room for contextualized observation, which we deliberately left open for serendipitous ethnographic encounters and the researchers' idiosyncratic sensibilities and thematic preferences.[25] In choosing our field sites we were careful to keep them comparable in terms of population size, the proportion of migrants in their populations, and the timing of their urbanization. Because the project framing was based on my fieldwork in Shenzhen's Pine Mansion, we expected to find wide variations. These expectations were mostly met, but the villages displayed more similarities than I had anticipated. Their governance institutions and hierarchical structures were strikingly similar, albeit with some variation due to differing administrative arrangements (chapter 1). The main difference we found was in the strength of the collective economy and, accordingly, the division of responsibilities between the former-village-level and upper-level municipal government authorities. Most notably, shareholding companies inherited from the rural and collectivist past are stronger and direct government control less present in Shenzhen than in the other two case studies.

This difference is related to another: although Shenzhen is larger, its rural past is far more present than that of Xi'an and Chengdu, cities that not only go back much further in time historically but were also prioritized for industrialization during the Mao era, while Shenzhen was industrialized only in the 1980s. Still, all three of the villages were rural until the twenty-first century, and their native inhabitants are former peasants who were recategorized as urban when the village became part of the expanding city. The difference may also be explained in social terms: like many other urban and rural villages in Guangdong Province, Pine Mansion in Shenzhen used to be a lineage village, most of its inhabitants being patrilineally related and considering themselves descendants of a common founding ancestor. Lineage ties tend to be stronger in South China than in other regions and therefore unsurprisingly play a more substantive role in Shenzhen. The presence of such "solidary groups" (Tsai 2007) may explain the distinct path followed by the Shenzhen authorities in allowing powerful shareholding companies, usually lineage based, to continue to exist after urbanization.

While Shenzhen's Pine Mansion is set apart from Xi'an's River Hamlet and Chengdu's South Gate in this respect, one important similarity between Pine Mansion and River Hamlet emerged. At the time of our fieldwork, both comprised a minority rentier class of native villagers and a majority population of migrant workers whose socioeconomic conditions were markedly lower than those of the indigenous villagers. Epitomizing a new model of urban migration in China, in South Gate Village in Chengdu the majority of non-native residents are white-collar workers granted local *hukou*. In Xi'an and Shenzhen, the native villagers kept the use rights to their land until very recently, well after administrative urbanization, while in the case of Chengdu most village groups relinquished their property rights at the moment of urbanization. In short, South Gate seems to have conformed very early to the top-down, new-style model of urbanization as a force for achieving middle-class prosperity.

There are only a handful of cross-city and cross-regional comparisons of villages-in-the-city in the literature using qualitative methods (Po 2008; Cheng 2012; Chung 2013; Smith 2014; Song 2014; Tang 2015; Wang 2017), which should not be surprising considering how difficult it is to take account of the multiplicity of factors involved in variation. Quantitative research isolating a limited number of variables to compare a large number of cases (e.g., Tsai 2007 on public goods in rural villages) is better suited for this purpose than an ethnographic approach. Multicase ethnography makes the best of the limited comparative potential of ethnographic case studies. It involves "thematizing the difference [between the sites] rather than their connections" and asking how that difference is produced (Burawoy 2009: 202–3). Case-oriented methods are aligned toward a comprehensive examination of historically defined cases and phenomena for their intrinsic value rather than testing propositions and assessing probabilistic relationships between variables.

This book does not provide a model based on a set of variables; rather, it accounts for the significant contrasts between the sites and offers context-sensitive generalizations—specificities of the local cultural, historical, and socioeconomic properties of the former villages and their inhabitants; municipal urban planning and city governance; and nationally defined ideological aims and legislative constraints. It looks at how the cases reflect a gradation of situations that stems partly from local variation in city history and socioeconomic circumstances and partly from their being at different stages within the wider evolutionary framework adopted by the Chinese state, which ultimately aims to totally dismantle villages-in-the-city. Government cadres' attitudes to the urban villages influence the pace and methods that they adopt and the resources they allocate.

We used a combination of methods to trace the histories of different public goods, their changes of status in the course of urbanization, and their provisioning paths: how and by whom the provision of public goods is planned, financed, distributed, and consumed. We collected urbanized villagers' accounts of the past and carried out short surveys at all three sites with natives and non-natives to get a more systematic sense of the social differences in access to publics goods such as healthcare, pensions, schools, and public transport, and we elicited opinions about existing public goods. We hung out in public spaces, where we had many informal conversations and met streetcleaners, children's carers, and volunteers for community activities and services. By taking regular walks we observed the state of the roads, the garbage collection, and the spatial distribution of cleanliness between neighborhoods and got a concrete sense of issues of remoteness from schools and public squares.

We also relied on data collected at different levels of the urban administration, including census and budgetary data, media reports, urban planning and renovation programs, audit reports, and legal documents relating to the collective economy and local *hukou* policy. We conducted interviews with local state cadres at the district and subdistrict levels[26] and with party secretaries and community workers at the grassroots, probing to discover which public goods they prioritized and why; to what extent they were responsive to local needs, the demands made of them, the evaluations they were subject to, and the objectives they had to fulfill; and how they met them. We asked them how they defined public goods and attempted to understand the dilemmas they faced in their daily work.

The project's comparative dimension required the preselection of a series of goods. We started out with the following list: health insurance and pensions, garbage collection, schools, cemeteries, public transportation, and parks and squares. Our premises differed from those of most economics and political science studies, which aim to modelize the mechanisms that ensure the efficient provision of public goods. We set out into the field without a predefined notion of which goods are intrinsically "public." We agreed on a deliberately eclectic list of goods in order to remain open to local, emic understandings of what counts as public goods. This allowed us to broaden the theoretical scope of our research by bringing together for analytical scrutiny the series of goods usually studied by economists and public administration studies (welfare, roads, garbage collection) and those favored by urban studies (roads, garbage collection, public spaces), as well as those far less often considered, although central to social reproduction (schools, cemeteries).

However, we left open the possibility that some goods might be absent or not relevant to residents, or that others might emerge as important in the course of the research. Strikingly, the only nonrelevant good at all three sites turned out to be public transport; instead, parking was a priority for residents. The wet market in South Gate (Chengdu) was an unexpected good. Public schools were an issue only in River Hamlet (Xi'an) and Pine Mansion (Shenzhen). Health insurance and pensions emerged as major issues but were hard to approach using ethnographic methods; I discuss them in chapter 1 in relation to social inequalities. Instead, care, particularly of seniors but also childcare, lent itself well to an ethnographic approach because, whether privately or publicly provided, it is largely performed in public space.

Book Outline

Chapter 1 introduces the field sites and focuses on two types of public goods: large-scale urban infrastructure and welfare (insurance and pensions). It locates the three urban villages in the cities of Shenzhen, Chengdu, and Xi'an and in the context of their different Mao- and reform-era industrialization and urbanization trajectories. Although all three have recently repositioned themselves as high-tech and service hubs and their *hukou*-granting policies have converged, the urban-rural integration paths they have taken and the types of rural to urban migration they have attracted differ. The chapter discusses the administrative reorganization that resulted from their legal urbanization and the consequences for the native villagers, notably in terms of the differing fates of the former village collectives. Inequalities between the welfare benefits of urbanized villages' native urbanites and new inhabitants also vary; these are starkest in Shenzhen and least in Chengdu, with Xi'an an intermediary case.

Chapter 2 retraces the changing provisioning and governance logics in the shift of regime from rural to urban. Even though circumstances are sometimes favorable to their de facto, if not de jure, persistence, one common that is systematically dismantled and dispossessed is communal burial land. The funeral reform in the Shenzhen and Xi'an case study villages was a violent decommoning that triggered recommoning mobilizations. The chapter compares two different ways of extracting market value and state revenue from the preexisting use-value of village goods: by letting an informal economy subsist in Xi'an's River Hamlet, and by luring the shareholding companies to sign urban renovation projects and expropriating the former village's self-funded school in Pine Mansion. While state provision of public goods in Pine Mansion is conditioned on this deal, South Gate's rapid transition from a village to an urban *shequ* through resettlement made way for a new tabula rasa allocation of public goods. Officials in Chengdu's already-redeveloped urban village of South Gate attune to the needs of its residents in a club-like manner. In this new, middle-class, resettled urban community, the authorities carefully alternate between privatization and public allocation of new urban social goods.

Chapter 3 focuses on the process of turning former peasant villages into urban neighborhoods conforming to the ideal of the civilized city, which is promoted against the threat of chaos: an urban landscape considered unruly because it is unplanned, and the presence of large, impermanent migrant populations in River Hamlet and Pine Mansion. This chapter examines the role of public goods that are closely associated with the discourse on urbanization as a civilizing process: urban infrastructure such as garbage collection and the maintenance of public order. The actors in the urban governance *wangge* (surveillance system) and *chengguan* (urban management) use these as governing tools. Infrastructure provision is graduated, in that it is constantly revised locally to accommodate both policies and campaigns decided by upper-level authorities and the local authority's vision not only of what remains to be done but also of what can potentially be achieved, based on its estimation of the community inhabitants' maturity in the urbanization-civilization process.

Chapter 4 looks at the provision of public goods and services, mainly care for seniors and cultural and pedagogic activities for all, through community-building projects. It also considers how the public good, in the singular and with a new philanthropic connotation, underlies this policy. Some community-building projects consist of charity events in which volunteers play an essential part; others are cultural events promoting traditional Confucian values, their overall goal being to shape ethical, self-governing citizens. Across our sites, such events are supported by unpaid and mainly female volunteer labor and by a competitive project-based allocation system that targets specific groups with the aim of integrating them into the community. And yet this moral governance is equally graduated, in that the charity events mainly cater for migrants and senior care is mainly performed by outsider volunteers for native beneficiaries.

Chapter 5 examines how the state asserts its presence in urbanized villages by shaping new public spaces that, in theory, are open to all. Whereas new modes of sociality are indeed taking shape around the use of public space in the model middle-class communities of Chengdu, in the Xi'an and Shenzhen case study villages sociality and the use of public space are largely segregated in practice. Native residents implicitly exert use right priority over newcomers, contravening state plans. However, newcomers who live in crammed apartments also appropriate public space by using it for care practices, thereby forming a social commons and making a claim on the state. These practices are also a way for those without hope of accessing urban citizenship to assert their membership of the community and claim a very different right to the city to that of its middle-class urbanites.

The conclusion recapitulates the book's arguments in favor of an anthropological, pragmatic, and historicized approach to social goods. Looking at actual provisioning practices avoids overstating the differences between commons and public goods, and allows consideration of the importance of both the state as a provider and its failings. Rather than taking the economists' classificatory approach, this approach examines their modes of provision, reveals how public goods are subject to commoning and clubbing practices, and uses rivalry and exclusion as analytical categories. Although Chinese citizens are no longer officially classified as either rural or urban, enduring legacies of this dichotomy weigh on the inequalities and tensions in China's urban villages. Finally, this book's pragmatic approach to graduated provision avoids some of the dead ends of the debate on whether or not China is neoliberal.

Notes

1. The "harmonious society" (*hexie shehui*) motto was adopted at the fourth plenum of the sixteenth Communist Party Central Committee in September 2004 (Ngok and Zhu 2010; Ngok and Huang 2014). Urban-rural integration (*chengxiang yitihua*) was first articulated in the New Socialist Rural Construction Program of the eleventh Five-Year National Economic and Social Development Plan (2006–10) (Ye 2009; Qian and Wong 2012).
2. New-Type Urbanization Plan 2014–2020, http://www.gov.cn/zhengce/2014-03/16/content_2640075.htm, China, 2014. It was tied with the Chinese government's twelfth Five-Year Plan.
3. The *hukou* is a booklet that records the details of an individual's identity and their registered residence. As part of the household residence registration (*huji*) system, adopted in 1958, each Chinese citizen is registered to one locality.

4. As per the definition of the National Bureau of Statistics (Liang and Ma 2004). They totaled 144 million in 2000, 221 million in 2010, and 375.82 million in 2020 (National Bureau of Statistics 2021).
5. By socialized reproduction I mean the way in which welfare, education, etc. (social goods, see below), are financed through channels of pooled-together contributions or taxes, which are meant (at least in theory) to ensure some amount of redistribution, in contrast to self-financed social reproduction.
6. China State Council, "Advice on Further Hukou System Innovation," issued 24 July 2014, http://www.gov.cn/zhengce/content/2014-07/30/content_8944.htm; China State Council, "Interim Regulations on Residence Permits" (Order No. 663), http://www.gov.cn/zhengce/2015-12/14/content_5023611.htm.
7. Focusing on welfare in China, Carrillo, Hood, and Kadetz (2017: 1–2) include under the rubric "social welfare" (*shehui fuli*): social insurance (*shehui baoxian*) such as retirement pensions, unemployment subsidies, subsidies for physical and mental healthcare, and maternity pay; social services (*shehui fuwu*), i.e., support for the elderly, the disabled, and the left behind, education, childcare, housing support, and legal aid; and social relief (*shehui jiuji*), i.e., assistance for vulnerable people and disaster relief. This book focuses on a limited number of items on this list and adds some urban public goods, such as parks and garbage collection; see below, "Comparing Three Urban Villages."
8. See Castells (1977) and Liu (2002) for critiques of "urbanism."
9. Beijing's famous Zhejiang villages, studied by Xiang Biao (2005) and Zhang Li (2006), are migrant enclaves formed in the second half of the 1980s on the outskirts of Beijing to house the inflow of migrants from Zhejiang Province. Although they prefigured the urban village phenomenon, they differ from it in that even if Zhejiang migrants initially rented apartments from native inhabitants, the latter did not build apartment buildings to accommodate more migrants. Urban villages are usually formed when native inhabitants build houses to host a variety of migrants originating from diverse locales. Urban villages in this latter and most widespread sense multiplied in Beijing from the 1990s onward.
10. Local governments used to control over 70 percent of the total revenue in China before 1994. After the budget reform, the central and local governments shared revenues almost evenly (Lin 2007). See also Wong (1997, 2018).
11. The latter expanded from 8,842 to 36,295 during 1984–2008, an increase of 310 percent (CSSB 2009: 367 cited in Lin and Yi 2011).
12. It is estimated that between 1990 and 2005, 30 percent of the increase in the urban population was due to migration, i.e., to people's changed registered residence, and up to 40 percent to the change in status of people residing in a locality that has become urban (McKinsey Global Institute 2009).
13. As well as the revised Constitution, the 1984 City Planning Ordinance, amended by the City Planning Act in 1989, established China's first comprehensive planning framework. While the act had jurisdiction over designated urban areas, the development of rural land remained under the control of the Planning and Construction Regulations on Villages and Townships (Chung 2009: 254).
14. See fuller discussion in Trémon (2022).
15. This book deals with public goods offered to the inhabitants of cities, which are subject to proximity constraints and therefore exclude potential users based on spatial distance. The public goods considered in this book should be accessible and available to all residents of a spatially limited urban community (*shequ*) if they conform to economists' nonexcludability and nonrivalry criteria.
16. An exception being Gidwani and Baviskar (2011: 43).
17. See also Sylvia Yanagisako's (2012) critique of the novelty of cognitive capitalism.

18. Kip et al. (2015: 15) identify potential commons based on what resource is being managed, the relations between commoners, and who is included in the community of commoners.
19. Public provisioning as distinct from publicizing, discussed in Trémon (2022).
20. On neoliberal urban entrepreneurialism in Western democracies, see Brenner and Theodore (2002); Harvey (2005).
21. Central Committee of the Communist Party of China's General Office, "Communiqué on the Current State of the Ideological Sphere," 22 April 2013. This communiqué (known as Document 9) was leaked and reprinted on the ChinaFile website, 8 November 2013, https://www.chinafile.com/document-9-chinafile-translation.
22. However, the effects of this evaluation system are not corroborated by Shih, Adolph, and Liu (2012).
23. Here he points to a clubbing logic that differs from commoning insofar as it gives access to club goods on the basis of ability to buy property in a gated community, for instance; nevertheless, it is true that once the rich have fenced off their community, nothing prevents them from managing their shared resources (gardens, public space, schools, etc.) cooperatively, outside market logics and state intervention, as a commons.
24. The choice of the term "governance" proceeds from the shift from "government" (*zhengfu*) to "governance" (*zhili*) in the Chinese authorities' discourse in the 1990s (Sigley 2007; Ngeow 2011).
25. Wang Bo has a specific interest in the anthropology of waste, which he studied in Tibet for his doctoral thesis at the University of Wisconsin, Madison, and Jessica has an inclination toward urban-rural integration politics, which she studied in Chengdu after the 2008 earthquake as part of her doctoral thesis in geography at the University of Toronto.
26. This book refers to the administrative level called *jiedao* (street) in Chinese as "subdistrict."

— Chapter 1 —

THREE VILLAGES-IN-THE-CITY

While the creation of "common affluence" (*gongtong fuyu*) and the development of a "moderately well-off society" (*xiaokang shehui*) have been the Chinese authorities' primary goals since Deng Xiaoping launched economic reforms in 1979, this ideal was to be achieved by allowing some to "get rich first" (Wong 2006).[1] However, the policy of uneven development can be traced back to Mao Zedong's prioritization from the 1950s to the 1970s of the industrialization of inner provinces over coastal ones (Naughton 1988; Yang 1990) and the redirection of agricultural surplus to the industrial sector in the same period (Knight and Song 1999).

Under Mao, the formation of a centrally planned socialist economy was coupled with policies curbing urbanization, enacted through the residence registration (*hukou*) system instituted in 1958 that recorded each household's place of origin and assigned them rural (peasant, *nongmin*) or urban (non-peasant, *feinong*) status. The near impossibility of converting one's rural *hukou* to urban *hukou* prevented migration to cities in the 1960s and 1970s (Chan and Zhang 1999). Furthermore, the Mao era was characterized by the establishment of a strong duality between urban and rural citizens in terms of their standards of living and the benefits available to them. Urban *hukou* holders, who were referred to as "those who eat state grain" (*chi guoliang*), were entitled to food rations and social services, including state-funded education and healthcare. Rural residents were organized into collectives that were expected to fend for themselves in terms of not only food provisioning but also providing their members with basic healthcare, education, and social services (Chan 2009). In short, there was a stark duality between the urban and rural public goods regimes (Solinger 1999; Smart and Smart 2001; Zhang and Kanbur 2005).

The spatial priority given to China's interior provinces in the collectivist era was reversed in the early 1980s, following the onset of economic reforms.[2] The first special economic zones (SEZ) were created along China's entire coast, starting in the southeast (Cartier 2001; Ong 2004). Since 2000, the bias in national economic development has been further entrenched with the redirection of capital investment from rural to urban areas (Ma and Wu 2005; Hsing 2006, 2008; Lin 2007, 2015; McGee et al. 2007; Huang 2008), especially large cities in coastal provinces. Elsewhere, particularly in the interior of the country, urbanization occurred well after the export-oriented light industry boom that fueled Shenzhen's growth. Today all regions of China, including its former hinterlands, are preoccupied with urban growth, and all its major cities compete for highly skilled migrants.

Rural migrants were allowed to register as temporary urban residents for the first time in 1985. They flocked to China's large cities, driven by a combination of pull factors including opportunities for employment on construction sites and in factories and the urban service sector, and push factors such as the state's disinvestment in rural areas and a more general sociocultural devaluation of rural life (Yan 2003). While their *hukou* status no longer served to prevent rural-to-urban mobility, it denied millions of migrants the welfare benefits and many social services provided in the localities where they lived and worked (Davis 1995; Yu 2002; Pun 2005; Wang 2005; Solinger 2006; McGee et al. 2007; Fan 2008; Chan 2012; Huang 2014).

The 2014–2020 National Urbanization Plan mandated the use of points-based schemes (*jifenzhi*) for the acquisition of local *hukou* in cities with a total population of over five million.[3] These schemes brought into effect the announced abolition of the rural/urban categorization and aimed at reaching the plan's goal of granting residency to a hundred million migrants while also capping the size of the population in larger cities. Points systems grant *hukou* to a predefined annual quota of migrants selected according to criteria that privilege those who are educated and economically successful. The consequences of these reforms include increased social polarization among the migrants who, no longer collectively excluded as rural *hukou* holders, are divided between white-collar migrant workers eligible for local residential status or hoping to achieve it one day (see chapter 5) and migrant workers from poor rural areas who live and work in informal conditions that exclude them from applying for points-based *hukou* and even a residence permit. This polarization is compounded in the larger cities by the continuing increase in the nonlocal *hukou*-holding population in spite of measures aimed at controlling their growth, and because of the selectivity of the points-based schemes.[4]

These recent policy changes aim to reduce the inequalities resulting from the legacy of the rural/urban duality, which is particularly strong in China's urbanized villages as this chapter shows. Other legacies are also at play in the urbanization of rural villages, and these combine with newer elements to produce what Andrew Kipnis calls "recombinant urbanization": the recombination of preexisting elements and external factors into new patterns (2016: 15–16). These combinations vary from one locality to another. This chapter introduces the three urban villages that the team studied in the cities of Shenzhen, Chengdu, and Xi'an and examines how local long- and shorter-term urbanization, *hukou*, and welfare policies interplay with legacies from the collectivist era and the sociospatial organization of former rural villages, resulting in different paths of village urbanization and population composition.

The three urban villages are set in one paradigmatic eastern coastal city, Shenzhen, and two interior cities, Chengdu and Xi'an. The first section locates the villages and contextualizes them within the geographies and histories of the cities of which they have become a part. The second directs attention to the contrast between native villagers' initiatives and top-down policies for the urbanization of their villages and provides an overview of their inhabitants, their residence and occupational patterns, and the proportions of natives to migrants in their populations. Next, I look at the varying degrees to which former villagers have lost their autonomy in the process of urbanization, how village institutions have been converted into urban ones, and which of these distribute welfare benefits, finding the strongest inequalities between natives and migrants where former village collectives are in charge. I conclude by highlighting the main commonalities and differences between the three cases, providing a framework for the next chapters.

A Variety of Chinese Urbanization Trajectories

In all three of the case-study cities, the municipal authorities (i.e., their mayors and party secretaries) have considerable leeway in setting goals and plans for urbanization and economic development, and in matters of *hukou* and welfare policies. Xi'an and Chengdu owe this power to

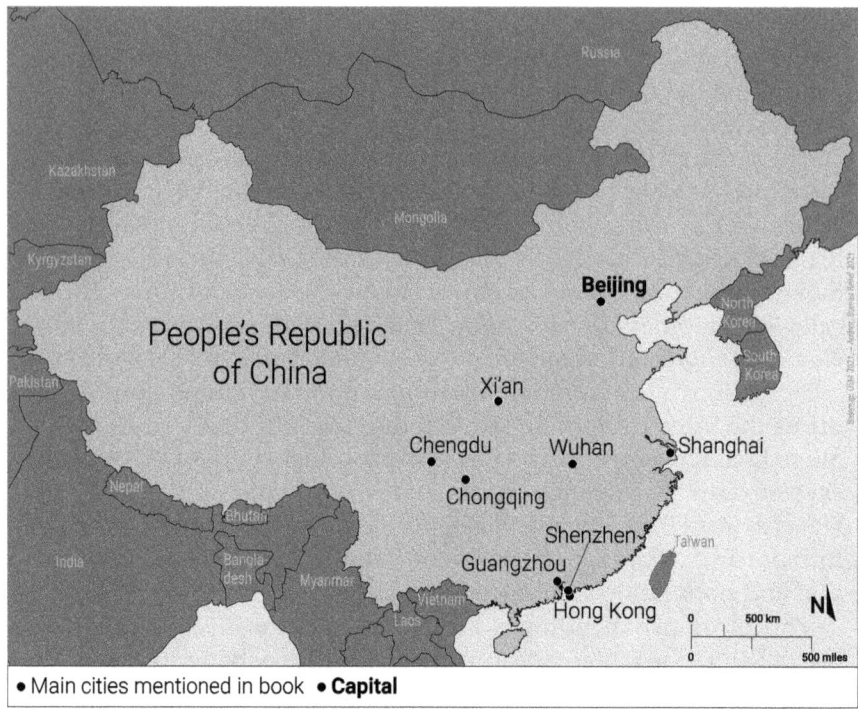

Map 1.1. People's Republic of China. © Bureau Relief.

their status as provincial capitals, while Shenzhen has the privilege of making its own rules and regulations as a special economic zone. Moreover, what Chan and Buckingham (2008) pointed out before the latest reforms has become even truer: the cumulative effect of the *hukou* reforms is not the abolition of the *hukou* but devolution of the responsibility for urban citizenship admission to local government.

They display differences resulting from their geographical positions and long-term histories, and from industrialization policies (or their absence) under Mao; however, they also tend to converge, due to the recent rebalancing of the reform-era coastal bias toward developing the interior. Shenzhen is a brand-new coastal city that embodies the spirit of China's early market reforms; the growth of its population and GDP has been so astonishing that it has led to the expression "Shenzhen speed" (*Shenzhen sudu*). Xi'an and Chengdu are ancient cities in China's interior provinces whose growth may be less spectacular than Shenzhen's, but whose recent expansion illustrates the policy of mitigating the imbalances resulting from uneven development across regions (Lim 2014a).

In Western Chinese cities such as Xi'an and Chengdu, much of the initial investment that spurred urbanization was prompted by the national Open Up the West campaign (*Xibu Da Kaifa*) initiated in 1999 to address the inequalities between Eastern and Western China through significant investment in infrastructure, education, agricultural modernization, and urbanization (Goodman 2004). Both cities strive for top spots as China's fastest-growing cities. Whereas Chengdu's rapid GDP and population growth and its success in attracting business investment has earned it a ranking as a "nationally central city," Xi'an has struggled to refashion itself and its regional impact as it has attempted to deindustrialize and develop tourism, commerce, and high-tech industry, and has been designated a "regionally central city."[5] The determination of Chengdu and Xi'an's governments to accelerate their urban development is comparable to Shenzhen's mission to maintain the speed of its economic growth by substituting high-tech industries for low-value manufacturing. All three aim to become global high-tech hubs attracting white-collar workers in a national competition that is constantly appraised and commented on in the Chinese media. The three villages-in-the-city reflect these long-term and recent processes.

Pine Mansion: An Industrial Village in Shenzhen

From its origins as a poorer marginal area in the wider Pearl River Delta region, Shenzhen became the fastest-growing area economically after China's reopening. It has a long history of human settlement and has been a strategic military and commercial frontier area throughout China's imperial history. Shenzhen was the name of the administrative seat of Bao'an County, a small town on the shore of the Shamchun (Shenzhen in Cantonese) River, which serves as the natural border between Hong Kong and mainland China. In August 1980, an area of 327.5 square kilometers was carved out of Bao'an County to create the Shenzhen City and special economic zone (SEZ). It was the largest and the most ambitious of the SEZs that opened up in China's southeastern coastal provinces after the start of the economic reforms. These zones were selected to test the decollectivization of agriculture, the granting of privileges to overseas investors and entrepreneurs, and the end of the "iron rice bowl," i.e., of guaranteed lifetime employment, reforms that would later spread to the rest of China (Vogel 1989; Sklair 1991; Ong 2006). The reforms turned the Pearl River Delta into the new "workshop of the world." Having transitioned from low-end, labor-intensive manufacturing to high-tech knowledge-based industries since the mid-2000s, the Shenzhen SEZ accounts for over 10 percent of China's exports and is estimated to produce 90 percent of the world's electronic goods (OECD 2017).

The export-oriented factories initially set up in Shenzhen attracted migrants from across China. In 1978 the town of Shenzhen had 27,366 inhabitants, and the population of the county surrounding it was 300,000–400,000. By 2020 the new city had a population of 17.63 million, of which 12.49 million (70.84 percent) had resident permits and only 4.14 million (29.15 percent) were urban *hukou* holders (Shenzhen Statistics Bureau 2021). Although the proportion of non-*hukou* holders among residents has declined (it had peaked at 76 percent in the mid-2010s), it remains the highest among Chinese cities. Leslie Sklair (1991) describes Shenzhen's growth as resting on a process of "temporary urbanization" in which most of the population growth was, and remains, the result of the presence of residents with temporary permits who can theoretically be sent home at any time. In 2008, Shenzhen pioneered a new type of permit no longer named "temporary," valid for ten years and for which all those who have worked for more than 30 days, hold property, or run a business in the city can apply.[6] In 2012, Shenzhen introduced a points system (*jifen ruhu*) institutionalizing the conversion process via which a permit holder could acquire a city *hukou*. This highly selective system ensures that an increase in the registered population will not result in greater pressure on the local budget (Zhang 2012). In addition to meeting the basic requirements, applicants must provide proof of consecutive registration of temporary residency and evidence of formal employment. Points are also scored based on age, level of education, the amount of capital invested in business, and whether property has been purchased. Applicants can apply if they match the qualification criteria and are granted a *hukou* transfer based on the available *hukou* quota. Such quotas allow governments in large cities such as Shenzhen to grant urban *hukou* to a small number of selected, high-income, educated migrants (see details in the section "Hopes of Accessing *Hukou*" in chapter 5).

Shenzhen's first districts—the four southern districts of Yantian, Luohu, Futian, and Nanshan (see map 1.2), planned by central ministries, were given extensive stretches of land on which high-rise urban residential neighborhoods and skyscrapers were built. Shenzhen's first mayor, Liang Xiang, requested soldiers of the Infrastructure Engineering Corps to build Shenzhen's first towers in Luohu District. In 2003 Shenzhen's city hall moved to Futian District, which became a business and administrative focal point. Shenzhen's first two metro

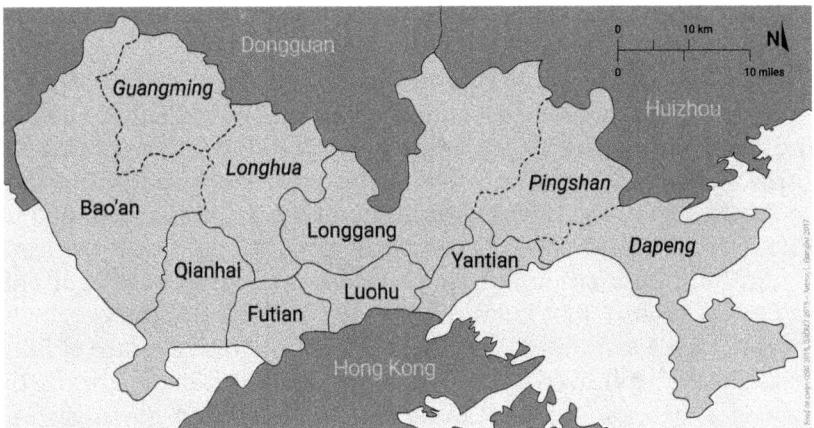

Map 1.2. Shenzhen's districts. Dotted lines: new districts created in 2010. © Bureau Relief.

lines opened in the same years. To establish the world-class status that it aspires to, Shenzhen hosted the World University Games in 2011, accelerating the extension and construction of new metro lines to catch up with the city's growth. Line 1 runs east to west for 41.04 kilometers, reflecting Shenzhen's east-west span, and stops at 30 stations.

Although Shenzhen has the reputation of being built from scratch, this is more myth than reality (O'Donnell 2001, 2017; Du 2020). The city has largely grown out of the unplanned industrialization and urbanization of the rural villages scattered across Bao'an County. The migrants who constitute 70 percent of Shenzhen's population have found affordable housing in these villages, the authorities having made no provision for accommodation except for requiring factories to provide dormitories for their workers (Song, Zenou, and Ding 2008; Cheng 2014). Shenzhen's four core districts contained almost a hundred rural villages that were administratively urbanized in the first wave of urbanization. There were many more in the rest of Bao'an County, which remained officially rural until 1993, when it was divided into the new urban districts of Bao'an and Longgang, which officially became part of Shenzhen city (see map 1.2). Although these two districts were separated from the SEZ by a barbed-wire border and checkpoints until 2010, their inclusion within the municipality and the proximity of the SEZ brought many changes to the villages long before they officially joined the zone or were urbanized. Their population growth was such that a year after they joined the SEZ, Bao'an and Longgang Districts were split into several new districts.

With the second wave of administrative urbanization in 2004, Shenzhen became the first "Chinese city without villages"; i.e., its entire *hukou*-holding population was urban. Pine Mansion, in the north of Shenzhen close to the border with Dongguan in former Bao'an District, now the new Longhua District, was urbanized as part of this second wave. It can be reached by the fast ferry from Hong Kong International Airport to Shekou Port and an hour and half on the metro, first from west to east on Line 1 and then northward to Line 4's terminus Qinghu, the administrative center of Longhua District, followed by a twenty-minute taxi ride or, since 2018, thirty minutes on a tram. Line 4 is being extended northward at the time of writing and will include a stop in Pine Mansion. Pine Mansion now has a modern high-tech industrial zone, but even before it was connected via the tram it had many small factories and workshops. The entire area has been heavily industrialized since the early 1990s, with two major plants, Foxconn Technology Group and Dongfeng Motor Company, only a few miles from the former village.

South Gate in Prosperous Chengdu

Chengdu is the capital city of Sichuan Province and boasts a settlement history dating back over twenty-three hundred years. Located in the fertile, well-irrigated Sichuan Basin, Chengdu owes its early prosperity to the agricultural productivity of the Chengdu plain, which is also known as the Land of Abundance. Like Xi'an, Chengdu was associated with economic backwardness during the heady economic reform period beginning in the late 1970s.

The initiation of the national Open Up the West campaign in late 1999 marked the beginning of a more dramatic sociospatial transformation in Chengdu, which offered companies seeking to move westward an abundance of developable land and cheap labor. Sichuan Province has been a key source of the migrant labor fueling the economic boom on China's east coast (Mobrand 2009). Chengdu officials used the new policy to position the city as a key growth pole and financial center in Western China, sparking a new round of extensive urban growth and intensive urban redevelopment (Meng 2001). With labor costs rising on the east coast, many companies turned toward Western China as a new investment frontier (Taylor, Ni, and Liu 2016: 180). Over two hundred Fortune 500 firms relocated their

Chinese headquarters in Chengdu, and by 2010 global analysts were hailing it as one of the world's fastest-growing cities of the future (Kotkin 2010). From 2000 to 2012 the city's GDP grew at an annual rate of over 15 percent.

Along with the nearby city of Chongqing, Chengdu aimed to form a core western urban agglomeration zone to rival the Yangtze River and Pearl River Deltas to the east, creating a new national growth pole and, eventually, a world-class metropolis (Fang and Yu 2016: 207). However the city's global ambitions were toned down with the 2012 arrest of Li Chuncheng, who had served as Chengdu's mayor and then party secretary from 2001 to 2011, on corruption charges. Li was considered responsible for Chengdu's development drive, having overseen a distinctive urban-rural integration policy (see below) and intensive urban development with a policy of renovating the old city that earned him the nickname Li Chaicheng, or "Li who demolishes the city." Under Li, the city experienced an extensive southward push to build high-tech development zones and the intensive redevelopment of older neighborhoods in the city core such as Kuanzhai Xiangzi (the Wide and Narrow Alleys) as commercial tourist attractions.

The city's primary orientation lies along its north-south axis. Its first and busiest metro line, which opened in 2010, runs through the traditional city center down to a string of high-tech parks, shopping malls, conference facilities, and luxury residential complexes in the city's southern development zone, Tianfu New District. The 2011 Master Plan reinforced the southern development drive by extending the growth corridor to over eighty kilometers in length, aiming to transform Chengdu into a "modern, international metropolitan city led by high-end industries, commerce, and logistics" (Miao 2019: 528). Like Xi'an, Chengdu has worked to position itself as an important overland logistics hub for China's Belt and Road Initiative.[7] A new railway cargo line connecting the city overland to Lodz in Poland via the Chengdu-Europe Express Railway was opened in 2013, and a second international airport was completed in 2020.

Like those in Shenzhen and Xi'an, Chengdu's officials are attempting to make the postindustrial transition by competing for white-collar migrant workers, offering preferential *hukou* schemes and policies based on a points system similar to that adopted earlier in Shenzhen. From 2000 to 2012 the city's population increased from 11.11 to 14.18 million (Qin 2015: 22). In 2020 Chengdu had a resident population of 20 million (compared with 16.58 million in 2019), including 16 million living in the central city's fourteen urban districts and cities under Chengdu's jurisdiction and four million living in the four rural counties (see map 1.3).⁸ The city's floating population is 8.4 million (42 percent of the resident population), of which almost 7 million are intraprovincial migrants. Compared with the sixth national census in 2010, the floating population increased by 4.28 million, an increase of more than 100 percent.⁹

Although Chengdu has similar selective *hukou* policies when it comes to migrants originating from beyond its jurisdiction, it stands in stark contrast with Shenzhen and Xi'an due to the inclusiveness of its local *hukou* policy. Owing to its nomination in 2007 as a "national urban-rural comprehensive reform pilot area," that is, a leading pilot region for the urban-rural integration policy, Chengdu anticipated the national reform by abolishing the dual urban or rural categorization of *hukou* in April 2011. All residents of Chengdu, whether in the city or the surrounding countryside, possess the same *hukou* status and enjoy equal access to social insurance programs previously only open to urban workers (Shi 2012).

As part of the pilot urban-rural integration policies, the city government in 2007 initiated a formal urban village renovation project to demolish and redevelop the final twelve remaining urban villages within the central city. In 2008 reconstruction after the Wenchuan earthquake also provided the municipal government with an opportunity to urbanize Chengdu's peri-urban regions with an urban-rural integration policy (Abramson and Qi 2011). In 2013 a roadmap and schedule for the coordinated development of Chengdu's urban and rural areas over the next five years were announced, partly as a commitment to equalizing living standards across urban and rural areas by reinvesting the revenue from state-led urbanization in rural communities in the form of public goods and services (Ye and Legates 2013). Chengdu's statistics stand out, in that they keep track of the evolution of the income gap between rural and urban residents with assessments of poverty alleviation, reemployment policies, and the degree of social insurance coverage.[10]

Located on the outskirts of Qingyang District, one of the five original urban districts just beyond Chengdu's third ring road (see map 1.3), South Gate Village is only a fifteen-minute ride from the center on the metro. Although most Chengdu residents still think of it as rural, South Gate is, however, the most urbanized of the three villages, both in terms of its urban outlook and the proportion of its urban-*hukou* holders.

River Hamlet: Small Informal Businesses in Deindustrialized Xi'an

Xi'an is the capital of Shaanxi Province in Northwest China. It served as the capital city for several dynasties from as early as the Western

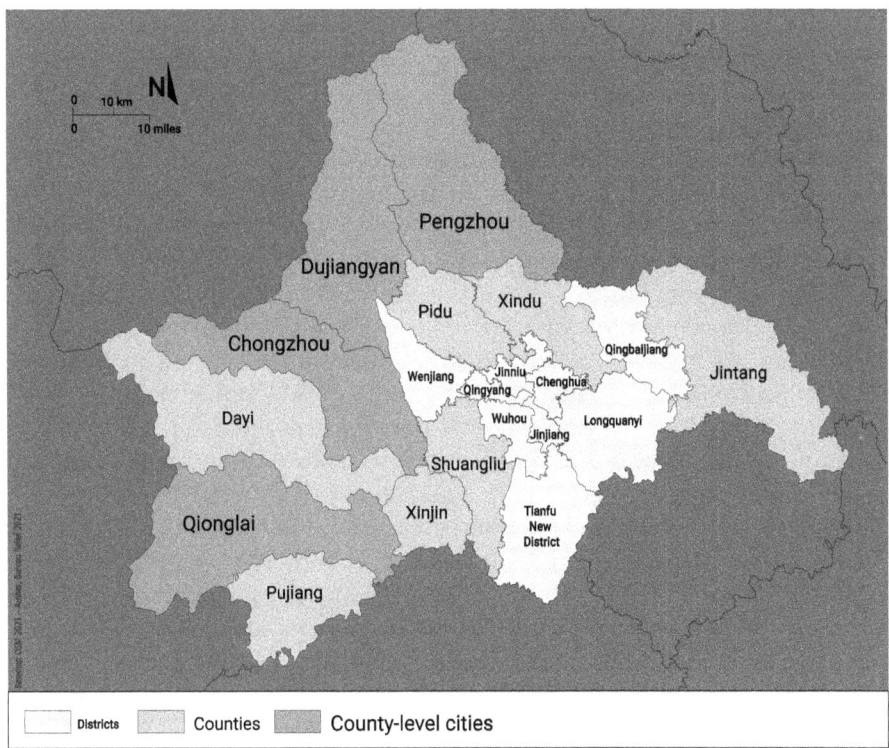

Map 1.3. Chengdu's districts and counties. © Bureau Relief.

Zhou (c. 1045–771 BC), but is most widely known as the burial site of China's first emperor, Qin Shi Huang (259–210 BC). As a major hub on the Silk Road heading westward out of China, Xi'an continued to serve as a cultural and commercial center throughout much of China's imperial era. It was designated an industrial city with a focus on textiles and precision instruments when the People's Republic of China was founded in 1949. When the special economic zones were established along China's eastern coast in the 1980s, industry in China's interior, including in Xi'an, suffered a sharp decline, and by the turn of the century most of Xi'an's textile factories, many of which were state-owned enterprises (SOEs), had closed, leaving hundreds of thousands of former state factory employees out of work.

The Open Up the West campaign did not spur the same rapid and dramatic economic growth and urban expansion in Xi'an as was seen in Chengdu. By 2015 the city had relocated all of its industry from the central city to industrial zones on the outskirts beyond the third ring road. Yet several issues still plagued the city, including poor air quality, the shoddy construction of the metro, and several high-profile corruption cases such as the illegal building of over a thousand luxury mansions in the Qinling foothills, a protected mountainous area south of Xi'an. Between 2006 and 2016 Xi'an underperformed in many key areas, including GDP, income growth, and infrastructure investment, leading some to describe this period as Xi'an's "lost decade" in comparison to the city of Chengdu.[11]

The Chang'an (Xi'an's historical name) China-Europe freight train was launched in 2016 as part of the Belt and Road Initiative.[12] Since 2016 Xi'an's policymakers have sought to leverage the city's advantages in science and technology research. Xi'an hosts several top science and technology universities and research facilities, including Xi'an Jiaotong University, Northwestern Polytechnical University, Chang'an University, and Shaanxi Normal University. Specializing in telecommunications and communication chips, the Gaoxin High-Tech Zone has attracted the headquarters of major international and Chinese companies such as Samsung, Intel, Foxconn, and Huawei. During the same period, Xi'an became known as a "famous social media" (*wanghong*) city due to its pioneering presence on new Chinese online video platforms and tourism forums such as Douyin and its partnership with the livestream app TikTok.[13] In 2018, with municipal GDP reaching RMB 800 billion (the highest growth in fourteen years), Xi'an was listed as a national central city.

This strategy of urban development through the upgrading of infrastructure and the economy was coupled with a new policy of awarding *hukou* to college graduates, professionals, and investors. The points system for *hukou* transfer was adopted in 2017. Xi'an thus joined many other cities in the nationwide competition for young, educated, white-collar workers.[14] In 2017 Xi'an ranked third for population inflow after Shenzhen and Guangzhou, and in the two years following, more than 1.15 million people became "new Xi'aners." Xi'an's population growth has been the highest of all Chinese cities between the two national censuses in 2010 and 2020.[15] The registered population has increased from 8.46 million in 2010 to 12.95 million in 2020 (a growth rate of 52.97 percent), and the floating population has more than doubled, from 1.72 to 3.74 million. Although a large number of migrants have not been able to access Xi'an *hukou* and have temporary resident permits instead, Xi'an's hukou is one of the most accessible, and the floating population is the lowest in percentage among the three cases (28.8 percent of the total resident population).[16] The vast majority are migrants from Shaanxi or neighboring provinces, making Xi'an a regional rather than a national labor market. These upgrading policies caused housing prices to skyrocket,

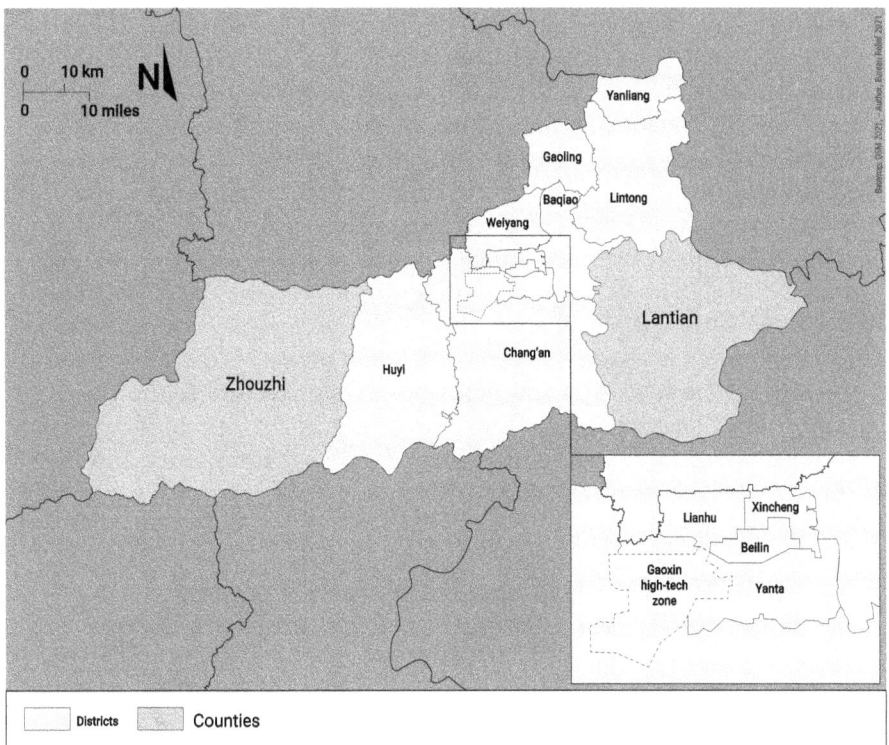

Map 1.4. Xi'an's districts and counties. © Bureau Relief.

doubling in 2016–17 and again in 2017–18, and led to a shortage of schooling and other public goods, putting further pressure on already marginalized social groups, mainly the rural migrants.

As in most Chinese metropolises, Xi'an's jurisdiction includes not only the built-up urban core, which is divided into urban districts, but also large areas of surrounding agricultural land in rural counties and towns (see map 1.4). Thus it is not surprising to note that 38.2 percent of Xi'an's legally registered residents were still classified as rural in 2004. This dropped to 31.5 percent in 2010 and 20.8 percent in 2020, suggesting a process of gradual urbanization within the wider city borders.[17] Xi'an launched a comprehensive urbanization plan in the early 2000s, converting agricultural land to urban uses through demolition and resettlement.

There are a dozen famous villages-in-the-city in the core of Xi'an, all located next to universities. Until the 1990s they belonged to the suburbs, but they became part of the city's core area when its border was extended from the second to the third ring road. River Hamlet was one such large village at the intersection between Gaoxin High-Tech Zone and Yanta District (see map 1.4). It was the largest of the twenty villages under the jurisdiction of a subdistrict of the same name, River Hamlet, in Yanta District, which became urban in 1988. In 2004 it became an "urban reform village" (*cheng gai cun*), i.e., a village scheduled for demolition and reconstruction. In September 2018, River Hamlet was transferred to Gaoxin Subdistrict in the High-Tech Zone, which had been coveting its land for years, and the villagers were evicted to make way for its demolition (see chapter 2). Between 2004 and 2018, with its cheap rents, fast food, and general liveliness, River Hamlet was seen as a paradise for many starting their first job or opening their first small business. Its proximity to the Gaoxin High-Tech Zone and Metro Line 3 opening in 2016 enabled an easy commute from work for employees of internet companies and biopharm research facilities, and for shoppers from all over the city.[18]

Collectivist Legacies, Population, and Housing Patterns in the Three Urbanized Villages

The rural past has left legacies that have "recombined" (Kipnis 2016) with villagers' own initiatives and municipal policies, producing distinct patterns of settlement and housing and populations with varying legal status and socioeconomic characteristics.

The retrenchment of rural villages under Mao went hand in hand with the maintenance of local structures, a state concession to community loyalties and traditional economic solidarities (Siu 1989; Shue 1980, 1984). With full collectivization from 1955, production teams (*shengchandui*) became the owners of collective land (Parish and Whyte 1978: 32), established at the level of small, "natural villages" (*ziran cun*) subordinate to the production brigade (*shengchan dadui*) at the administrative village (*xingzheng cun*) level (see table 1.1).[19] Although, to be built on, agricultural land must first be converted to urban use or expropriated by the state, the collective owners of rural land have relative freedom regarding how they use it. Because rural land in China belongs to collectives, villages close to expanding cities have generally started urbanizing in advance of administrative urbanization. In the reform era the collectives, which morphed into village-level enterprises, have been the main agents of rural industrialization along with government township enterprises (Oi 1989; Chen 1998; Pei 2002).

In all three of the village case studies, urbanization has occurred in such a way that the native villagers' socioterritorial organization

Table 1.1. Village and *shequ* economic and administrative organization, 1950s–today.

	Village (*cun*)/Urban Community (*shequ*)	Village/Urban Community Subdivisions
Collective economic organization (1950s–1982)	*Shengchan dadui* Production brigade	*Shengchandui* Production team
Administrative organization (1950s–2004)	*Xingzheng cun* Administrative village *Cunweidahui* (abbrev. *Cunweihui*) Village assembly	*Ziran cun* Natural villages *Cunweihui* Village committees
Administrative organization since legal urbanization in 2004	*Shequ dangqun fuwu zhongxin* Party Service Center for the masses	*Shequ jumin weiyuanhui* (abbrev. *Juweihui*) Residents' committees

of the collectivist era has endured, albeit to different degrees. The importance of shareholding companies and other former village institutions, and the degree to which native villagers in urbanized communities continue to identify with their former village although it no longer officially exists, varies according to the extent, modalities, and timing of the expropriation of village land, both collective agricultural land and individual land (Tang 2015). Apart from collective land, in the early years of postreform urban growth, village households generally retained the use rights to their individual housing and homestead farming plots (*zhaijidi* and *ziliudi*). These plots of land have also undergone varying fates, reflecting the degree of the villagers' control over urbanization.

Pine Mansion in Shenzhen: Rentier Natives, Factory Workers, and Self-Employed Migrants

While Pine Mansion village, whose territory covers 3.2 square kilometers, has physically disappeared, its agricultural fields replaced by factories and residential buildings, there is a striking continuity from the pre-collectivist period to today in its territorial-social structure. Everyone who originates from Pine Mansion strongly identifies with their *cun*, which refers to both the former administrative village of Pine Mansion as a whole and to each of its seven "natural village" subdivisions, which became seven production teams in the 1950s (table 1.1). Native villagers introduce themselves by saying they are from this or that *cun* (natural village) or *wei* (neighborhood, residential clusters of aligned houses), both terms referring to the same units and used interchangeably. Six of these *wei* used to be (and still are, to some extent) inhabited by members of different segments of the dominant Chen lineage, whose members are Hakka speakers.[20] Among the natives there is also a very small minority of Cantonese speakers, most of whom belong to a much smaller lineage, the Huang, whose members live in the seventh *wei*.

Pine Mansion now has seven small shareholding companies at the neighborhood (natural village) level, and one large one at the higher, *shequ* (former administrative village) level. The shareholding companies draw rental income from industrial and commercial real estate on the land to which they have collective use rights. The larger shareholding company has bought sections of collective land from the smaller companies and holds use rights to what has become a medium-sized industrial zone on the former village's outskirts, its headquarters located in one of a pair of eight-story buildings in the heart of the old village, the second of which is occupied by the community center. They embody civil society and administrative power, respectively. While *shequ* employees are directly appointed by the upper municipal level, company leaders are elected by the shareholders. However, their concurrent powers are not of the same scope: the shareholding companies are owned by the native villagers, while the community center is concerned with all of the *shequ*'s residents, natives and non-natives alike (see next section).

This shareholding system was first introduced in Guangdong Province in the early 1990s to securitize collective assets (Po 2008) when income from industrialization started to grow; it spread to other regions in the 2000s (Po 2011; Tang 2015). According to elderly Pine Mansioners, living conditions were extremely harsh in the wake of Deng Xiaoping's reforms. Massive emigration greatly reduced the labor force, hampering teamwork as each team was left with only a few workers, mainly women whose husbands had left for Hong Kong. The families survived thanks to remittances and plots of homestead land (*ziliudi*) allocated to them by the brigade, on which they grew vegetables, sweet potatoes, and sugar cane. Farmland was decollectivized in 1981 with the adoption of the Household Respon-

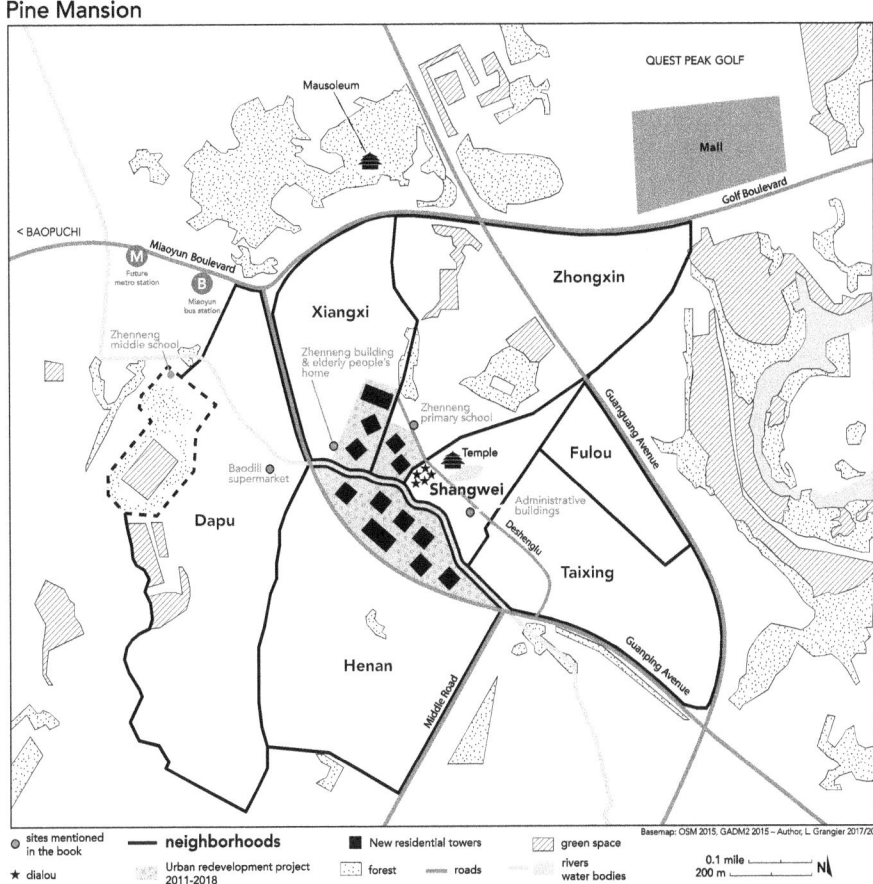

Map 1.5. Pine Mansion, Shenzhen. © Bureau Relief.

sibility System, which made each household responsible for the cultivation of its own plot of land (*zerentian*).²¹ The Mao-era collectives had become empty shells.

In the early 1990s collectives resurfaced with the creation of economic development companies (*jingji fazhan gongsi*) in which the villagers held shares, and they also gained the right to undertake nonagricultural activities. Part of the former collective agricultural land was then redistributed among the villagers by drawing lots. By 1994 most villagers had built four- or five-story houses on these plots and moved from the old compounds to these new modern buildings, often occupying one floor and renting the others to migrant workers. The new residential areas around the core of the old village are named after each of the seven original *wei* or natural villages, preceded by *xin* (new); e.g., "xin Xiangxi," and so on. In short, there has been centrifugal expansion: the *wei* have expanded beyond their original limits onto the land that their inhabitants used to cultivate.

The shareholding companies started building factories and dormitories on their collectively held agricultural land. The village shareholders called for investment and financial support from kin in Hong Kong and overseas, and pooled their money to build the factories, which they rented to Hong Kong and Taiwanese corporations. This process continued even after the village's urbanization in 2004, when the development companies were renamed cooperative shareholding companies (*gufen hezuo gongsi*). In the 1990s, the large village cooperative was forced to sell a significant portion of its land in the northeast of the village to a state-owned company, which two years later sold part of it on to a private foreign company for development into what has become one of the world's largest golf courses and a shopping mall (see map 1.5), and the rest to a state-owned agro-industrial company, both at a much higher price. In 2004, as with most villages urbanized in the second wave, the Shenzhen government did not expropriate individual residential and farming plots. It took over only part of the former collective land, and this was mainly unused forest and hilly land for which the shareholding companies received forty-six RMB per m^2 in compensation. The villages' companies, and those in the Pearl River Delta region more generally, retained collective use rights (*jiti tudi sheyong quan*) on the remaining land (Yan, Wei, and Zhou 2004; Tan 2005; Tian 2008; Po 2008; Chung 2013).

Only the natives were entitled to a share in the reformed shareholding companies. The condition for becoming a shareholder was local peasant residential status before urbanization in 2004. In Pine Mansion, those eligible included the Chens and the Huangs, along with their wives who originate from other nearby villages.[22] Thus, in Shenzhen, administrative urbanization in 2004 gave rise to a new category of people called "native villagers" (*yuancunmin*), whose local *hukou* was changed from peasant to urban and who received shares in the reformed shareholding companies. According to Shenzhen regulations, all those with *hukou* registered elsewhere are to be excluded from this official category, but in Pine Mansion, some downtown Shenzheners who left the village and changed their *hukou* before 2004 (i.e., those with commercial or urban administrative careers) were entitled to buy a share. They paid a much higher price than the 1,000 RMB paid by those who had cultivated the land for their entire lives.[23] The concern about equality is all the more understandable as companies distribute not only annual dividends that can amount to several thousand RMB a year from the richest companies but also social benefits (*fuli*).

According to the last detailed official census in 2010, the population of 59,980 residents of Pine Mansion included 1,441 or 2.4 percent local *hukou* holders or "native villagers." Many Pine Mansioners do not have to work for a living and display the idleness that had become a sign of status by the early 2000s in other formerly rural villages in the area (Chan, Yao, and Zhao 2009: 293); Siu calls their native inhabitants "Maoist landlords" (2007: 334; see also Liu 2009). They collect rent on their apartments, leaving them plenty of time to sit outdoors, chatting with fellow native villagers and playing mahjong. Those who live in the village appreciate their quiet and comfortable community, where everybody knows everybody else. Wang Cuichun, a former peasant whose husband lives in Hong Kong, declared, with her friends nodding in agreement: "Here we have freedom: we're used to rural village life (*nongcun*), there's more space. In the city, in Shenzhen and Hong Kong, the houses are very small." The native villagers persist in speaking of Pine Mansion as "their village" (*women cun*), both to distinguish it from the city of Shenzhen, even though they are formally Shenzheners, and to refer to their close-knit, face-to-face community within the wider urban community (*shequ*) with all its new inhabitants.

The non-native and non-*hukou*-holding population is younger and far less homogenous than the native population. The 2010 census registered 11,881 factory workers, mostly in their twenties and living in factory dormitories and old houses. The redevelopment of the village has visibly reduced their number, although some factories remain.[24] Pine Mansion's temporary resident population is increasingly composed of white-collar employees and small-business entrepreneurs; they run grocery and vegetable stores, canteens and restaurants, garages, and factories producing goods for larger subcontracting factories. About a third originate from other localities in Guangdong Province or nearby Guangxi Province; the rest have migrated from China's inner provinces, mainly Sichuan, Jiangxi, Anhui, Henan, Hunan, and Hebei.

South Gate in Chengdu:
Resettled and Commercial Residential Communities

South Gate community was established in June 2004 and covered an area of 1.6 square kilometers prior to its division into two communities. The village's original territory was probably larger, but with urbanization the state immediately expropriated all village land. When Jessica Wilczak started her fieldwork in Chengdu, where she had already carried out her doctoral research (in a different site), South Gate community had just been divided by carving out 0.75 square kilometers in March 2017 to form North Gate community (see map 1.6).

In 2018 the North Gate community website listed a population of 19,645 people, of which 10,415 were permanent residents and 9,230 floating population. The South Gate community website numbered its own population at 19,945, with no breakdown into registered and floating populations.[25] South Gate community consists of two resettlement estates for former farmers (*anzhi xiaoqu*) and seven commercial estates (*shangye loupan*); North Gate community comprises two resettlement estates for former farmers and six commercial estates: while this reflects the rapid expansion of commercial housing in Chengdu (Yang et al. 2017: 84), clearly the division was done in such a way as to keep a balance between native and non-native villagers as part of Chengdu's effort toward urban-rural integration.

For the sake of simplicity, unless differentiated, the former village of South Gate and resulting urban communities of South Gate community and North Gate community are referred to collectively in this book as South Gate. South Gate's communities are primarily residential: other than small shops, restaurants, and medical clinics there are no big employers or factories in the area. Before urbanization in 2004, most of South Gate's residents lived in *linpan*, a settlement pattern unique to the Chengdu Basin consisting of clusters of three to ten courtyard-style houses (*yuanzi*) hedged by tall groves of bamboo and surrounded by small plots of agricultural land. For the most part they grew staples such as rice, wheat, and rapeseed for oil. Vegetables were largely grown for home consumption. Some families also kept cows and sold the milk to a privately run commercial dairy in the village. The land use was mostly residential or agricultural, interspersed with a few small enterprises such as commercial garages. In other words, South Gate was visually quite rural before its formal urbanization in 2004. It was not entirely an agrarian economy, however: by the 2000s most of its young people were working or studying in the city, and some households rented space to migrants from other areas.[26]

South Gate Village is part of a zone referred to as a mixed urban-rural border area, in which resettlement housing represents two-thirds of residential land use for resettlement in Chengdu city (Yang et al. 2017: 85). Unlike Pine Mansion and River Hamlet, South Gate's legal urbanization involved its immediate physical transformation. Similar to the process Zhang, Wu and Zhong (2018) describe in Ji-

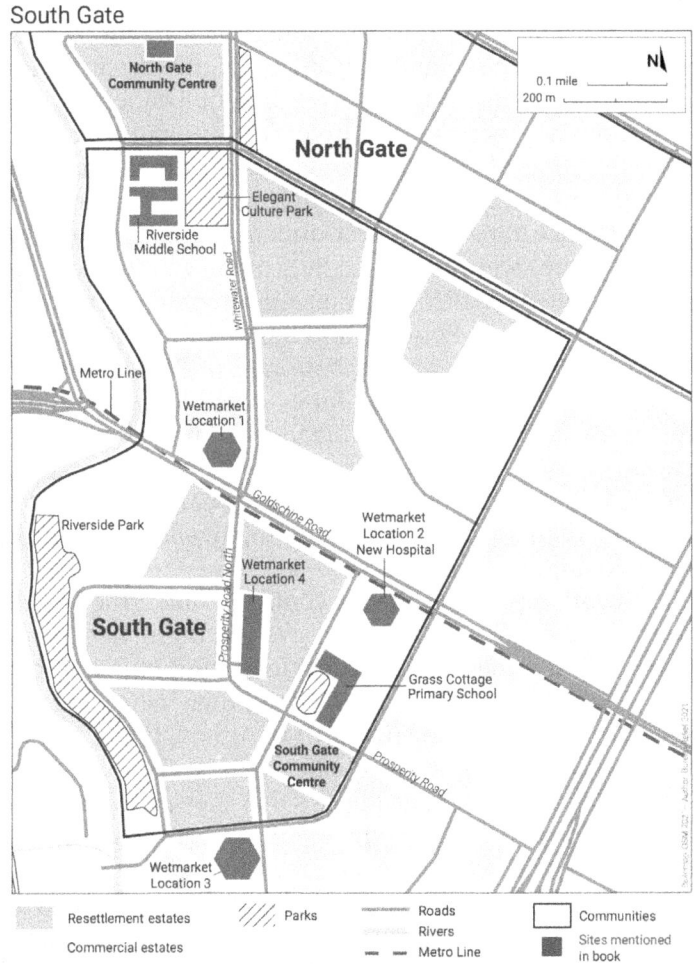

Map 1.6. South Gate, Chengdu. © Bureau Relief.

angsu, another region known for its proactive urban-rural integration policies, it was urbanized in a sweeping, top-down fashion under a policy of "large-scale demolition and construction" (*dachai dajian*). Village land was requisitioned by the municipal government and auctioned off to developers. In contrast to Pine Mansion and River Hamlet, the South Gate villagers lost their use rights on all of their collective agricultural and individual residential and homestead land. However, in return they received apartments in new resettlement estates built on plots of land belonging to the five former production teams (*shengchandui*), meaning that members of former teams were often resettled in the same buildings. Therefore, much as in Pine Mansion and River Hamlet, connections among people of the same production team remained strong even after urbanization, and former villagers continued to refer to different locations in the community by team numbers; for example, "on Number 3 team's land."

The construction of the resettlement estates took several years, during which the villagers had to arrange their own accommodation, often renting space in nearby as-yet-undemolished houses. Once the resettlement estates were complete, they organized the decoration of their new apartments, which in China are generally sold without fixtures such as appliances, flooring, and lighting. Only native villagers received a subsidy of a few tens of thousands of RMB for this; women who had married into the village, for example, were not eligible for this subsidy. By 2008 most of the villagers had moved into their new apartments, which were allocated based on the number of household members at a rate of 35 m² per person. This meant that most families received more than one apartment, and many ended up renting the extra space to migrants from other areas.

Although both types of estate are conflated under the term *xiaoqu*, or residential area, native villagers are distinguished from nonvillagers largely by their place of residence and ownership status. Resettled villagers do not receive deeds of ownership, and this is a widespread problem in China (Ong 2014). Although they are allowed to rent it out, native villagers on resettlement estates do not own their property. The absence of deeds implies that they are prevented from selling the apartment units on the open market, although they are often traded on the black market at a reduced price.[27]

The resettlement housing estates on which the former villagers live are also visually distinct from commercially sold housing. Those in the North and South Gate communities are complexes of a dozen or so low-rise five- or six-story walk-up buildings. Visually, they resemble the work-unit (*danwei*) housing built in the heyday of state socialism. The commercial estates, by contrast, are collections of four- to twelve-story high-rise apartment buildings with elevators. Their occupants are a mix of Chengdu urbanites and white-collar migrant workers. Although some low-income rural migrants rent apartments or rooms in the resettlement estates from former villagers, the distinction between the low-rise resettlement estates for former villagers and the high-rise commercial estates for white-collar workers is clear-cut. However, there is one hybrid exception: Benevolence Garden is a large, recently completed resettlement complex for villagers from other demolished villages in Chengdu. Some of its apartments are for sale on the open market, with the price per square meter about half that of nearby fully commercial estates due to unclear ownership rights.

Today South Gate looks like a fairly middle-class residential community. There are no traces of the rural village apart from some murals depicting former village life in the community center and a few unoccupied fields that have yet to be developed and are being used as informal community gardens.

River Hamlet (Xi'an):
Rentier Natives, Migrants, and Retired Factory Workers

In 2018, when Wang Bo started his field research in his natal city Xi'an, the native villager population of River Hamlet was around 5,000 and that of migrants was about 70,000. River Hamlet's earliest inhabitants migrated from river villages in Jiangsu to Shaanxi province during the Ming Dynasty in the fourteenth century. In recent decades River Hamlet, which covers an area of 2.474 square kilometers, has seen an influx of both rural laborers and new white-collar urbanites into the commercial residential estates springing up next to the village on sold-off land. The number of 70,000 temporary residents is an underestimate, because many rural migrants do not hold permits and stay only for short periods, frequently changing their accommodation. The popular saying is that River Hamlet has around 300,000 people. A community center officer explained that "only the long-term residents in River Hamlet are counted, for social welfare distribution purposes."[28] In addition, the sheer number of daily visitors to River Hamlet can reach the tens of thousands as both white-collar workers and rural migrants come from the surrounding area to buy food and other goods, to network, or simply to get a haircut.

The native or original villagers are spread across five natural villages (*ziran cun*) corresponding to the five production teams (*shengchan dui*) of the collectivist era, grouped at the administrative village level as a production brigade (*shengchan dadui*) (table 1.1). River Hamlet is not unified around a majority lineage, like Pine Mansion: the native villagers have a wide diversity of surnames. The scope of social interaction and reciprocity ties through gift-giving in life-cycle rituals was, and still is, largely restricted to the natural village—i.e., team—level. Prior to the village's demolition in spring 2018, wedding and funeral ceremonies were held in public spaces, often in makeshift tents in narrow alleys away from the main street (see map 1.7).

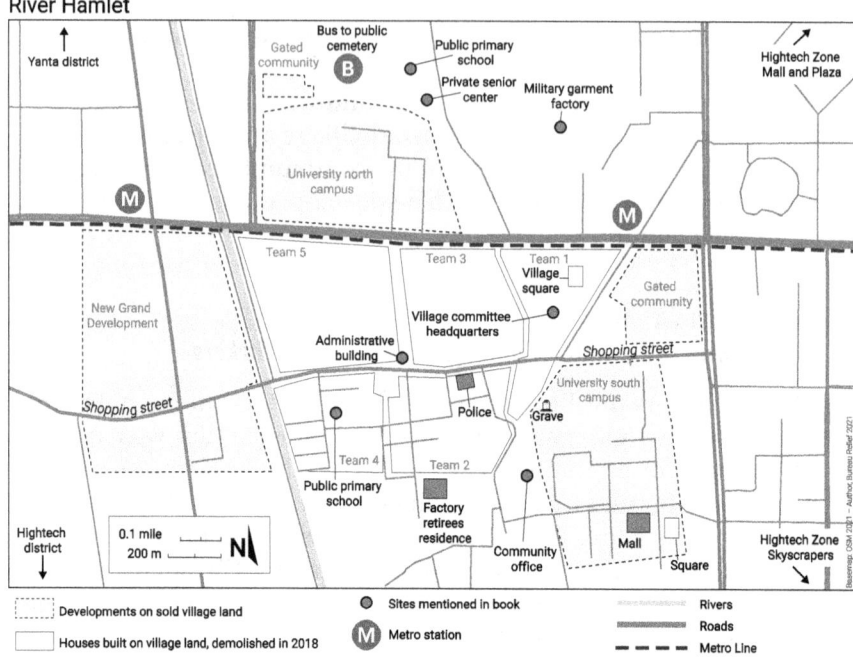

Map 1.7. River Hamlet, Xi'an. © Bureau Relief.

After it became an "urban reform village" (*cheng gai cun*) in 2004, River Hamlet's village committee gradually sold much of its collective land to developers for factories, colleges, a wastewater treatment plant, and metro and road construction. By 2017, some of the old village houses built on such formerly agricultural land had already been demolished. Although deprived of their collective assets, the villagers accumulated wealth individually from rent for well over a decade. Like the situation in a Beijing urban village described by Zhan (2018: 1537), "as the ordinary local peasants [had] little access to benefits from their collective land, they [devoted] all their money and energy to the informal rental business on their own housing plots." Ignoring state planning regulations, they rebuilt their own houses with six, eight, or even ten floors and let them to rural migrants; from former farmers they became the propertied rentier class.

While many of the elderly remained in the rebuilt village homes collecting rent on apartments, shops, and vending places in public spaces, most of the younger villagers purchased apartments in the commercial gated communities nearby. Not only younger native villagers but also many well-to-do migrants live in the gated communities on commercial estates, most of which are outside River Hamlet, because the apartments are of a higher standard and living in a gated community is a sign of status. Poor migrants rent apartments on the main street and in back alleys, where many run shops, restaurants, and hotels, which are often unlicensed.

Until it was fully demolished, River Hamlet was a paradise for many rural migrants who opened their first small businesses there, and for students and young graduates in their first job, attracted by the cheap rent and food, good transport connectivity, and general liveliness of the area. Students and young graduates living in precarious conditions have become popularly known as "ant tribes" (*yi zu*) after Beijing professor Lian Si (2009) coined this term to describe the ways in which these hardworking yet underpaid young people congregate in urban villages. Some urban villages in Shenzhen and Chengdu are likewise populated by large sections of young people, but this is not the case of South Gate and Pine Mansion, which are not close to universities and/or high-tech zones, and rather accommodate families with young children. The Hong Kong–based Phoenix Television station produced a 2011 documentary series on the young residents of Xi'an's urban villages.[29] One of these was a college student who tutored computer graphics students part-time to help with his daily expenses and his own tuition. He lived in a six-story self-constructed building with a view of a new high-rise building under construction. He had come from a very poor village, and his dream was to finally leave rural life behind and start a family in the city with his girlfriend.

Mrs. Cheng, the owner of a handmade jewelry business, had arrived in Xi'an in 2001 at the age of just nineteen from the neighboring Shanxi Province. For several years she had rented, from the small village committee, sidewalk space on which she set up a tiny makeshift table to show her elegantly crafted handmade bracelets, necklaces, and earrings. When Wang Bo met her, she was renting a shop on the main street, still from the small village committee. She rejoiced: "You never have to worry about a lack of customers, they come to you in their hundreds every day."[30] She noted that if she had not been willing to pay the rent for the sidewalk, another vendor would have been quick to take her spot. With business that good, living in precarious conditions and paying the native villagers for the use of a piece of public space was tolerable.

Besides the native villagers and rural migrants, River Hamlet's population included a few dozen long-term urban *hukou* holders. They had been workers in the formerly state-owned military garment factory (see map 1.7) before migrating to Xi'an in the 1940s and 1950s, and were among the minority who had transferred their rural *hukou* to urban *hukou* under Mao. Now retired, and some of them very old, they still lived in several factory dormitories that had been left standing, although the factories are no longer in use. The dormitories they used to live in are still unofficially considered to belong to them, both in their own eyes and in those of the government. They were quite isolated and did not socialize with the elderly native villagers.[31]

Of the three cases, River Hamlet conforms best to the negative image of the *chengzhongcun*, villages-in-the-city, as chaotic, unruly, crime-ridden areas. Its thriving informal economy was connected to the existence of gangs involved in sex trafficking and other illegal activities. Indeed, local scholars have commented on the vibrant "gray economy" in these locations, "gray" signifying tax evasion and illegal activities such as gangs and prostitution (He et al. 2012). Police cars patrolled River Hamlet after dark, and gamblers hid their money away before the police arrived. At night the back alleys were lit by the red lights of brothels, from which prostitutes beckoned to potential clients. Despite its rougher side, River Hamlet was popular among many newcomers, who affectionately called it Little Hong Kong, referring to the vibrant yet violent city depicted in the movies they had grown up watching. River Hamlet's violent and insecure atmosphere increased when the municipal authorities announced its full-scale demolition and replacement with plazas and high-rises (see chapter 2). The state-run media justified the demolition by depicting the urbanized village as overrun with vicious criminals and riddled with security concerns.

Administrative Arrangements and Welfare Provision

Administrative urbanization entails a loss of power for village inhabitants. The village committees (*cunweihui*), autonomous mass organizations via which villagers manage their own affairs and meet their own needs, are not part of the state apparatus.[32] Once a village becomes an urban jurisdiction, its committees are replaced by residents' committees (*juweihui*), which, however, have much less say in their community's affairs as community management falls to the new *shequ* office. Communities (*shequ*) are the lowest level of governance in urban China, with a hybrid position at the intersection of administrative power and civil society organizations (Derleth and Koldyk 2004; Ngeow 2011; Heberer and Göbel 2013; Audin 2017). They are governed by the higher-level subdistrict ("street") office (*jiedao banshichu*), which is under the jurisdiction of the district (*qu*), itself directly answering to the city administration (*shi*).

In the collectivist era, the production brigade provided the disabled and the elderly, especially those lacking familial support, with material assistance known as the "five guarantees" (*wubao*), which consisted of food, clothing, medical care, housing, and funeral services. The collectives also funded a cooperative medical scheme (CMS) for agricultural workers. Both systems fell apart following decollectivization (Duckett 2011; Qian and Blomqvist 2014). Although health and social insurance have been extended since 2003 with the goal of universal coverage, this was based on a strategy of "stratified expansion" (Huang 2020: 42). The CMS was replaced by the New Rural Cooperative Medical Scheme (NRCMS) in 2003, and new funding mechanisms for the Five Guarantees were established in 2006.[33] From 2009, a New Rural Pension Scheme (NRPS), based on both individual contributions and government subsidies, was gradually extended (Frazier 2010; Zhang, Luo, and Robinson 2019) (apart from a pilot program based on individual contributions that lasted just a few years in the 1990s, there were no retirement pensions in rural areas until 2009). On the whole, rural welfare benefits were and remain generally lower than those paid to urban hukou holders, as many scholars have noted (Chan 1994; Cheng and Selden 1994; Selden and You 1997; Solinger 1999; Smart and Li 2001; Wang 2005; Zhang and Kanbur 2005; Wu 2009a, 2009b; Whyte 2010; Hsing 2012).

With urbanization (in 2004 in the cases considered in this book), the former villagers as new urban residents were to be covered by urban welfare benefits, i.e., the state should start funding retirement pensions and increase social and health insurance provisioning. The urban healthcare system, which was reformed in 1995, is managed by local governments and applies to all urban hiring units, including state-owned and private enterprises, government organs, and social enterprises (Wong, Lo, and Tang 2006). The Basic Health Insurance is composed of personal medical accounts (both the hiring unit and the worker are required to pay premiums) and local government-run socially pooled funds. Urban social insurance (pensions, unemployment subsidies), made mandatory in 1998, is likewise funded by multiple channels, and enterprises of all ownership types must contribute. It was only in 2011 that the inclusion of rural migrant workers in the urban social insurance system was mandated by the social insurance law, which also facilitates social insurance fund transferability between rural and urban jurisdictions (Shi 2012). Recent studies show that informal employment is becoming a more important factor than *hukou* in access to social insurance (Cheng, Nielsen, and Smyth 2014). Indeed, in recent years there has been mounting pressure from the central authorities on municipal governments to increase the number of *hukou* transfers, thereby further increasing the size of the population eligible for the urban public goods regime. Furthermore, the recent reform of resident permits aims at "promoting basic services and facilitating full coverage of the permanent population," including non-hukou holders.[34] However, its consequences in terms of access to urban welfare benefits for temporary residents are so far unclear.[35]

In general, China's municipal governments are inadequately funded to cover the number of public functions they are expected to perform. They resolve this contradiction by setting up elaborate points systems, as discussed in the first section, and by leaving village collectives or private employers in charge, resulting in inequality between the native and migrant populations. Of the three urban villages considered in this book, this is starkest in Shenzhen.

Powerful Shareholding Companies in Pine Mansion, Shenzhen

On April 1, 2004, Pine Mansion's villagers became urban citizens of Shenzhen; their *hukou* was converted from a rural to an urban one (a process called *nong zhuan fei*). Before that date, Pine Mansion had been administratively autonomous, run by the village head and village committee assembly (*cunwei dahui*). A twelve-year transitional phase saw the gradual transfer of power from village institutions, residents' committees (RCs), and the elected village head to municipal administration.

Urbanization has created a duality of power with increasing subordination to the municipal power hierarchy. Initially the locus of the new municipal power within the *shequ* was the workstation (*gongzuozhan*) (Zhang and Yan 2014), which, in the first years after urbanization, was ruled by the former village head, a Chen. When I (Anne-Christine) arrived in Pine Mansion for the first time, in 2011, he held the position of workstation head in tandem with the community's party secretary, a Huang (the main native minority lineage). The two positions were merged in 2012 and a vice-position was added. Huang became workstation head while remaining the *shequ*'s party secretary, and was reappointed to this double position in 2013, with a native Chen in his forties as vice-head and vice-secretary. In 2017 the latter was appointed workstation head and party secretary while Huang was elected as head of the large shareholding company (see below). In short, the main leadership positions of party vice-secretary, community center head and vice-head, and head of the large shareholding company rotate among the same native villagers.

In 2016 the transitional phase came to an end, and the workstation was renamed the Community Party Service Center for the Masses (*shequ dangqun fuwu zhongxin*). The community center employs sixty people in different departments: family planning, urban management (*chengguan*), social affairs; conflict resolution (*weiwen*), labor supervision, petitions, and "information" (propaganda), reflecting the mix of functions allocated to community centers (Xu, Gao, and Yan 2005). Chen Pine Mansioners head several of these departments, including the most strategic, social affairs and urban management, while other less strategic and more subordinate positions such as those of social workers appointed by the district are staffed by natives Shenzheners originating from other urbanized communities. The renaming of the community center signaled the beginning of a policy of charitable service and activities oriented toward the migrant population (see chapter 4).

The native villagers thus hold important positions in the community center. In addition, they govern two types of institution that represent former village power in the urban community: the Chen lineage foundation, discussed in the next chapter, and the shareholding companies and residents' committees. Pine Mansion's seven neighborhoods are covered by three residents' committees (RCs), one consisting of two small shareholding companies, and the other two comprising three. Mr. Chen, the head of a shareholding company and of an RC, explained that RCs have been marginalized (*bianyuan hua*), with "many of their responsibilities" transferred to the community center. In fact, the RCs' functions are nominally the same as those of the community center, but they have little in terms of resources with which to execute them. Until 2016 the RCs received subsidies from the district, including "vitality funds" for organizing activities and money to pay their employees' salaries. Funding now goes only to the community center (see Audin 2017 on a similar process in Beijing).

The RCs' functions have therefore been reduced to only "very small-scale things," as the same RC head explained, such as the delivery of tenancy certificates for native residents. Although the residents' committees have lost power to the municipal administration, their close links with the shareholding companies keep them running. All three RC heads (*zhuren*) are also elected directors (*dong-*

shizhang) of a small shareholding company.³⁶ Chen made it very clear that the RCs do not receive enough from the government to cover their needs, and therefore the shareholding companies have to make up the losses from their own budgets (Jiang [2005] describes a similar situation elsewhere in Shenzhen). They provide everything from office space to drinking-water fountains, and systematically appoint shareholding company employees to simultaneous company and RC positions.

The native villagers still enjoy considerable autonomy, thanks to the economic power derived from their collective land use rights. In urbanized Shenzhen villages, the former village collectives, which are now shareholding companies, are responsible for paying villagers' pensions and social and health insurance. This is the main change brought by legal urbanization: previously there were virtually no social benefits. Women aged over 50 and men over 60 now receive a pension of about 2,500 RMB per month from the company in which they hold a share. Wang Cuichun, who married in the village in 1972, lives with her grandson in a house in Xiangxi. She holds a company share, and her grandson has inherited one from his grandfather (her father-in-law). She emphasized that her retirement pension is higher than that of her husband in Hong Kong.

Pine Mansion's large shareholding company provides social insurance (*shebao*) and health insurance (*yibao*), buying them in and providing them directly to their shareholders or reimbursing those shareholders—mainly the self-employed—who purchase their own insurance. This phenomenon, which prevails in the Pearl River Delta, has been characterized as the creation of mini welfare states funded by village shareholding companies (Chung and Unger 2013: 35). In 2018, all-inclusive insurance (*zonghe bao*) covering health and social insurance cost the shareholding company about 900 RMB per person per month. The amount increases every year, accompanied by a gradual upgrading of the insurance coverage. None of the ordinary villagers know precisely how it works, and the shareholding companies provide very little information about the system.

Non-natives are excluded from this urban public goods regime run by the former village collectives. Of the seventy-five non-native non-*hukou* holders I surveyed with the help of a student assistant, a high—and probably disproportionate due to the way we targeted respondents in the public square—number (thirty-three) of respondents were over fifty years old; eleven said they were retired, but none received a retirement pension; some worked outside the home, but most (twenty-four) cared for their grandchildren (see chapter 4).³⁷

South Gate, Chengdu:
Serving the Middle Classes and Integrating Newcomers

Chengdu's approach to urbanization with almost instant large-scale demolition and resettlement meant that institutional transformation in South Gate village was also fairly rapid. Until 2004 the village was run by a villagers' committee with an elected village head and a party secretary, the latter often being the real locus of power. When the village became an urban community in 2004, the villagers' committee became a residents' committee, although the party secretary remained the same. No proper village shareholding company similar to those in Shenzhen was formed. However, after their resettlement, the South Gate villagers continue to receive small dividends of a few hundred RMB per year, much less than in Pine Mansion, from the small amount of real-estate income drawn from former collective land. The residents' committees collect rent from the shops on the ground floors of the relocation estates, where members of each production team are housed together. To this extent the residents' committees act exactly like Pine Mansion's small shareholding corporations, although they do not provide welfare benefits.[38]

In 2008 the relocation estates and some of the commercial estates were finished, and residents began to repopulate the area. A "Community Party Service Center for the Masses" (hereafter, community center) was built in South Gate, prefiguring the type of community center to be set up almost ten years later in Pine Mansion. The community center in South Gate is a composite unit that centralizes functions that in Pine Mansion are dispersed across the community center, the shareholding companies, and the RCs (and also, as discussed in later chapters, the lineage foundation).[39] The center has taken over even more functions from the RCs than that in Pine Mansion: it includes offices for family planning, social affairs, and conflict resolution, also issuing identification and household registration certificates for all inhabitants (a function of the RCs in Pine Mansion) and providing a clinic, a reading room, and meeting rooms and classrooms for various cultural activities and social clubs. However, unlike Pine Mansion, it does not include an urban management (*chengguan*) unit (see chapter 3).

The increasing population of South Gate community led to its division into North Gate and South Gate communities in 2017. Mr. Wang, a native South Gate villager who had worked at the original community center since its creation, was selected as party secretary to the newly created North Gate community. He lives in the South

Gate residential area. Mrs. Gu, a native of the nearby city of Chongqing who had been employed as a community worker in South Gate for two years previously, was appointed party secretary to South Gate community. Although Secretary Gu is not a native villager, she speaks the local dialect and understands village dynamics. Despite her dedication and qualifications, however, she is not well-liked by the former villagers, who compare her unfavorably to the North Gate party secretary.

Both party secretaries have master's degrees in agricultural science from Southwest Agricultural University, and both were fairly young at the time of their appointment, with Wang in his early forties and Gu in her late twenties. They combine an understanding of the communities' rural roots with a recent move to recruit more youthful and professional community workers. The new North Gate community center is located in the part of the resettlement estate allocated to the former Number 5 production team to which Secretary Wang belonged. The new head of the North Gate community residents' committee, Mr. Xu, in his late thirties and a former villager, has a university degree in design and worked in design before taking up his position in the community in 2017. While ensuring a certain amount of continuity in social organization, the new community centers mark the change from rural to urban life. In most villages the village committee headquarters are fairly functional, with meeting rooms, offices, and possibly a small reading room. The new community centers in North and South Gate villages are not only administrative centers but also active social hubs (chapter 5 and the conclusion).

Former villagers occupy a number of positions in the community center, and although the center is open to all, attendance is dominated by the native villagers, who generally express satisfaction with their urbanized living standards. As in Xi'an, their urban status allows them to sign up for a basic urban pension and medical and social insurance schemes, managed at the level of the subdistrict rather than by the shareholding companies as in Pine Mansion. It proved difficult to obtain precise data on social insurance during surveys of native villagers in all three cases, as many did not know how much they were paying or for which type of insurance. This was true not only of former farmers but also of older people who had previously worked in an urban *danwei* (a state factory or administrative work unit), who just said that the *danwei* took care of it.[40]

Most of South Gate's immigrants are middle-class white-collar workers and have earned or are in the process of earning local *hukou*; they sign up to private insurance schemes, or their employer pays for them. Some have come from other cities where they have access to pensions and insurance, while others are from the countryside, mainly in Sichuan Province. Many immigrants have brought their parents to the city with them to care for their children, and these often betray the rural roots that their children have escaped. Most of these elderly temporary residents with rural backgrounds have no pension.

River Hamlet, Xi'an: Dispersed Natives and Excluded Migrants

As in Pine Mansion, in River Hamlet the district government did not take over the village's land upon urbanization in 2004. Unlike in Pine Mansion, however, due to River Hamlet's transitional status as an "urban reform" village, most villagers retained their original rural *hukou*, and the village committee (*cunweihui*) remained in place.[41] This arrangement was an early indication that the district government was willing to impose change only gradually on River Hamlet. In the year it became an "urban reform village," the River Hamlet Village Shareholding Company was established, staffed with elected members of the village committee. Although it was modeled on Shenzhen's shareholding companies, its main purpose is to facilitate land transfers between the village and the district government and to distribute compensation.

The purpose of the River Hamlet shareholding company is not to finance welfare provision under an urban public goods regime, as in Shenzhen. The original villagers retained their non-urban *hukou* and were given shares in the shareholding company, which provides minimal social benefits. Rural status is desirable because of the associated use rights to collective land: those who change to an urban *hukou* lose these rights, and thus their shares in the company. Sometimes even when a household has bought urban property elsewhere, they have registered it in the name of just one of their adult children, so that the rest of the family can continue to enjoy their rural *hukou* and thus claim company dividends of around 2,000 RMB per year, as well as income from renting out their own real estate built on collective land. For elderly people, the informally employed, the unemployed, and children, who cannot obtain urban *hukou* via formal employment, their rural *hukou* is a source of income (on other similar cases of resistance to becoming urban, see Smart and Li 2012).

The River Hamlet inhabitants' welfare benefits such as free medical care differ widely.[42] Native villagers have two options: to register as urban residents without formal employment and receive the minimum medical insurance from the municipal government—not an attractive option, as it means renouncing their share in the shareholding company—or to register as urban residents and see the responsibility for such benefits transferred to the employer, an option that is attractive only for stable employees. *Hukou* holders receive full medical insurance benefits through their employers, as required by urban labor laws. The community center processes the benefit transfers from the government to employers. As of 2018–19, the monthly per capita municipal government's contribution to the city's minimum medical care plan (*chengzhen jumin dibao*) was less than two hundred RMB, reflecting the minimal care it provided, whereas the average amount paid by employers for "five insurances and one pension," *wuxian yijin*, the same as all-inclusive insurance, *zonghe bao*) was at least four hundred RMB.

Integration into the urban government scheme is the new policy, although its actual implementation is slow, as it requires putting demographic data into the system, which was still ongoing at the community center in 2019. This slowness is a source of concern for rural migrants who hold temporary permits, because they are not entitled to medical care for urban residents as long as their medical insurance cards are registered in rural areas of Shaanxi or neighboring provinces, leaving them the option of either attending the rare clinics and pharmacies that accept province-wide insurance cards or not being reimbursed for their medical expenses.

Elderly people who had lived in factory dormitories before River Hamlet's urbanization (see previous section) received benefits from the private contractor to whom the state's pension scheme had been sold when the factories were shut down. The contractor had to commit to pay workers an amount calculated based on the number of years they had worked before retiring. These state-guaranteed pensions were barely enough to live on, even in the inexpensive urban village, and feeling abandoned, retired workers vented their resentment of the guarantee system that had been such a source of pride and security for those retiring in the socialist era. Workers who had not reached retirement age when they were laid off had no option but to find employment with a pension and healthcare insurance.

From 2004 onward, the River Hamlet shareholding company, unlike those of Pine Mansion, gradually sold off the village's agricultural land to real-estate developers via of the district government. The transactions were rapidly completed to facilitate several major projects, including a university campus, a wastewater treatment plant, a riverbed extension project, and a residential development.

In contrast to Pine Mansion, there was a lack of accountability from elected leaders and a lack of solidarity among River Hamlet's villagers, who were strongly divided across and within the five natural villages. As Lily Tsai (2007) has demonstrated, there is a strong correlation between the presence of solidary groups, leaders' accountability, and the level of public goods provision (see also Song 2014; Zhu and Cai 2016). River Hamlet villagers elected ten representatives, two from each natural village, to sit in the village assembly. The competition for seats was fierce, because whoever was elected would have a role in shaping how compensation would be paid to individual native villagers and in negotiating with developers and the district government on the terms of their relocation.

Villagers complained that the transaction processes were opaque. Wang Bo found only one detailed account of how the revenue from a land sale had been divided among the villagers: in 2012 a large piece of land (540 mu) was sold to the district for 335,000 RMB per mu for the construction of a college campus. Each household received 300,000 RMB. Families with only one child or with two daughters received extra money to reward their obedience to the one-child policy, and the remainder was distributed among the senior villagers, comprising men over sixty and women over fifty. The land was sold to the college campus at a suspiciously cheap price, suggesting that part of the money was pocketed. A rumor circulated that the village leaders had exchanged land for promotion to government positions or other under-the-table favors. The rumor became a scandal in 2016 when a real-estate developer was exposed as the niece of a high official who had benefited from the sale of land. Worse still, not only did the below-market price resulted in the River Hamlet shareholding company making less money than it could have, but the A4 sheet that was posted in front of its headquarters, listing the financial records of the shareholding company, revealed that the company's finances were in deficit because it had invested poorly, including in illicit mountain villas that were demolished in 2017.

The tension between the villagers and the administration was high, exacerbated by increasing administrative intervention from above as a result of the village's urban reform status. The village committee kept regular staff in charge of party outreach and women's affairs—that is, party member recruitment and occasional checks on birth control. In 2013 illicit parking became a severe problem as migrants and customers parked their scooters in the village's narrow alleys, blocking the passage of former native villagers' cars when they visited their parents and friends in the village. The village committee decided to establish an office for the imposition of fines, thereby challenging the authority of the subdistrict and the police station, which was only fifty meters from the village office. The office was soon closed down.

Commonalities and Differences between the Three Urban Villages

The distinctive features of the three villages-in-the-city largely reflect the urbanization trajectories of the cities of which they have become part. This is particularly clear in the case of Shenzhen, a city whose growth owes much to the industrialization and urbanization of its constituting blocks, formerly rural villages. Although the core of Shenzhen has been partly state-planned and state-built, state investment, especially in the northern part of the city, which joined the special economic zone late in the process, has been almost nil until very recently. The urbanization of Xi'an and Chengdu has been planned and state-led far more than that of Shenzhen. Chengdu's proactive urban-rural integration policy and the voluntarist policy of the local state (the municipality), which saw rapid top-down urbanization with almost simultaneous rebuilding and the top-down resettlement of rural villagers, is quite distinct. While Chengdu's and Xi'an's authorities have made increased efforts to catch up with the pace of China's urbanization, Xi'an's River Hamlet has more in common with Shenzhen's Pine Mansion regarding the leeway left for former rural villagers to shape their urban village spaces.

Xi'an and Chengdu are more welcoming of migrants than Shenzhen, which has the highest proportion of migrants of the three cities, as reflected in the differences between the three cases summarized in table 1.2, below. Pine Mansion has the highest proportion of temporary residents. In all three cases, native villagers constitute a very small minority; the difference, however, is that in Chengdu's South Gate a large part of the incoming population is made up of white-collar workers who have been granted urban *hukou*, whereas in Shenzhen's Pine Mansion most temporary residents have their *hukou* elsewhere, although the proportion of *hukou*-holding white-collar workers is increasing. Xi'an's River Hamlet is in an intermediate position with an incoming population partly of new white-collar urbanites granted local *hukou* and living in the new gated communities and partly of blue-collar workers, small entrepreneurs, shopkeepers, and owners of small restaurants, most of whom are rural migrants, who were expelled in the winter of 2018–19 in a sudden crackdown on the urban village's informal economy (see chapter 2).

The three cases have all retained some form of collective social organization inherited from the Maoist rural past, i.e., the production groups and brigades, which continue to frame native villagers' sociability. This accounts for their enduring identification with "the village," in the sociological sense of a social collective that has its reference point in a given territory (Feuchtwang 1998: 48) and must be understood in the context of the villages having physically morphed into urban neighborhoods. In Shenzhen and Chengdu this sociological and territorial continuity is very strong, with native villagers coexisting on plots of land that they previously cultivated collectively, while in Xi'an they live scattered across the former village and on nearby new commercial estates.

There is an even greater contrast between the roles of the former villages' institutions. In Pine Mansion, the powerful village shareholding companies have retained collective use rights to former agricultural land, which they have converted to urban use. The creation of the shareholding companies with the village's urbanization has emphasized territorial bonds and given importance to the new social category of "native villager," which defines one who is entitled to a share of the shareholding companies and the welfare benefits that they distribute. These collectives coordinate their own projects and continue to subsidize residents' committees, although the latter's responsibilities have been partly transferred to the community center. In South Gate, all of whose land was expropriated early on by the state, the collectives did not become formal shareholding companies, and while the villagers had little say in the top-down urban redevelopment of their village, they did benefit from relatively good compensation and continue to receive dividends, the only remaining collective source of income being rent from shop spaces on the resettlement estates. Social welfare is distributed by the local state.

Xi'an is once again an intermediate case: the local state distributes basic welfare benefits because there is a lack of collective revenue, but villagers are strongly encouraged to take up formal employment in the commercial sector and move over to employer-funded pensions and insurance. Whereas, as in Shenzhen, individual villagers have until recently been left relatively free to run their own local informal rental economy, adding extra stories to their existing homes or building taller buildings in order to rent housing to rural migrants, there has been little collective organization at the scale of the former administrative village, with much of the former collective agricultural

Table 1.2. Summary of the main characteristics of the three case-study villages-in-the-city.

	Timing and Governance of Urbanization	Proportion of Temporary Residents	Power of Village Collective Economy and Persistence Village Institutions
Pine Mansion, Shenzhen	Gradual, bottom-up	High	Strong shareholding companies, weakened village institutions persist
South Gate, Chengdu	Strong, top-down	Low	Weak shareholding companies, village institutions dissolved
River Hamlet, Xi'an	Gradual, top-down	High	Weak shareholding company, weakened village institutions persist

land gradually sold off to developers, leaving villagers and migrants vulnerable to the sudden, brutal eviction that took place in 2018.

The next chapter discusses the recent redevelopment projects via which Xi'an's River Hamlet and Shenzhen's Pine Mansion are intended to catch up with model urban villages such as Chengdu's South Gate, and takes a closer look at the new urban public goods and what remains of the collective past.

Notes

1. Deng's frequently quoted slogan in the 1980s was, "Let a portion of the people get rich first" (*Rang yibufen ren xian fuqilai*).
2. The Four Modernizations (of agriculture, industry, national defense, and science and technology) were announced on 12–18 December 1978, at the third plenum of the eleventh Central Committee of the Chinese Communist Party.
3. New-Type Urbanization Plan 2014–2020, article 7, http://www.gov.cn/zhengce/2014-03/16/content_2640075.htm. China, 2014; China State Council, "Advice on

Further Hukou System Innovation" issued 24 July 2014, http://www.gov.cn/zhengce/content/2014-07/30/content_8944.htm.
4. The gap, mentioned in the introduction, between the urban population share and the share of the population holding *hukou* in a city has increased in ten years, between the two national censuses. In 2010 the difference was of 17.19 percentage points between the two, and in 2020 the difference had widened to 18.48 percentage points. In other words, the population of city dwellers holding *hukou* in the city where they live has grown more slowly than the population of city dwellers without *hukou* (Cheng and Duan 2021: 288). Moreover, although the plan's goal of granting *hukou* to an additional 100 million people has succeeded, another aim—namely, to bring down the percentage of the migrant population without access to urban social benefits from 17.3 percent in 2012 to 15 percent in 2020—has failed. This book explores some of the reasons for this failure, although more research will be needed.
5. In 2010 the Ministry of Urban-Rural Development published a "Development Guide for Urban and Rural Planning" outlining how provincial cities could strengthen their competitiveness by considering social, economic, and ecological development. http://www.gov.cn/flfg/2010-06/30/content_1641639.htm.
6. Note that a precondition is to have official registration, i.e., *hukou* and a birth certificate conforming to family planning policy. This excludes a significant number of the Chinese population who do not have official registration.
7. President Xi initially introduced the Belt and Road concept in 2013, expanding on the idea of the ancient Silk Road's trade route to strengthen the region's infrastructure and economy and connect China to Asia, Europe, and Africa. See Summers (2016) on the importance given to major urban nodes in this spatial configuration.
8. Chengdu bureau of statistics, http://www.cdstats.chengdu.gov.cn/htm/detail_180293.html. The resident population reached 20 million in 2021.
9. Chengdu Bureau of Statistics, 27 May 2021, http://www.cdstats.chengdu.gov.cn/htm/detail_385112.html.
10. Chengdu had already implemented a lowest-living-standards guarantee system for its urban inhabitants in 1997, which was extended to its rural areas in 1998. https://www.ucl.ac.uk/dpu-projects/Global_Report/pdfs/Chengdu.pdf.
11. "A Tale of Two Cities: Xi'an vs. Chengdu: Who Is the First City in the West?" *Research on City Industry Dynamics Blog*, 18 July 2019, https://zhuanlan.zhihu.com/p/74196256.
12. See this chapter, note 7. "The China-Europe Railway Line Chang'an Provides Substantive Freight Services," Xinhuanet.com, http://www.xinhuanet.com/2020-07/22/c_1126269690.htm.
13. Anonymous, "Douyin zhi cheng – Xi'an" [Tiktok city Xi'an], 10 June 2018, https://k.sina.cn/article_1887344341_707e96d502000aq87.html?from=news&subch=onews
14. "Xi'an: Nearly 3 Years after the Implementation of the New Household Registration Policy, the Average Age of the Registered Population Dropped by One Year," *The Paper*, 28 June 2019, https://www.thepaper.cn/newsDetail_forward_3789900.
15. Chen Jie, Li Zehui, Du Bohan, "Ten-Year Population Changes in "Double Ten Thousand" Cities," 20 November 2021, http://m.caijing.com.cn/api/show?contentid=4821585.
16. "The Main Data of the Seventh National Census in Xi'an Announced That the Permanent Population Increased by 52.97 Percent," 30 May 2021, http://sx.sina.com.cn/news/b/2021-05-31/detail-ikmxzfmm5628577.shtml.
17. Ibid.
18. Wang Bo, *Final Report on Fieldwork* (hereafter *Final Report*), 31 October 2019.
19. In 1958 the Great Leap forward introduced self-sufficiency and collectivization on a larger scale: that of the commune (*gongshe*). Each commune included an average of ten to twenty production brigades and one hundred production teams, involv-

ing about fifteen thousand people (Oi 1989: 5). Following the major economic and demographic disaster this caused, the communes were reorganized into small cultivation teams (*xiaozu*) that became the basic units of collective ownership and management while remaining under the supervision of the production teams and brigade. However, it was only in 1983 that government administration was separated from economic management (O'Brien 1994: 37; see also Shue 1984: 259). Administrative villages (*xingzhengcun*) then returned to the forefront.

20. The Hakkas constitute an ethnolinguistic group, but they are Han and do not figure among the official ethnic minorities ("nationalities") recognized by the Chinese state. Chengdu and Xi'an are located in provinces that have significant ethnic minority (not Han Chinese) populations, but these were absent in both South Gate and River Hamlet.
21. Eight *fen* (0.8 *mu*: 1 *mu* = 0.0667 hectare) of land were allocated per person. *Tian* land (as in *zerentian*) was for rice, and *di* (as in *ziliudi*) for vegetables, sweet potatoes, and sugar cane.
22. Although there is continuity between the lineage structure (its genealogical and territorial subdivisions) and the shareholding companies, lineages have not remained unchanged in the process of morphing into collectives under Mao and into shareholding companies today (see Zhao 2014; Zou 2014; Trémon 2022).
23. For more details and analysis of shares and the moral economy underlying their distribution, see Trémon 2015 and 2022.
24. Updated data were not yet available at the time of my last stay in 2018.
25. North and South Gate community websites, date, and link not disclosed for anonymization.
26. Jessica Wilczak, *Chengdu: Initial Assessment Report*, 8 April 2018, and *Final Research Report* (hereafter *Final Report*), 30 July 2019. The remainder of this section is based on this latter report.
27. See blog post by Fang Tianxia on *Baike Baidu*, 12 May 2019, "What's the Difference between Shequ Housing and Commercial Housing? Regrets after Buying a Resettlement House," http://baijiahao.baidu.com/s?id=1652047187009326504.
28. Interview by Wang Bo, 26 September 2018.
29. *Chengzhongcun Li de Qinchun* [Youthful years in the urban village] (2011).
30. Interview by Wang Bo, 5 May 2019.
31. Wang Bo, *Final Report*, 31 October 2019.
32. Article 2 of the Organic Law of Villagers' Committees (1987, revised 1998). Their full name is *cunmin weiyuanhui*. They have broad powers and limited but real autonomy from the rural township governments that sit above them (O'Brien 2001: 416). Elections were introduced to clarify the authority of village leaders (O'Brien 1994). See this chapter, note 20.
33. State Council, Regulations on the Work of Providing Five Guarantees, 2006, http://www.lawinfochina.com/display.aspx?lib=law&id=11892.
34. Article 1 of the Interim Regulations on Residence Permits, which came into force in January 2016, see this chapter, note 6. It extends the type of permit introduced in Shenzhen as early as 2008 to all Chinese cities.
35. The research project looked only at pensions and insurance schemes and did not include *dibao* (minimal living guarantee). For recent research on *dibao*, see Gustafsson and Deng (2011), Solinger and Hu (2012).
36. In recent years, the party-strengthening campaign has led to stronger control over who can be elected. All elected leaders must now be members of the CCP, and party branches must be established in each shareholding company. This caused the 2018 elections to be delayed because of the lack of party members in Pine Mansion.

37. I conducted the survey in March and April 2018 in Pine Mansion with the help of two students originating from Shenzhen. We conducted 126 surveys in total with 60 men and 66 women. Among the 51 natives surveyed, 9 did not hold local *hukou*; they had lost it after moving to Hong Kong and did not get it back when they returned after living there for several years.
38. Unless otherwise stated, this section is based on Jessica Wilczak, *Final Report*, 30 July 2019.
39. The actual term is Community Party Committee, Commission for Discipline Inspection, Residents' Committee and Community Party Members Service Centre (*shequ dangwei, jiwei, juweihui, he shequ dangqun fuwu zhongxin*). As this is rather cumbersome and does not reflect the wide range of services these centers provide, I simply call them community centers.
40. Jessica Wilczak, *Survey Report*, 19 January 2019, and *Final Report*, 30 July 2019.
41. Unless otherwise stated, this section is based on Wang Bo, *Final Report*, 31 October 2019.
42. Survey conducted between December 2018 and January 2019 by Wang Bo and two students; 163 responses were collected among 69 local urban-*hukou* holders and 94 nonlocals. Wang Bo, *Mid-term Report on Fieldwork*, 29 March 2019.

— Chapter 2 —

FROM VILLAGE COMMONS TO URBAN PUBLIC GOODS

As villages are made administratively urban, the paths by which public goods are provided are diverted from their previous grassroots organizations. The state takes over the provision of most social goods, previously provided by the villages themselves, in a process of transition from village commons to a state urban public goods regime. Legacies from China's collectivist era, notably its rural/urban dualism in matters of landownership and responsibility for providing public goods, shape this process. While they were classed as rural, village communities largely financed their own infrastructure and other public services, and this persisted when rural villages started physically urbanizing and even after they had become urban communities (*shequ*).

When villages are administratively urbanized, in theory they should be funded by municipal public finance because their collectively owned land, previously a source of revenue used to fund village social goods, is now state-owned.[1] However, due to the budgetary scarcity resulting from China's centralized fiscal structure and its downward devolution of responsibility for provisioning, city governments have limited means with which to compensate for land expropriation and finance urban public goods. City governments are responsible for financing over 80 percent of all government spending on social welfare and services, including healthcare and pensions (Wong 2010; Huang 2020). As there is no nationally standardized institutional process whereby local governments can obtain funding from higher levels, city governments end up passing the fiscal pressure even further downward, expecting district and urban community administrations to assume the considerable burden of providing services and welfare with inadequate funding.

One way out of this difficulty is to redevelop the villages-in-the-city. Redevelopment projects replacing former village houses or unplanned buildings with newly planned residential complexes generate funding for municipal governments from auctioning off land leases to developers, and income from leasing the land. This approach, in which existing buildings and sometimes entire neighborhoods are demolished to make way for new development, was common in many urban development projects in China at the turn of the twenty-first century (Wu, Zhang, and Webster 2013). Although it has come under fire for its harmful social and environmental effects (He and Wu 2005; Shin 2009; Ye 2011; Xie and Han 2014; Yang 2020), and measures have been adopted to guarantee better compensation terms and render the governance of such projects more inclusive (Ye 2014; Lin, Hao, and Geertman 2015; Lin 2015; Zhang and Tochen 2016), the practice remains widespread.

Such redevelopment happens in different ways and at different speeds, reflecting the differences across the three cases outlined in chapter 1. In South Gate in Chengdu, the local municipal government paid for the former villagers' resettlement while drawing tax revenue from new commercial estates built on leased-out former village land that was freed up by substituting village houses with resettlement estates. In River Hamlet in Xi'an and Pine Mansion in Shenzhen, partnerships with commercial developers save the government money, as they are responsible for compensating the villagers for their holdings. Starting in 2011, the former village of Pine Mansion in Shenzhen underwent the same kind of erasure as South Gate did in Chengdu, with the total destruction of the old village center to make way for a new urban environment. In 2018 the parts of Xi'an's River Hamlet that had not already been redeveloped shared the same fate.

Redevelopment projects are based on the expectation that rebuilding neighborhoods wholesale will purge them of their unruly landscapes and undesirable rural migrant populations to bring about well-functioning, proper urban communities inhabited by law-abiding and well-educated middle-class citizens. They rest on teleological imaginaries of modernization mixed with a form of social eugenics. However, such projects can be successful only with a certain amount of investment in parks, transportation, and schools to make them attractive to future buyers.

A focus on public goods permits examination of the entanglements, both collusive and antagonistic, between communities, the state, and capital (Kalb 2017: 70; Kalb and Mollona 2018: 9). This chapter shows how public goods provisioning is highly conditional on the path followed by individual villages-in-the-city; municipal authorities start putting their hands into their pockets only when the redevelopment plans are launched. Another less widespread but still significant means of triggering the transformation is for the state to expropriate existing village social goods based on village commons and convert them to urban public goods to create favorable conditions for forthcoming redevelopment projects. It also happens, however, that villagers manage to safeguard their commons by bringing them into at least apparent conformity with new urban public goods standards. Such strategies for commoning public goods require villagers to cooperate in ways that make them strong enough to negotiate with state authorities, as Elinor Ostrom's (2015) work has shown, or to navigate the gray zones of state policies.

As the previous chapter began to show, the stronger the village collective and the longer it remains in place, the greater its involvement in the provision of public goods, including welfare benefits, community office space and staff, and public infrastructure. More generally, in villages-in-the-city the endurance of communal village sociability and organized groups such as former rural collectives (cultivation brigades turned into shareholding companies) shapes the path of the statization of public goods provisioning. This chapter takes a closer look at this changed provisioning path. Susana Narotzky (2012: 78) defines provisioning as "a complex process where production, distribution, appropriation and consumption relations all have to be taken into account, and where history defines particular available paths for obtaining goods and services." This emphasis on the historically framed paths of provisioning lays the foundation for this chapter, which describes the transition from village to urban public goods. How are state public goods substituted for village commons? In this shift from rural to urban, what types of public goods are prioritized? What remains of former villages' social goods, and which new urban public goods come to the fore? What chance is there for ordinary citizens, including both former villagers and new inhabitants, to shape and make claims about which public goods should be provisioned by the state?

To answer these questions, this chapter first examines the changes to one of the most important village commons: collective tomb land. Burial sites are generally among the first targets of urbanization planning, and the land is cleared by transferring the remains of the dead to public cemeteries. The villagers of Pine Mansion and River Hamlet found different ways of coping with this state-imposed obligation. The second section follows this comparison with a close look at the urban redevelopment projects spearheaded by the two villages' local municipal governments. This was a far more cooperative process in Pine Mansion than in River Hamlet, not only because Shenzhen's redevelopment policy lends more importance to grassroots communities' agreement to such projects but also because Pine Mansion's preexisting commons created favorable conditions for the extraction and generation of exchange value to benefit the natives, the state, and the real-estate developer. I further explore this by turning to wet markets, parking space, and schools, typically new urban public goods catering for middle-class consumers. Examining the principles underlying decisions to privilege private or public provisioning, I highlight how local governments tune into and prioritize middle-class demands following a clubbing logic in which provisioning is graduated according to class divisions. In all, this chapter shows how graduated provision is differentiated along class lines and according to the evolutionary stage the authorities judge an urban community to have reached.

Circumventing or Coping with State Policy: The Expropriation of Tomb Land

The existence of ancestral tombs in urbanizing villages constitutes an obstacle to urbanization planning. China's exponential urban population growth and sprawl has led the state to generalize and speed up its nationwide funeral reform (*binzang gaige*), whose stated goals are to "eliminate superstitious activities (*mixin huodong*) in funeral customs" and to "build a socialist spiritual civilization." These goals have been on the Communist Party's agenda since cremation was established as a national objective in 1956, but under Mao it was mainly achieved in urban areas (Whyte 1988).[2] This reform is ideological, in line with the Chinese state's official atheism and condemnation of the superstitious beliefs and practices associated with burial. However, the timing of its implementation shows that it is mainly about freeing up land for economic development. The means are equally revealing: the state promotes the exhumation of remains and their cremation and transfer to large, state-run public cemeteries in hilly outlying zones. Although the state rhetoric considers the break from ancestral worship a necessary step toward proper urban behavior, it tolerates what it sees as superstitious activity as long as this is performed in the new cemeteries. These cemeteries allow a spatial economy of scale, as there is generally one cemetery per urban district rather than tombs scattered throughout the urbanizing villages.

In both Pine Mansion and River Hamlet, the relocation of graves was the most violent measure that the state imposed on the former villagers; by comparison, their own relocation to more comfortable modern apartments rendered the destruction of their old village houses acceptable. The funeral reform is itself based on a "violent abstraction" (Loftus 2015) insofar as it aims to replace burial places that are meaningful and crucial to communities' social reproduction with abstract, homogenous, urban space (Yang 2004). In the exhumation of the tombs, the violence of the land requisition was compounded by the violation of values fundamental to social reproduction across generations and beyond death. The reform clashes with the widespread principle that a deceased person must rest in the earth, as expressed in the phrase *rutu wei'an* (literally "enter the earth to [be] at peace"), and must receive postmortem ritual care to enable them to become a proper ancestor and not a hungry and potentially harmful ghost (Ahern 1973; Wolf 1974). In Pine Mansion and River Hamlet, relocation far from the village territory represented a threat, as the villagers worried that this would discourage their descendants from carrying out the necessary ancestor worship. The reform also goes against the idea that animates burial practices and ancestral worship rituals, namely that the ancestors can be all the more beneficial to their descendants when they are buried in sites endowed with good geomancy (*fengshui*). Ancestors who are properly cared for and receive regular ritual attention are expected to be benevolent toward their descendants and ensure their fertility and prosperity. It is therefore important to bury a dead relative at a propitious site whose geomancy will canalize the vital essence or *qi*, held in the bones, which is a source of vitality and fertility for their descendants (Feuchtwang 1974; Bruun 2003).

"The totalitarian impulse in China leads to ideological claims that the only soul that should be celebrated is that of the Party itself" (Kipnis 2021: 110). With urbanization, the Chinese state is becoming increasingly involved in the governing of funerary affairs. Yet as Andrew Kipnis (2021) notes, although unified state rule and total party monopoly of power are the political ideal, this is contradicted by various government departments and local governments pursuing their own interests. Native villagers in Pine Mansion and River Hamlet drew upon their former village-level social resources and called on government officials' shared cultural understanding to negotiate the transition from village tombs to urban public cemeteries. In Pine Mansion they mobilized to save their most important tomb, that of the ancestor who had founded the village, from destruction by building a mausoleum over the tomb and using legitimization strategies to make the mausoleum acceptable to the authorities. The former villagers of River Hamlet, however, had no option but to accept the transfer of their ancestors' remains to the public cemeteries, although some managed to take advantage of negotiations over a redevelopment project to obtain free transport to the cemetery.

The Pine Mansion Mausoleum: Commoning a Public Good

The Pine Mansion Chen lineage built a mausoleum around the tomb of their founding ancestor Chen Zhenneng at the end of the 1990s. At that time Pine Mansion was still officially a rural village, but Bao'an District, in which it was located, had been incorporated within the Shenzhen municipality in 1993, thereby becoming urban. This accelerated the urbanization of the rural villages that until then had been outside of the original special economic zone, which explains why, in 1997, the Shenzhen municipal authorities drastically implemented the national funeral reform regulations that had just been issued by the Chinese State Council. A decision was made to achieve 100 percent cremation across Shenzhen within ten years and to prohibit burial (*tuzang*). Moreover, the authorities ordered that all buried remains were to be exhumed and cremated, and the ashes scattered or stored at an official public cemetery.

Pine Mansion's tombs, like those of all the surrounding villages, were scattered across the hills around the village on land held in common by the collectives. The new municipal policy intended to concentrate all the dead's remains in one public cemetery per urban district, requiring the rural villages within Shenzhen to relinquish what the government saw as a waste of space. A government team came to Pine Mansion in 1998 to proceed with the exhumation, threatening that villagers who did not comply would lose their shares in their cooperative companies. I estimate that about a thousand graves were dug up and the remains cremated and placed in urns that were stored in the ancestral temple until the construction of the mausoleum was finalized two years later, when they were placed within it.

In 1997 a Pine Mansion Chen, a retired high-level government cadre, took the lead in the collective mobilization to build the mausoleum, using his connections in government, in the construction industry and among the overseas Chens. The latter set of connections allowed the speedy mobilization of the diaspora in Asia Pacific and Northern and Central America, and the swift collection of over a million RMB in a few months to build the mausoleum (see Trémon 2015 and 2022 for details). The cadre's connections—and, as he confessed, the bribery of district-level officials—ensured that the site was listed by the Heritage Bureau as one of Bao'an District's heritage spots (*wenwu dian*). This public recognition of its importance ensures its protection. It is worth noting that Pine Mansion is not the only Shenzhen village where an ancestral tomb has been accorded heritage protection, demonstrating that district governments have shown some leniency regarding such initiatives.

The mausoleum was a clever solution to a double challenge: to protect the remains of the founding ancestor, and to store the ashes of those deceased that they had not been able to avoid exhuming and cremating. It was built over the founding ancestor's tomb, keeping his remains entire and undisturbed; the aisles of the three-story building provide storage space for the funeral urns of the Chens and the non-Chens who also participated in the fundraising. The mausoleum is officially called the Pine Mansion Historical and Memorial Hall, although I have rarely heard it called by this name: generally the word *lingyuan*, meaning "mausoleum" or "cemetery," prevails.[3] The village leaders played with the official definition of "public cemetery" where the funeral urns were to be stored, cleverly dealing with the government authorities by using the gray zones and interstices of the funeral reform. As the reform commanded that urns be placed in public cemeteries, the community created its own. Allowing non-Chen native villagers to store their dead's funeral urns in the mausoleum prevents it from appearing to be a private family site.

The ancestral tomb and now the mausoleum are, with the temple, the locus of a collective gathering and annual sacrifice to the ancestor. The Chen lineage foundation (*jijinhui*), which draws an income from real estate initially built with overseas and Hong Kong funding, pays for lineage and village activities: the annual worship ceremonies and sacrifices at Chunfen, the spring equinox (20 March on the solar calendar), and the ancestor's birthday on the twentieth day of the ninth lunar month.[4] Each of these rituals is followed by a collective meal in which the entire lineage participates. The mausoleum also serves as a columbarium where individual villagers go to worship their personal ancestors, in contrast to the common ancestor, at Qingming, Tomb-Sweeping Day, on 5 April. On each of these occasions Pine Mansioners and visiting relatives from downtown Shenzhen and Hong Kong bring the urns outside—unless it is raining,

Figure 2.1. Mausoleum in Pine Mansion, Shenzhen. © Anne-Christine Trémon.

in which event the ceremony takes place inside the mausoleum—to perform the ritual offering of food and drink and to burn paper offerings of clothes, passports, and money. They also light firecrackers, in open contravention of the banners hanging in front of the building requesting that people pay "civilized" (*wenming*) respects to the ancestors.

The mausoleum can be regarded as a new village-level public good. The Pine Mansioners' success in providing this for themselves is clearly linked to the predominance of the Chen lineage in the village. The lineage structure not only fosters political unity (He and Xue 2014) but also is a powerful channel for maintaining relations with the diaspora overseas and in Hong Kong (Trémon 2022), and increasingly in downtown Shenzhen. This success can also be understood as resulting from the importance attached to the village as the place of one's roots in the context of Pine Mansion's long migratory past. This makes maintaining the village as an anchorage point for the diaspora essential, the growing trend of Pine Mansioners moving to Shenzhen and other major cities only increasing this need.

While in the past each family took care of its own gravesites, and only the maintenance of the founding ancestor's grave was financed by the foundation, the building of the mausoleum has required and entailed a communalization of management in a commoning strategy. The mausoleum's maintenance and management are ensured and financed by the lineage foundation, which allows all community members, including native non-Chens, to place the urns of their deceased in it free of charge. With the loss of autonomy brought about by legal urbanization, the Chen lineage foundation remains important in maintaining the village commons and creating new village public goods.[5] Pine Mansioners have thus created a public good for themselves that, while limited to native villagers, is more accessible than the official public cemeteries, which are hugely expensive, with an individual plot costing 100,000 RMB, plus 600 RMB a year in administration fees. Their creative use of the term "public cemetery" has allowed Pine Mansion's former villagers to mitigate the new state regulations and urban exigencies by skillfully commoning their own public good.

Negotiating Access to Displaced Tombs: River Hamlet

The funeral reform was mandated in Xi'an in the early 2000s but has only been strictly enforced since 2010. Xi'an's municipal authorities required that all remains in the urban districts be dug up, cremated, placed in urns, and stored in the designated rural public cemeteries.[6] Unlike in Pine Mansion, where the lineage foundation provided free space for urns, the River Hamlet shareholding company purchased a large area in one of the public cemeteries and sold plots and tombstones to individual River Hamlet households. The plots were expensive and the cemetery, sixty kilometers from the city center, is hard to access. Most of River Hamlet's elderly villagers do not drive, relying entirely on public transport, which does not connect River Hamlet with the cemetery.[7]

Some of River Hamlet's former villagers managed to negotiate a free bus service to the public cemetery. In 2015 the leaders of one of the village's neighborhood collectives (Production Team Number 5) were negotiating on a project for the redevelopment of land on the northern periphery of the former village, on which their original rural homes stood (see map 1.7). Negotiating over their compensation for this project, which entailed the loss of collective use rights to their land and the removal of their ancestors' tombs, the former villagers managed to add the condition that the developers pay for a twice-yearly bus service to the public cemetery. Since 2015 the native villagers have used this at Qingming and on the day of the Winter Clothes Festival on the first day of Lunar October, the tenth month of the lunar/agricultural calendar (*nongli*). This festival is popular mainly in the colder northern part of China, as the burning of colorful offerings of paper clothes is believed to keep the ancestors warm over the coming cold months.

The distance between the city and the public cemetery makes it barely accessible to the former villagers and thus not really a public good, as it excludes everyone without a car or a driving license. The transport service negotiated by the dispossessed villagers facilitated their access and smoothed the transition. During their negotiations with the developers, mediated by the district government, the native village leaders emphasized the traditional cultural ties that they had maintained with their ancestors and demanded that access to the public cemetery remain available to all. They proposed that native villagers from other nearby villages should also be able to use the bus service rather than reserving it for themselves exclusively—although the buses depart from the gated estate where they have been resettled (see map 1.7). The developers conceded to their demands. On the day of the first visit, three buses waited at the community gate. Some sixty native villagers, most of them elderly, got on the buses, appreciating the comfortable seats and the company of family and fellow villagers. They spent a few hours at the public cemetery buying flowers, burning paper money, and eating lunch together. Some attempted to burn paper money offerings but were stopped by guards shouting over loudspeakers, so they dumped the offerings on the garbage pile. When the villagers' allotted time was up, the bus drivers started hurrying passengers to get back onto the bus. Confused and lost, some frail elderly people just got to the bus in time for the return trip.

Paradoxically, as in Pine Mansion, this collective bargain resting on a public-private partnership increased the commonality of the villagers, who had previously visited their relatives' tombs individually. Another case of native River Hamlet villagers losing their ancestral land was a different story. In the center of the village, where many still lived, there was a small plot of land where some thirty tombs remained. The headstones were marked with names and dates, and one or two had elaborate biographies signaling the status of the deceased. In 2015 the subdistrict government and community office attached a notice of eviction to the iron gate giving access to this plot of land, requiring that the native villagers involved accept the relocation of the headstones and the tombs beneath them, with specific rules for compensation. The eviction notice regarding the tombs was reiterated from year to year until it was announced in October 2018 that the villagers would also be evicted from their houses. By April 2019 the demolition was complete, and the contents of the collective graveyard had been transferred to a public cemetery outside of the city.

The villagers defended their ownership of this plot of land, claiming that the ancestral graves were pivotal to receiving good fortune from the ancestral spirits. They attempted to resist the cremation of the remains, insisting that worship continued through the medium of the ancestral bones. Their claims were also voiced within a framework of a moral economy of relations with the dead and their postmortem reciprocal obligations to them. The native villagers insisted that they had received the land as a gift from their ancestors in the expectation that they would continue to worship them; the removal and relocation of the ancestral graves would disrupt this gift relationship and risk losing the ancestors' protection. In other words, they asked for recognition of the graves' significance in their own social reproduction.

The clearing of central River Hamlet was far more brutal than that of its northwestern part, and there was no room for negotiation (see next section). The evicted villagers now have to visit public cemeteries far away, using their own means of transport; they also have to pay an expensive cemetery maintenance fee, whereas in the past access to the village tombs was free. These two eviction processes occurred in River Hamlet only three years apart. Between 2015 and 2018 Xi'an saw a fourfold rise in the price of real estate due to urban expansion and development. This increased potential economic value accounts for why the eviction in 2018 was far more brutal than that in 2015. Furthermore, while the minority of relatively fortunate villagers had first been relocated to commercial buildings constructed on the land where their family houses had previously stood, those evicted in 2018 found themselves dispersed across the city, losing the territorial bond that is central to community life.

Urban Renovation Projects

This section continues the comparison between River Hamlet and Pine Mansion. In the redevelopment projects, whole areas of urban villages are physically transformed from village settings to urban neighborhoods with residential tower blocks and shopping plazas. In outlying villages on the rural peripheries of cities, the process of urbanization entails the city government's expropriation of village agricultural land for urban construction. The villagers are resettled elsewhere or on another part of their former land, as happened in

South Gate in Chengdu (chapter 1). Many central villages that find themselves engulfed by an expanding city core urbanize spontaneously (Shen, Wong, and Feng 2002), illegally building houses on agricultural land in the absence of formal land conversion. While such illegal de facto land use conversions are often legalized after the fact (Po 2012: 2018), they allow the government to impose redevelopment projects with compensation rates far below the market value of the land. This happened in River Hamlet, while in Pine Mansion the strength of the collectives, backed by Guangdong Province's policy on cooperative projects, gave the native villagers much more power to negotiate the deal and the terms of the compensation. He and Wu (2005: 16) note that in most cases residents are presented with a fait accompli in the form of a finalized redevelopment plan announced by the government and the developer. However, a more collaborative process prevails in Guangdong Province (Ye 2014; Li and Liu 2018).

During the transitional period following administrative urbanization, River Hamlet's informal economy was tolerated by the municipal authorities as not only a necessary evil but also a source of revenue. This very informality, however, was the reason the municipal and Party leaders used to crack down on the bustling urban village and the livelihoods of many of its inhabitants. During the short-lived period of prosperity that had arisen from the informal economy, the village collectives had provisioned certain types of social goods, including the maintenance of public roads, policing of parking, and a reliable public minibus service, all with little interference from officials and administrative bodies. In Pine Mansion the village collectives, mainly the shareholding companies, had long been providing their own public goods when the redevelopment project started.

Cracking Down on Counterfeit Goods and Unsafe Buildings in River Hamlet

Until it began in November 2018, River Hamlet's native villagers and migrants did not expect the district government to go ahead with the demolition.[8] This expectation may have been supported by the fact that they had received indications of official recognition of their thriving shopping street (see next chapter). Moreover, the special office set up in 2004 that turned out to be in charge of the demolition and redevelopment of River Hamlet was a temporary branch of the Gaoxin High-Tech Zone district government, three administrative levels above the village committee; the villagers may simply have been ignorant of the scope of the plan.

The Management Methods for the Reconstruction of Urban Villages in Xi'an (Xi'an shi Chengzhongcun Gaizao Guanli Banfa) were issued in 2007 "in order to promote and standardize the transformation of villages in cities, speed up urbanization, improve the living environment, and improve the living standards of residents ... in accordance with the city's actual conditions."[9] This decree established an office responsible for the management of the city's urban village reconstruction at the municipal level. While each district is responsible for the transformation of the urban villages within its jurisdiction, district-level urban village reconstruction offices "accept the guidance of the municipal urban village reconstruction office." In other words, this is a centralized, top-down process. The municipal urban village reconstruction office, in conjunction with the municipal planning administrative department, formulates a special plan for urban village reconstruction in accordance with the overall city and land-use plans. All urban villages within the second ring road are included in the urban village reconstruction plan, and those outside the second ring road are included after the district urban village reconstruction office reports on them to the municipal urban village reconstruction office and receives the latter's approval.

The redevelopment of villages-in-the-city that pose "hidden dangers to social public safety" must take place within a given time limit (article 9 of the Management Methods decree).[10] The district government used this provision to crack down on central River Hamlet in a way that left no room for negotiation and reduced compensation to the minimum. As noted in the previous section, one redevelopment project had already taken place in 2015 in the northwestern part of the village. This part of River Hamlet was very attractive to developers and new buyers due to the presence of a kindergarten and a primary school. The project was carried out with relatively good terms for the native villagers, who have received more than one apartment each in compensation for the loss of their own houses and the floors they rented out. In this redevelopment estate the underground parking is underused, because while households may own several apartments and their allocated parking spaces, many do not own a car.

Prior to the demolition and redevelopment of the urban village center—that is, the largest part of River Hamlet (map 1.7)—the municipal government had allowed an informal and barely regulated economy to thrive in blocks that had been built unofficially. Sales of counterfeit goods, which are very popular among urban consumers, had begun to mushroom in rural and county-town street markets, as well as in villages-in-the-city because of the laxer regulation and cheap shopfloors and street space. In River Hamlet, numerous stalls and stands occupied the sidewalks of the two-kilometer-long shopping street, reminiscent of the farmers' markets that the villagers had regularly attended in the past. The majority of the shops sold counterfeit goods or copycat (*shanzhai*) brands.

Xi'an's municipal authorities were ambivalent about this informal economy. They appreciated the economic growth generated, along with these enclaves' functional role in housing a large population of migrant laborers. Villages such as River Hamlet were providing inexpensive housing and livelihoods for migrants—generally rural blue-collar workers and starting white-collar youths—as they struggled to house themselves and their families. They referred to River Hamlet as inexpensive and welcoming. The hotels and apartments for rent offered subpar services at bargain prices. As they did not provide hot water, public bathhouses run by private owners were common. The lack of municipal guidelines on sanitation and construction codes contributed to the existence of piles of waste in the alleys and the tangled power lines lying exposed on overburdened trees.

There was no official public transport serving River Hamlet either. While the city-run bus system connected the major roads around the commercial street, it did not reach River Hamlet's shopping area. Instead, individually run tuk-tuks and fifteen-seater open electronic minibuses, funded entirely by the village collectives (former production teams), connected one end of the main street to the other, day and night. These served both the native villagers and anyone living in or visiting the neighborhood for the low fare of two RMB per ride, in this way constituting a self-provisioned village public good. Although a couple of minibuses broke down over time due to wear and tear, the system worked smoothly. The minibus drivers were paid and the buses maintained by the collective based at the headquarters of Team Number 1. Visitors often associated the experience of using this style of public transport with the unique village-in-the-city lifestyle enjoyed by River Hamlet residents. Some long-term residents living near the commercial street noted that "the minibus is where the city ends and the village starts." In the absence of state provisioning, the village's self-provisioned public transport benefited both the people and the local economy. Besides this, four of the five former production teams (see chapter 1) operated large public fields as parking lots, some of which included a car wash and repair center. This was a profitable business until the eviction.

From 2004, the year of administrative urbanization, the commercial landscape of River Hamlet gradually changed from shops selling

Figure 2.2. Minibuses in River Hamlet, Xi'an. © Wang Bo.

mostly counterfeit goods to upmarket shops selling more expensive products. Yet both old and new businesses were granted licenses by the local department of commerce for taxation purposes. Even the small businesses selling counterfeit goods were granted certificates and licenses by the district government, despite their obvious infringement of intellectual property. The subdistrict recognized the bustling food scene in the form of a golden plate with the inscription "Xi'an Good Eats Street" displayed on the wall next to the police station.

This legal gray zone resulted in a vibrant commercial and social space that delayed the demolition: as one commentator wrote, "The demolition of River Hamlet has been rumored for more than ten years. Yet more and more people have gathered here, and coupled with the development of the city, the surrounding area has become increasingly mature. Whether in terms of demolition costs or social stability, it is becoming harder to demolish."[11] "If it wasn't demolished then, how can it be demolished now?" was the question circulating widely among residents. However, the gray zone also ended up justifying demolishment of the area by the municipal government, which cited intellectual property infringement and violation of the building code. The lure of taxing small shop owners became less attractive in the eyes of the district authorities than that of taxing the mall established a few hundred meters east of River Hamlet, which had few customers. Therefore, the small businesses, even though they were paying taxes, began to be seen as a hindrance to larger-scale revenue-raising urban development. The prior recognition of the lively street market was forgotten, and the government used the presence of counterfeit goods, gambling, and prostitution as evidence of its chaos and backwardness. Once the benefits of the informal economy and unplanned neighborhood had dwindled, the district government showed little tolerance for them and launched the demolition. The demolition campaign was presented partly as a crusade against counterfeit goods, but mainly as the necessary removal of unsafe buildings that posed a fire hazard and did not conform to electricity and other urban building codes. Professionals in uniform showed up with heavy-duty mechanical diggers and scraped away the buildings in their entirety. The minibus was discontinued after the River Hamlet villagers living in this central part of the former village were displaced.

Xi'an's policy has been hailed as a model (*moshi*) for its highly effective citywide compensation scheme, with a single standard written into the urban renewal decree stating that the owners of all demolished buildings were to be fully compensated for the first floor, with a lower rate for any building space considered illegal, i.e., above the second floor.[12] As most of the remaining native villagers had drawn their main income from renting out the additional floors they had added, they lost their livelihoods. For example, Mrs. Li was born in 1947 and was native to River Hamlet. Her natal natural village was only a kilometer from the self-built house in which she lived with her husband. The house was conveniently located in an alley just fifty meters from the entrance of the main street, and she rented her apartments for less than the price of accommodation on the main street. All her relatives whose houses had been demolished in 2015 were living in gated communities. Her son and daughter both lived elsewhere in the city, visiting her and her husband occasionally. In 2018, with eviction orders issued daily, Mrs. Li lost her temper, complaining, "What I experienced when I was eighteen years old has come back!" She was comparing her situation with the Cultural Revolution (1966–76), when violence was rife.[13] She was also concerned about the personal safety of the two young female tenants remaining in her house. After dark they were followed and harassed by security guards. This became truly frightening once the powerlines were cut, leaving the village road in complete darkness. The two tenants finally decided to leave for elsewhere, and like other native villagers, Mrs. Li lost her rental income. In contrast to her natal family relatives, who had received a compensation deal that included several apartments prior to the inflation of Xi'an's housing prices, she was told that she would receive only a small payment. It was nowhere near enough, due to the soaring cost of real estate, to buy an urban apartment within reasonable distance of the former village.[14]

Cooperative Real-Estate Development in Pine Mansion

The shareholding companies of Pine Mansion finance welfare benefits such as pensions and social and health insurance, while the lineage foundation funds scholarships for young Pine Mansioners who gain a place at university. Both contribute to the Chen lineage's ritual expenses. Until the early 2010s, the former village institutions also financed village infrastructure including road maintenance, sewage, and electricity, as well as private security guards. Indeed, the main reason the Shenzhen municipal government refrained from taking over the collectives' land at the time of urbanization was so that they would remain responsible for providing public goods (Zhu 2004; Po 2012: 2841). Some Pine Mansion leaders made it clear that in some cases, their decisions to allocate money were responses to a lack of government funding. For instance, the newly appointed vice-head of the workstation, a Chen in his late thirties, explained that both the shareholding companies and the lineage foundation fund public facilities when the municipal government is slow to approve a request or lacks the resources to do so. In short, the collectives and the foundation co-finance public facilities in the absence of or to complement government funding. This has changed, however, over the past ten years, with increased government involvement and improvements to roads and public transport tied to the urban redevelopment projects.

The desire to build Shenzhen into a modern metropolis led the city government to include villages-in-the-city in their overall city planning. In March 2005 the Shenzhen government announced their reform, and the Shenzhen City Planning Bureau initiated the Master Plan for Villages-in-the-City Redevelopment (2005–10), followed by the 2011–18 and 2019–25 Master Plans.[15] As in Xi'an, village redevelopment thus follows a state-led paradigm (Chung 2009); it is planned by and through government institutions. This top-down perspective does not rule out community participation: in Guangdong Province, the Three Olds Redevelopment (*sanjiu gaizao*) policy allows villages to negotiate directly with developers for market-price compensation, and the village collectives thus work out tripartite deals with the municipal government and developers (Ye 2014: 134; see also Wu 2002; Hsing 2006).[16] According to the procedures adopted by the Shenzhen municipal government (cited in Chung 2009), the development of villages-in-the-city must be initiated at the community level through shareholding cooperative companies (*gufen hezuo gongsi*), the former rural collective units (chapter 1). The companies work on the redevelopment plans in close collaboration with the developer and district government. Over two-thirds of each of the participating companies' shareholders must vote in favor of the plan for it to be approved by the municipal government.

The emphasis on community participation in Shenzhen is not just due to the government seeking to avoid social conflict. In contrast to Xi'an, Shenzhen has a policy of legalizing illegal buildings in urbanized villages, triggering a large wave of further illegal building (Wang, Wang, and Wu 2009). Moreover, as the shareholding companies have retained the collective rights to their land, the redevelopment projects ensure the partial transfer of land use rights (*shiyongquan*) from collectives and individuals to the municipal government at little or no cost to the latter, because in such projects the real-estate developers assume financial responsibility for compensation costs. The land on which redevelopment takes place becomes state-owned urban land. This transfer thus takes place years after administrative urbanization, which in theory should have resulted in such a change at the time. The process of urban renovation is ultimately one of transferring land rights from collectives and individuals to the municipal government by way of a developer (O'Donnell 2012). The state benefits from such programs insofar as it takes over the use rights from individuals and companies and leases them to real-estate companies; in Pine Mansion, the district government will receive payment for the use rights at a rate of two hundred RMB per square meter, as well as future taxes from the real-estate company.

Besides the promise of financial gain from the rising real-estate prices and the developers' individual remuneration of local shareholding company leaders for their work in planning and in persuading fellow villagers to accept the compensation terms, the main means of pressurizing the shareholding companies to engage with the redevelopment projects was the poor state of their finances. In the wake of the 2008 global economic crisis, the shareholding companies saw their income shrink as a result of declining real estate rents, as many factories closed or negotiated discounts on their monthly factory rent. In Pine Mansion, as could be seen on the bulletin boards on the street in front of the office buildings, the shareholding companies were all in deficit except the larger, *shequ*-level company. According to an employee of the subdistrict collective property bureau in 2012, 90 percent of the 108 (11 large and 97 smaller) shareholding companies (*gufen gongsi*) in the subdistrict were in deficit.[17] The fact that their leaders owed their election to their largesse to shareholders worsened the small companies' financial condition, noted the same employee (see Xue and Wu 2014 for a similar situation in nearby Dongguan). In about 2010, Shenzhen's city officials started contemplating changes to the regulations governing shareholding companies to put a definitive end to what was left of the rural collective economy based on territorial and kinship ties. As I have shown elsewhere, the blame was put on the perceived traditionalism and backwardness of lineage ties, seen as contrary to Shenzhen's push for modernity (see Trémon 2015, 2018 for details).

However, the municipal and district governments did not reform the shareholding system itself but instead took measures to ensure that the companies reinvested part of their earnings in more profitable ventures by imposing the reinvestment of a minimum percentage of income in upgrading industrial buildings and by ordering industrial redevelopment, shutting down the old first-generation factories built in the 1980s and replacing them with commercial or residential real estate or more profitable high-tech industries.[18] This process is ongoing. The government uses specific funds to upgrade factories managed by small shareholding companies, and the redevelopment projects are a further means of reaching this goal.[19] The leaders of the shareholding companies have been pressured into engaging with the redevelopment projects to increase the companies' income and allow them to continue paying welfare benefits to their shareholders. This was clearly stated by several Pine Mansion leaders, heads of shareholding companies, and members of the lineage foundation. "Our task is to increase value as much as possible in order to be able to increase the level of welfare (*fuli*) delivered to our shareholders," one retired but still influential village head told me. Furthermore, there is a clear concomitance between these urban renovation and redevelopment programs and the local state's greater participation in financing public goods, thus alleviating the strain on company budgets.

Li and Liu (2018) argue that such projects do not conform to an "urban growth machine" model (Molotch 1976; Jessop 1999; Logan and Molotch 2007 [1987]). It is true that shareholding company leaders are under pressure to engage in such projects, a top-down dimension that is absent from the growth machine model, in which actors willfully coalesce based on their best economic interests. However, Jessop (1999) argues for retooling urban growth theories by bringing in structural constraints and state power: what we have here is a coercive growth coalition, led by the entrepreneurial state (see also Guo et al. 2018). Moreover, even if ensuring growth and generating value are meant to serve their community's welfare, this does not contradict the fact, further shown in chapter 4, that the company leaders represent the interest of the rentier class (native share- and property-holders) in driving up real estate prices.

Their central role in the negotiation process and their ownership of land-use rights affords the shareholding companies real bargaining power. Pine Mansion was scheduled for demolition and reconstruction in three phases: 2011–18, 2018–26, and 2026–34. The first phase involved three shareholding companies with use rights to the former village center surrounding the ancestral temple. It saw the tearing down of the village's old low-rise tile-roofed houses, which the natives had rented to migrant workers, and their replacement with three high-rise blocks of luxury flats, one for each shareholding company involved, that were completed in 2018. The first floor of each block is a commercial concourse, and each block will be partially topped with a roof garden. The redevelopment project also included the demolition of the first- and second-generation two-story factories concentrated in the former-village center, often beside the tiled houses, or their conversion into restaurants, lending them a postindustrial feel. New third-generation factory buildings have been constructed to replace these in the industrial zone on land owned by the larger shareholding company. The next two phases involve land owned by the remaining four shareholding companies as well as privately owned residential land, formerly collective land that was converted and distributed among native villagers in the early 1990s (chapter 1). By 2018, all the buildings in the remaining old and new neighborhoods, including those most recently constructed, bore the sign *chai*, signaling their imminent demolition, with the exception of a private kindergarten and two more recent factories.

Villagers who owned houses in the area scheduled for demolishment in the first phase had to choose between two options. Either they received financial compensation of 4,600 RMB per square meter plus compensation for their loss of rental income, the majority of these houses being the old-style ones with tiled roofs that were rented to migrant workers, or they could exchange their house for a future apartment, provided they were willing to pay for the extra square meters, as the new apartments are a minimum of 60 square meters. For a house with a tiled roof, or *wafang*, they received 160 percent compensation: that is, a ratio of 1.6 square meters per square meter.

Not all the native villagers are able to buy a house. There is a clear contrast between high-income earners, many of whom live outside the village and have been able to take out a loan to purchase the extra square meters (at less than the price set for second-wave buyers), and native villagers living in the village on lower incomes and still fairly well-off, but for whom the cost is too high. Mrs. Wang took the monetary compensation for the loss of her husband's old house, which she had been renting to migrants at one hundred RMB per month before it was torn down during the redevelopment of the village. She has no other rental income, having sold another building, which she had built for her son, to pay his gambling debts and possibly also her own. Some of the native villagers who opted for compensation considered it too low and were angry that the shareholding company leaders had been unable to negotiate a better package, accusing them of taking bribes of money and gifts from the developer to encourage them to accept the rate offered. Another reason voiced by native residents for taking the compensation rather than buying an apartment, besides not being able to afford it, was their loss of the right to use the land, which they resented, while the upper-middle-class buyers were confident that the state would never expropriate their property. On the whole, however, despite the anger expressed about the company leaders, the promise of increased dividends ensured that the majority voted for the projects. The exact percentage of land-use rights that the shareholding companies have retained with the redevelopment is unclear, as company leaders' answers to enquiries about this were vague and contradictory, but what is certain is that they will continue to earn a rental income from shops and restaurants, the area of which has been greatly increased by the operation.

Gentrified Middle-Class Public Goods

New urban public goods—wet markets, parking space, and schools—emerge from the gentrification of the urbanized villages, attracting middle-class residents who define themselves first of all as consumers and aspire to social mobility. This section shows how provisioning is graduated, and examines in what situations and according to what rationales the provisioning of these social goods is private or public.

South Gate in Chengdu embodies the authorities' ideal of a harmonious urban community populated by middle-class inhabitants, which was reached very quickly as a result of a voluntaristic policy of rapid demolition of former village houses and the resettlement of the native villagers who had lived in them side by side with the new middle-class incomers. Chengdu is distinct from Xi'an and Shenzhen in that its urbanization has been accompanied by significant investment in public infrastructure and service provision. It was in Chengdu that we found the local authorities most attentive to the needs of the community and most behaving along club-like logic (see introduction, "Clubbing and Commoning"). In an interview, South Gate's party secretary identified the wet market and parking as the community's two most pressing issues. On the one hand, some of the public goods that were previously central to rural peasants' livelihoods are still important, although their functions have changed, as in the case of the wet market, where the peasants used to sell their vegetables and now, as urbanites, they buy them. On the other hand, a need for new public goods reflecting new urban middle-class consumption patterns and lifestyle has emerged: parking space is a typical example.

Returning to Pine Mansion, its primary school, which has an excellent reputation, was one of the major factors behind why this community was one of the first urban villages in that area of Shenzhen to engage in redevelopment. Long self-funded by the local community and its diaspora, it is now funded by the provincial and district governments, which have invested in its extension. The school constitutes a major asset in the redevelopment project. This is an instance both of conditional provision and of how value can be extracted from a preexisting commons and turned into both a source of revenue for the state and exchange value for future apartment owners—middle-class native villagers and newcomers.

In Chengdu, the solutions brought to the wet market and parking issues, considered together, resemble Ostrom's (2010) notion of a "polycentric provisioning system," that is, a system of governance in which citizens, enterprises, and the state cooperate in the management of a common-pool resource at multiple scales within a metropolitan area. However, while wet markets are provided as part of a state system of supervised prices, parking space is delivered as part of the market system. In Shenzhen, the provision of primary education follows a mixed public-private model; but even when provisioning is public, as when the government disburses money to extend existing public schools, such extensions are tied in with redevelopment programs. Echoing David Harvey's critique of polycentric governance and its underlying clubbing logics (2012: 81–82), in both Chengdu and Shenzhen, these public goods are delivered to satisfy the social reproduction needs of the middle classes.

South Gate: The Wet Market

The South Gate website describes the community (*shequ*) as "having grown from a rural community more than ten years ago into a complex new community where urban and rural residents live together in a prosperous, inclusive, secure, and stable manner." A 2018 post from North Gate *shequ*'s website describes it as a "typical mixed community, in the process of transforming from a rural into an urban community."[20] Since urbanization, the community leaders have been working with the city to build a market offering inexpensive products in a move echoing the subsidization of food prices in urban areas in the Mao era. Access to a wet market can be a decisive factor in the value of housing in any urban Chinese community. Moreover, in a new urban community populated by residents with rural roots, the opportunity to purchase fresh, affordable produce is generally appreciated by those who attended the village or township markets in the rural past. When South Gate was officially urbanized in 2004, there was a wet market close to Goldshine Road, the major road bisecting the community. Today the only reminder of this is the South Gate Agricultural Market bus stop. In 2007 the market was moved to a new location on the opposite side of the road so that a commercial apartment complex could be built on the site. In 2017 the market was moved again, this time to a location south of the South Gate resettlement estates for former villagers, to make way for the construction of a public orthopedic hospital (see map 1.6). In 2018 this third site too was razed, the market vendors being moved to empty stores on the ground floor of one of South Gate's resettlement estates. Neither the vendors nor the residents of the apartment complex found this last solution satisfactory: the vendors were unhappy because they were paying higher rents than before, and the residents objected to the noise and poor sanitation associated with the sale of meat and vegetables. This sequence of moves suggests that the government was playing a game of cat and mouse with the market vendors, but in fact the opposite is true. Every move was facilitated by the community leaders and required negotiation with each of the small farming groups (*xiaozu*, subdivisions of the production teams) that held the property rights to each piece of land that the market occupied.

In the summer of 2019, North and South Gate each set up a temporary morning market on the squares facing their community centers, selling vegetables and simple food such as tofu and noodles. In North

Gate, this is a people's livelihoods (*minsheng*) project set up directly by the community (*shequ*) and benefits farmers facing financial hardship in nearby rural counties in Chengdu (see chapter 4 for livelihood projects). The relatively low prices also benefit the residents, making this morning market a real success. South Gate community is collaborating with the Yimin Vegetable Market Company, a state-owned enterprise, to build a new market using the same, yet again empty, stores. As a state-owned enterprise, Yimin's mission statements include public welfare (*gongyi*) and the people's livelihoods (*minsheng*). It works directly with local farmers, and collaborates closely with the city government, to guarantee food safety and prices. In 2019 there were around sixty such Yimin markets in Chengdu, with plans to expand to three hundred over the next three to five years.

These projects point to the government's active role in urban food supply on multiple scales. It closely resembles the state's monopoly of vegetable retail in socialist urban China (Zhang and Pan 2013), when wet markets, or *cai shichang*, were run by municipal governments as a public service. Most Chinese cities whose boundaries include wide swathes of surrounding rural land were largely self-sufficient in terms of vegetable production, with municipal vegetable companies managing their supply and distribution across the city. While most cities have since privatized these systems and lost their agricultural self-sufficiency, Chengdu has maintained a relatively strong local food-supply system (Lang and Miao 2012). The state has stepped back in recently to address food safety concerns and rapidly inflating food prices since the early 2000s (ibid.), the latter being a common complaint heard on the streets at the time of fieldwork.

South Gaters displayed an ambivalent attitude toward wet markets in the context of efforts to build a modern, "civilized" city. When asked directly where they preferred to shop, many survey respondents, even those in the lowest income brackets, answered that they preferred the supermarkets because the quality of the products is more reliable. But they are also much more expensive, and such statements were belied by the intense busyness of the vegetable stalls, particularly before lunch and dinner. The need for a wet market only became acute after South Gate's former villagers were urbanized, as previously many households had been able to grow their own vegetables. The new wet-market customers include residents of both the resettlement estates and the commercial housing complexes. It is a public space where all three groups—former villagers, low-income migrants, and middle-class urban *hukou* holders—congregate.

Parking in South Gate

Unlike the wet markets, the parking issue does not have socialist roots. When the area was urbanized in 2004, the developers planned for less than one car per household, but today most have more. The lack of parking is experienced most keenly by residents of the commercial housing complexes: apart from the large, recently completed Shanshang North and South Gate complex, the resettlement estates (*anzhi xiaoqu*) for former villagers are five-story walkup buildings with a much lower resident density than the commercial estates. Moreover, as the regulation of space on these resettlement estates is much less strict than that for the commercial apartments, residents can park aboveground inside the walled estate. This is not an option on the grounds of the commercial complexes, which are carefully manicured and regulated. Most parking is in underground parking lots built about ten years ago, when not all families had a car. The available space is for less than one car per household. With the rapid pace of economic development in Chengdu, only ten years later most households have at least one car, creating a severe shortage of parking spaces.

The space opposite the community center on the most recently vacated wet market site was temporarily converted into a rough parking lot with a toll gate, but this space was soon closed again due to construction. A green space beside the river (see chapter 4) is often occupied by parked cars, and when that is full, residents have to park on the street. The street spaces are managed by private firms on contract to the municipality. They are overseen by parking attendants, usually working around the clock in teams of two, carrying hand-held machines on which to register the arrival of each car and print out receipts for the drivers. They set up an area on the sidewalk with a large umbrella and an old sofa or chairs where they can rest, although they are generally busy registering cars as they arrive and collecting fees from the departing drivers.

The government had previously provided guidelines on parking charges in the city, including for residential and street parking. At the beginning of 2015, in response to a series of decrees issued by the National Development and Reform Commission, the price of residential parking in Sichuan Province was liberalized. In fact it is difficult to imagine how a free market exists for residential parking spaces, which are fixed in supply with few alternative options for residents. Real-estate developers in China often also operate subsidiary property management companies that maintain the buildings and facilities once the apartments have been sold. The number of parking spaces is obviously fixed to the initial design of the apartment complexes. They are either sold separately from the apartments or rented to homeowners, and the property management companies charge an additional monthly maintenance fee for them.

Here is where the free-market element comes in: homeowners' committees can choose the organization that manages their parking spaces, which can be the original developer/property management company or a third-party parking-service provider.[21] But the initial government announcement caught South Gate's homeowners' associations by surprise, and there was confusion about the legal ownership of different facilities within the residential complexes. Although the liberalization decree was guided by free-market ideology and its tenet that competition might lower parking fees, it in fact brought about widespread fee increases resulting in conflict. One resident reported that his parking fees had risen from 200 to 600 RMB per month in the five months following the 2015 announcement. Homeowners in Chengdu's Hongfengling community were informed that their parking fee of 200 RMB per month would rise immediately to 500 and eventually to 700 RMB. This caused the tension in the community to erupt so severely in street protests that the police were called in. After a series of heated negotiations between the homeowners' committee and the developer, the latter eventually lowered the price to 350 RMB per month.

As with the wet markets, parking was not merely a local issue. Yet unlike the price of food, a basic necessity, the government seemed reluctant to regulate parking prices, possibly in order to limit the surge in car ownership, but also because of the prevailing idea that middle-class citizens should self-organize in homeowner committees and pay fees for status goods such as green space and parking spaces on residential estates (*xiaoqu*). In Shuangliu County, where Chengdu's airport lies, abusive practices by management companies were reported in the *Chengdu Business Daily*. The management companies blamed the developers and said that they were only collecting fees. A staff member at the Price Bureau admitted the government's helplessness: "This is national policy. It's just the law of supply and demand. If there's no monopoly, the Price Bureau has no grounds for intervening in market behavior."[22] The same district, however, soon set up a tiered pricing system for parking in public space.[23]

In South Gate, community leaders worked with property management companies to devise various solutions. One property management company instituted an app that allowed residents with parking spaces to rent them to other residents or their guests when they were not using them themselves. But this was clearly not a long-term solution. South Gate party secretary Gu explained that community leaders have little influence over land-use planning, which is decided by the municipal planning bureau. "We can collect residents' opinions and make suggestions to upper levels," she said. "They don't require us to, but we do. And they don't necessarily listen to what we say."[24] However, in the context of community-building and the emphasis on urban communities' economic self-sufficiency (chapter 5), the community was eventually authorized to turn a plot of land earmarked for a public park into a parking space—an income-generating venture. Moreover, their primary mandate to prevent social unrest attuned the community leaders to their middle-class residents' claims.

Pine Mansion's Public School

Schools have become prized public goods that add value to urban redevelopment projects (Zhu 2002, 2004; Wu, Xu, and Yeh 2008; Xu, Yeh, and Wu 2009). Among all public goods, schools are often a key factor in making a residential area attractive to middle-class buyers, an education-driven type of gentrification and middle-class reproduction that Wu, Zhang, and Waley (2016) call "jiaoyufication" (*jiaoyu* means education) (see also Wu, Edensor, and Cheng 2018; Trémon 2023). This section focuses on the story of the primary school in Pine Mansion, Shenzhen. It is worth considering in some detail as the most striking example of a formerly rural village good being converted to an urban public good catering to the middle class, involving the extraction of value from a preexisting commons.

Since the 2008 nationwide abolition of all tuition fees for the nine years of compulsory education, all children, including migrant children, are entitled to receive primary and middle schooling free of charge. Before this, migrant children either stayed with their grandparents in their home villages or enrolled at private schools, for which their parents had to pay. Increasingly they are admitted to public schools, but these are often underfunded, and competition between schools has deepened the inequality between the wealthy natives and newcomers who access the top schools and the poor—largely migrants—who attend less-popular schools (Lan 2014; Zhang 2016; Dong and Goodburn 2020).

In Xi'an, River Hamlet's public primary school opened up to migrant children in 2010. The school is poorly funded, the resources allocated to it still based on the officially registered local *hukou*-holding population and insufficient for the needs of a larger population. Most native River Hamlet couples with children have either purchased or rented apartments in the catchment areas of better schools to secure school places; most migrants with less purchasing power do not have this option. In Chengdu, education is by far the most frequent topic of conversation among the middle-class mothers of South Gate's commercial estate. Many of these new urbanites expressed concern that allowing their uneducated parents to care for their children may harm the latter's development. Reassuringly, their children are able to attend the well-funded schools that have been built at the same time as the resettlement and commercial estates: Grass Cottage Primary School in South Gate community, and Riverside Primary and Middle Schools in North Gate community (see map 1.6). Grass Cottage Primary School is a branch of the original primary school of the same name in the city center, which has an excellent reputation, rendering South Gate attractive to many young families seeking to buy an apartment.

Pine Mansion's primary and middle schools also have excellent reputations, especially the former, which has provincial status.[25] Pine Mansion's primary school was established by the Pine Mansion Chen lineage community in 1914 and upgraded later using income from several rounds of local and overseas fundraising. It was taken over by the Communist government after 1949, although the lineage village community continued to manage it. In 1987 a new call for funding was put out to the diaspora that enabled the construction of a new, larger school building. The school also resumed its original name (it is named after the Chens' founding ancestor, Zhenneng).

In 1997 the people of Pine Mansion heard of district government plans to close it and merge it with a school in a nearby village. When the Chinese state introduced reforms to expand and strengthen its educational system in the 1980s and then decentralized their administrative and financial responsibilities to local government, many schools were closed under a school consolidation policy in which local education bureaus tied investment in new facilities to the closing of small schools (Kipnis 2006). Merging schools was a way for district governments to save money through economies of scale and to meet municipal and provincial requirements and targets regarding school size and facilities.

Because the Pine Mansion school bears the name of the Chen founding ancestor and was built by their forefathers, the Chens and their allies found the idea of closing their school unacceptable and mobilized to defend it with an open letter of protest (*gongkaixin*) to the district government. The government gave the village a year to build a school conforming to the new higher standards; otherwise, the merger would go ahead. The village leaders appointed a preparatory committee (*choubei weiyuanhui*), which launched a funding campaign. In just a few months they had collected over 2 million RMB (Trémon 2022). It was only after the old building had been destroyed, the new school building finished, and the merger canceled that the municipal government and two state-owned enterprises based in Shenzhen granted the project almost a million and 700,000 RMB respectively, which were used to equip the new multistory building with multimedia teaching rooms, a library, a large dormitory, basketball and volleyball courts, football grounds, and even a ping-pong room.

The government had struck a sensitive chord with Pine Mansion villagers when they threatened to close a school that, while it had nominally belonged to the state since the early 1950s, they still considered lineage property. In this way the district government was able to compensate for its lack of resources by relying on citizens' private investment. The primary school was already formally a public school, although the village committee had been paying half the teachers' salaries. It moved up the ranking from a local school in 2000 to a municipal one in 2003, and, shortly after the village was urbanized in 2004, the school became entirely government funded, which allowed it to reach the highest level as a provincial school in 2005.

Today the school has over nine hundred students, only 10 percent of whom are the children of Pine Mansion Chens. Along with all public schools in Shenzhen, it was made entirely free of charge in 2015 and is now run by the district's Bureau of Education without input from the Chens. Most of the pupils are from migrant families who score sufficiently in the points-based system, which resembles the city's points system for accessing *hukou*, although it is a little less selective; points are earned by proof of a contract to work in the area, a residence permit, a certificate of housing in the desired school's catchment area—in addition to which the school place allocated to the apartment or house must be available—and, since 2018, the number of years for which the applicant has contributed to social insurance.[26] This excludes migrants who do not have a work contract, have a low-income job, or have arrived only recently.

Education is a type of good that may seem less conditional upon redevelopment plans than other public goods such as roads and public transportation. The Guangdong provincial government and Shenzhen city government have made concerted efforts to promote free public education over the past two decades. An increasing proportion of the city's public expenses is devoted to education, and the number of public kindergartens and secondary and vocational schools has increased. However, the number of primary schools has remained stable over the past three decades, in spite of population growth. This is due to the municipality's preference for subsidizing private primary schools and its policy of merging and extending public primary schools.[27]

The recent extension of Pine Mansion's primary school bears a close relationship to Pine Mansion's redevelopment and is a clear instance of how the government conditions the provision of public goods, in this case education, and its public expenditure on economic growth, principally through the generation of value derived from real estate (Trémon 2023). The school was one of thirty-five being extended in Shenzhen in 2018, all in redeveloping communities. The district government has spent 58 million RMB on doubling the school's surface area and increased the number of classes from twenty-six to sixty. On its completion in 2020, Pine Mansion's extended school had places for an additional 1,530 students.[28] A year after the village was urbanized in 2004, the district government assumed full responsibility for the teachers' salaries and the school's functioning and maintenance, and negotiated with the village collectives for the transference of their use rights to a piece of land adjacent to the school to the district's Bureau of Education as part of a plan for the school's future extension. Significantly, this was decided only after the collectives had signed the redevelopment contract; construction of the new building began twelve years later when the first phase of the village renovation was almost complete. The developer used the proximity and extension of the provincial primary school in sales literature illustrating the attractiveness of the future neighborhood.

In April 2018, a visiting UK emigrant who had been a major donor to the school in 1997 and his brother-in-law, the community-center employee in charge of social affairs, were discussing, over morning tea, whether this deal with the Bureau of Education had been a good one. They could have built factories on it instead of leaving the piece of land next to the school unused for so long, the UK visitor complained. His brother-in-law replied that this school was an important sales argument for the new buildings and raised the value of the apartments. Many locals have opted for apartments in the new buildings as compensation for their old houses, which have been torn down. In short, the school and its future extension were major factors in the price of the new apartments to be sold and the amount the developer would pay the government for leasing the use rights to the land.

Graduated Provision

The rationale behind China's urban redevelopment has changed from "the elimination of dilapidated housing estates as a means of social welfare provision to state-sponsored property development as a means of growth promotion" (He and Wu 2009: 291). Such urban redevelopment often involves local government and the private sector working in partnership to create prestigious urban spaces that tend to be too expensive for the existing communities (Zhu 2002, 2004; Wu and Yeh 2008; Pow 2009; Yeh and Wu 2009; Miao 2011; Ye 2014). While economic growth thus mainly takes the form of maximizing value derived from real estate, all three cases show that the maximization of real-estate value as an instrument for capital accumulation is linked to welfare and public goods provision in a mode of governance that ties the provision of public goods to the generation of value.

Provision is therefore graduated—i.e., differentiated—along class lines and according to the stage an urban community has reached in the authorities' evolutionary thinking, which combines civilizational discourse on the need to rid villages of their rural backwardness with developmentalist thinking in terms of value-generating potential. This combination is particularly visible in the way in which the funeral reform was implemented. The civilizational discourse legitimizes the authorities' aggressive policy of clearing burial sites and cremating the exhumed remains, although it is obvious that what is really at stake is clearing the way for urban development. The villagers' dead relatives, buried on geomantic sites that bestow good fortune on their descendants when they are ritually cared for, are transferred to state-operated, distant, and impersonal public cemeteries. While River Hamlet's villagers in Xi'an were only able to negotiate transport to these remote sites, the Pine Mansioners in Shenzhen found a clever way of maintaining their cremated ancestors' remains within the limits of their village territory, succeeding in commoning a public good and making it free and accessible to all native villagers.

Changing provisioning paths follow the pace at which urban communities are being redeveloped. The authorities allow unplanned urban villages' informal economies, which are mainly based on rents from real estate for native villagers and from small vending businesses for migrants, to thrive as long as they continue to generate value, but when this value drops below what could be expected from the surrounding city's real-estate boom, as it did in Xi'an, or falls due to the impact of the global financial crisis on export manufacturing, as in Shenzhen, they resort to the demolition and rebuilding of entire areas. This not only deprives migrants of their livelihoods and native villagers of their rental income but also puts an end to village public services and infrastructure, such as roads and transportation, funded by village collectives. The state then steps in to provide adequate infrastructure as a necessary investment to attract developers and new residents.

Graduated provisioning is perhaps best illustrated by the case of Pine Mansion's public primary school, which was a village commons until it was taken over by the state. State funding turned it into a public good, but a conditional one: access is open to *hukou* and non-*hukou* holders alike, but not to poor migrant workers, and the school's extension was conditional on the shareholding companies' acceptance of the redevelopment project. Graduated provision clearly prioritizes middle-class residents in a residential clubbing logic that privileges the idea of the self-governing middle class while tempering potential sources of social instability. This is most obviously the case in Chengdu, where the socialist tradition of regulating prices was reinvigorated to fund community-scale wet markets and guarantee affordable food. Yet the funding was implemented via a competitive, project-based system of allocating funds that sets communities in competition with one another. Before addressing this in chapter 4, chapter 3 takes a closer look at the relationship between urban redevelopment and governance through provisioning.

Notes

1. China's land ownership system defines urban land as owned by the state and rural land by collective units (see chapter 1).
2. The funeral reform dates back to the Republican era. In the 1930s the Nationalist government sought to replace the complex funeral rituals with the simple wearing of a black armband. The Communist Party continued and amplified this reform by requiring its members and ordinary citizens to simplify their funeral practices.
3. The same strategy was pursued with the Confucius Temple in northwest China, which is officially "a public site dedicated to cultural education" (Jing 1996: 64–67).
4. The Chen lineage foundation originated in Hong Kong in 1961, with Pine Mansion Chens who had fled the village during the Great Leap Forward, and was brought back to Pine Mansion in the early 1990s. Although unregistered, it is tolerated by the authorities due to its part in building relations with Hong Kong and the philanthropic nature of its activities, which its leaders emphasize, downplaying its role in ancestral rituals.
5. See Zhu and Cai (2016) on the role of informal institutions such as lineages in public goods provision in Guangdong Province.
6. Xi'an Municipal Funeral Management Implementation Measures (Amended in 2004), http://www.fsou.com/html/text/lar/172461/17246143.html.

7. This section is partly based on Wang Bo's draft paper for the panel on urban public goods at the EASA conference, "From Ancestral Tomb Land to Public Cemeteries in Urban China," 21 July 2020.
8. Unless stated otherwise, this section is based on Wang Bo's *Mid-Term Report*, 29 March 2019, and *Final Report*, 31 October 2019.
9. Xi'an Municipal People's Government decree, Administrative Measures for the Reconstruction of Urban Villages in Xi'an, 17 September 2007, article 1. https://baike.baidu.com/item/西安市城中村改造管理办法/532287?fr=aladdin. These measures replaced the Interim Measures issued on 4 April 2003.
10. Ibid.
11. Article on Fangxun.com, 2018, exact reference not given for reasons of anonymization.
12. The second floor was included in the "Rules for the Management of Urban House Demolition and Relocation in Xi'an City," Municipal People's Government, 21 April 2004, https://baike.baidu.com/item/西安市城市房屋拆迁管理实施细则/551220. Article 7 of the 2007 Administrative Measures (see this chapter, note 9) excludes the second floor. According to Wang (2008), one characteristic that, although present in other cities, is particularly strong in Xi'an, setting its "model" apart, is the important leeway left to developers by the city government. Wang presents this as a way of "reducing social problems" (2008: 47), because developers are thought to have more funds for compensating villagers for the expropriation of their houses.
13. She was not the only one. Several respondents to Wang Bo's survey made similar allusions to the Cultural Revolution. Wang Bo, *Survey Report*, 29 March 2019.
14. Wang Bo, interview with Mrs. Li, 10 December 2018.
15. The two latter Master Plans change the approach to a more ecological and heritage-friendly vision that avoids systematic demolition (see Du 2020 and Zhan 2021). Pine Mansion is unaffected by these plans, but note that the native Chens have been careful to protect their most valuable, lineage-related sites (Trémon 2022).
16. An example of Chinese experimental governance (Schoon 2014), this pilot program is based on shared interests among stakeholders (the local state, the market, and communities) who share the revenue generated by land transactions.
17. Interview by Anne-Christine Trémon, 9 July 2012.
18. This is known as the 6+1 policy of industrial real-estate upgrading. See http://www.sz.gov.cn/cn/xxgk/xwfyr/wqhg/20130118/.
19. The improvement in the shareholding companies' financial situation might also be due to the increase in capital resulting from the joint ventures they have operated with investors, offering low rents in exchange for a gradual transfer of capital.
20. References not given for reasons of anonymization. This section and the next are based on Jessica Wilzak's *Final Report*, 30 July 2019, and on the paper she gave at the panel on Urban public goods at the EASA conference, "Not Just Growth: Rethinking China's Urban Governance through Public Goods Provisioning," 21 July 2020.
21. Based on their shared interests as property owners in commercial housing estates, private citizens establish homeowners' associations. Many studies highlight how these necessarily involve some amount of self-governance and thereby challenge the authority of the residents' committees and subdistrict offices. However, the associations are not always successful in getting quality services in return for the maintenance fees they pay the private management companies, and in poorer neighborhoods, commercial property management often fails because residents do not pay fees—or have not set up a homeowner association. See Zhu (2007); Read (2008); Zhang (2010); Tomba (2014); He (2015); Wu (2018); Yip (2019).
22. Wang Chun and Fan Jijun, "Housing Estates New Parking Fares Have Been Released and They Have Tripled. The Price Department Recommends Using Contracts to Agree on Parking Prices," *Chengdu Shangbao* [*Chengdu Business Daily*], 8 July 2015,

https://sichuan.scol.com.cn/cddt/201507/10215901.html. On the parking problem, see also Anonymous blogger, "Chengdu Has the Greatest Volume of Commercial Real Estate, Parking Difficulties Urgently Need to Be Solved," *Weibo Keji*, 21 December 2015, http://www.parkbobo.com/front/news/1/29.html.
23. "Important! Shuangliu Parking Fees to Be Adjusted! Give Us Your Opinion!" *Kuaibao*, 11 December 2019, https://kuaibao.qq.com/s/20191211A0J83200?refer=spider.
24. Interview by Jessica Wilczak, 23 July 2018.
25. Guangdong's schools are ranked as local, municipal, and provincial according to their size and the quality of their infrastructure. Their ranking determines their funding, which varies according to the level of government providing it. Provincial schools receive local, municipal, and also provincial funding, and are therefore the best-resourced and most prestigious.
26. If the apartment owner uses the school place for his own child, it will not be available for the tenant. This generates conflict between many owners and tenants.
27. Following a model of mixed public and private provision that resembles that in the neighboring city of Dongguan (see Wang 2016).
28. Longhua District Development and Finance Bureau website, date and link not disclosed for anonymization.

— Chapter 3 —

CREATING VISUAL AND PUBLIC ORDER

Underlying the current teleological vision of China's urbanization-cum-modernization is the longer-standing notion of the threat of all-consuming chaos. Continuous action is required to subdue it and generate spatial order (Lewis 2006: 2).[1] Despite the overnight redefinition of villages as urban following an administrative fiat, the prevailing idea is that the process whereby rural villages are naturally absorbed into the city's forward march, leaving behind the undesirable chaotic characteristics of their rural past, will be slow. Urbanized villages have earned a reputation as chaotic (*luan*), insanitary, disorderly, and unsafe, perceptions linked to the stigma associated with their mixed population of former peasants and large proportion of floating migrants, and to the fact that they were initially excluded from the urban planning taking place around them due to their rural status.

Such village enclaves are thus considered transitional; however, their transition is hindered by a variety of factors. Since legal urbanization in 2004, efforts in Shenzhen and elsewhere have been directed at incorporating issues such as migrant control and public sanitation into the urban governance system (Chung 2010), not just on the city scale but also at the most local level: that of the urban community, or *shequ*. The slow and uneven pace of their actual urbanization further fuels the civilizational discourse, which continues as long as urbanized villages display characteristics of their transitional state, signaling the threat of chaos. The previous chapters have shown that this is particularly the case in Pine Mansion in Shenzhen and in River Hamlet in Xi'an.

This chapter explores infrastructure provision practices and the accompanying rationales by which local authorities attempt to achieve their civilizational ideal. It examines the role of public goods that are closely associated with the broader Chinese discourse on urbanization as a civilizing process: garbage disposal, electricity, sewerage, street lighting, greening, cleaning, and security to maintain order and resolve conflicts.

The focus here is on infrastructural public goods that create visual and public order. Although security may not appear to fit the usual definition of infrastructure, its implementation in China's new urban communities is performed by two units, the *Chengshi guanli zonghe xingzheng zhifa ju*, or City Urban Management and Law Enforcement Bureau, colloquially called the Chengguan, and the *Wangge guanli zhongxin*, or Grid Governance Center, known as the Wangge. These two units work together in close cooperation and with partially overlapping mandates. Both are responsible for maintaining visual and public order; while the Chengguan works by direct intervention, the Wangge applies a system of grid governance, a web of surveillance that is both digital and human. While infrastructural improvement is a goal within China's wider national modernization project, it is also an instrument for reaching another goal that the Chinese state sees as a high priority: the maintenance of order. Provision of the above infrastructural goods performatively shapes the new urban environment as a primary means of bringing the civilized urban community into being.

A substantial body of scholarship has devoted attention to the role of infrastructure in urban politics (among many others, Graham and Marvin 2001; Swyngedouw 2004; McFarlane and Rutherford 2008; Collier, Mizes, and Von Schnitzler 2016; Anand, Gupta, and Appel 2018). McFarlane and Rutherford (2008) call for a closer examination of political infrastructures, i.e., the specific ways in which infrastructure, and particularly sanitation infrastructure, matters politically. Historians have pointed out the close relationship between the broader project of modernity and the shaping of the modern metropolis. Public health and hygiene have been shown to be of particular importance to this project. Hygienism, which first emerged in urbanizing European and colonial settings in the nineteenth century, brings together concerns with order, policing, civic consciousness, and a particular kind of aesthetic.

Moreover, homogenous infrastructure was a historically important part of the modernist ideal of the uniform, spatially integrated, equitably serviced city, in which public goods were defined on the basis of nonexcludability and universal service obligations (Graham and Marvin 2001: 52, 80). In Western Europe and North America, privatization and reduced state spending, in contrast to state and municipal authorities' earlier universalizing commitments, have increasingly fragmented infrastructure since the 1980s, leading to "splintered urbanism." Enclaves such as business zones, technopoles, and gated economies in which the rich live apart from the poor concentrate investment in infrastructure that is disjointed from the wider urban fabric, creating urban "archipelago" economies (Graham and Marvin 2001; Swyngedouw 2004). However, the urban fabric has always been fragmented and urbanism splintered in many cities in the Global South (McFarlane and Rutherford 2008: 370; see also Gandy 2006; Coutard 2008).

In China the party-state upholds a modernist commitment to improve and provide equal access to urban public goods. Yet city infrastructure planning and resource allocation have mostly been carried out with little regard for the needs of many residents because only the de jure urban population is considered in budget allocation. This chapter further highlights the graduated temporality and spatiality of governance in Chinese cities, and particularly villages-in-the-city, which are seen as passing through a transitional phase. Paradoxically, to reach the modernist goal of the integrated city, some are singled out as "model villages" whose outward appearance is the subject of intense attention, as in the cases in Chengdu and Shenzhen discussed below. Because such model villages are supposed to set the standard for surrounding neighborhoods and illustrate governmental policy goals both visually and materially, infrastructural interventions in such cases are often designed to hide from view what is considered unseemly.

Examining the ways in which infrastructural public goods are provisioned as part of the civilizing discourse on urbanization requires a closer look at the actors in urban governance and their governing techniques (such as points systems of reward and punishment, house visits, and campaigns) and technologies (e.g., databases, and connecting or cutting off sewerage systems).

The points systems, house visits, and campaigns are governing techniques inherited from the collectivist Mao era, when members of the production brigades were rewarded for their labor in the fields with work points (*gong fen*).[2] The house visit (*jiafang*) is a monitoring method widely used by social workers and also by teachers, who visit their students' parents' houses (Bakken 2000). House visits were practiced under Mao during mobilization campaigns (Perry 2019). The political campaign (*yundong*) is a technique by which the party-state in the Maoist era mobilized a target population (cadres/intellectuals/peasants/the people) to perform political purges or to launch and apply a new policy (Hertz 1998). Campaigns are still widely used, with slogans remaining a central component (Trémon 2018); however, their political dimension has decreased, and their role in policy implementation, especially in aligning local officials' compliance and enforcement behavior with the regulatory demands of the central government, has grown (Zhou 2012; Liu et al. 2015).

Infrastructure is used as a technology of rule by, for instance, cutting off sewerage services or demolishing unsightly buildings to compel citizens to accept the changes forced upon them. Infrastructure can also be a technology of subjectivity (Ong 2006), insofar as its use in the production of a civilized, productive, clean, and healthy city drives the urban environment and the city's moral condition into relation with one another (Joyce 2003; Otter 2004.)

Such micro-infrastructural governing techniques and technologies are "micro" both temporally and spatially, as they can be decided and put into practice very swiftly, targeting specific locations. They therefore offer some flexibility and allow local leaders leeway in their use of them. When a change in policy is decided from above, campaigns quickly follow suit. Infrastructural upgrades in model villages, which are often experimental and ephemeral, can be used to stage adherence to upper-level government initiatives, in particular for the visits of higher officials, as described below.

The use of terms such as "technologies of power" and emphasis on their micro-dimension follow Foucault, but this chapter is also influenced by Laura Nader's view that we must study "invisible and visible aspects of power working vertically through institutions and ideas" (1997: 712).[3] The cases I describe display how governance is graduated; that is, constantly adjusted locally both to policies decided by upper-level authorities and to local authorities' vision of not only what remains to be done but also what can potentially be achieved based on the community inhabitants' "maturity"—their location in the evolutionary scheme of things. As a result, considerable variation can be found between both these urbanized communities and their subcomponent neighborhoods, although the governing techniques used are remarkably similar.

This variation is moreover situated within the same overarching framework of community-building (*shequ jianshe* or *shequ yingzao*), a concept that emerged in urban China in the 1990s at the same time as that of party-building (*dangjian*). Both are at times conflated as "community party-building" (*shequ dangjian*), revealing their close interrelationship. They were articulated as the CCP was transforming itself from a revolutionary to a governing party (Ngeow 2011), its market reforms resulting in the privatization and closure of many state-owned enterprises. Community-building was piloted throughout the country in the 1990s, and in 2000 a Ministry of Civil Affairs document announced that it would become national policy to "support and ensure the rule of law and the fulfilment of responsibilities by community residents' committees."[4] The main goal of community-building is to create self-governing communities (*shequ*); that is, to enhance their governability (Nguyen 2013). Communities are not expected to self-govern in the political sense: they are expected to act autonomously while still under state control (see chapter 4). Middle-class citizens are the primary targets and instruments for achieving this controlled autonomy.

Along with expanding services to people in need of social assistance, dealing with family planning issues, and promoting community culture, two of the community-building policy goals are the beautification of the community landscape and upholding the public order.[5] Public order and visual order are seen as intrinsically related public goods. Community center (*shequ zhongxin*), public order (Chengguan), and grid (Wangge) employees closely monitor both the population and the urban environment. They conduct swift infrastructural interventions, cutting off access or putting new facilities into place, and they discipline via reward and punishment. I first look at how the beautification of the community landscape involves achieving a clean, green, and sanitized community. However, even in the most orderly community, attention to cleanliness and order varies depending on the neighborhood's sociospatial characteristics and the timing of policies and mobilization campaigns.

As the next section describes, the Chengguan's sanitization and policing of the urban community entails eliminating everything it considers messy, disorderly, and escaping control, especially where a large share of the population consists of floating migrant workers whose daily activities, such as street vending, threaten to disrupt the community's visual order. In the most extreme case, cutting off utilities facilitates eviction. The third section deals with the Wangge's role in the surveillance of the floating population and in preventing conflict between migrants and the native population to secure social stability. I conclude, by closely observing what is lacking in a community, where problems might arise, and what is in need of repair or elimination, by highlighting how all these actors practice gradual infrastructural governance, a form of sometimes brutal, albeit finely tuned, provision in which both spatial and temporal flexibility are key.

Beautification and Cleaning Campaigns

This section looks at the civilizing discourse in cleaning and greening policies in urbanized villages. Cleaning includes both garbage collection and removing litter from the streets and sidewalks. Greening, consisting mainly of planting trees and vegetation along sidewalks, is tied to cleaning as part of the goal of an orderly visual appearance. None of the three sites participates in a green community program, yet greening is clearly a preoccupation.[6] The constant adjustments to the governance of the villages-in-the-city are clear to see. There is considerable variation in the degree of intervention depending on the prevailing housing system in Chengdu's North and South Gates, and on the timing of the ongoing redevelopment projects in Pine Mansion in Shenzhen. The fine-tuning approach to cleaning and greening moreover requires a flexible workforce, as illustrated by the case of River Hamlet in Xi'an where, in the absence of a clear division of duties between government units, workers bear individual responsibility for the community's outward appearance.

Chengdu's Park City Plan

Linking visual order with social order, a real-estate agent warned Jessica Wilczak not to rent an apartment in Benevolence Garden, South Gate's hybrid resettlement-commercial estate, because of security concerns there. He related a story about trees in a recently landscaped part of the estate being uprooted and stolen. "How can it be safe," he asked, "if they can even steal the trees?"[7]

Urban greening and beautification projects have become progressively more sophisticated in Chengdu since the city's development began to take off in the late 1990s. Public parks and urban landscaping are now no longer simple amenities or even markers of urban modernity but part of an overall aestheticizing of the urban environment intended to signal the city's postindustrial status, attract white-collar workers, and support competition on the world stage for "global city" status. In 2008, the city government announced a new strategic plan, the World Modern Garden City Plan (*Shijie Xiandai Tianyuan Chengshi Guihua*). The name of the plan refers to well-known modern garden cities such as Singapore, but also to the early twentieth-century British planner Ebenezer Howard, who envisaged a network of small, agriculturally self-sufficient garden cities closely connected to their rural hinterlands. Chengdu's Garden City Plan thus connected the city's urban-rural integration project with its efforts to compete on the global stage (Wilczak 2017). However, the plan, which was associated with Chengdu's ambitious municipal party secretary Li Chuncheng, was quietly forgotten when Li was investigated and eventually charged in 2012 under Xi Jinping's anticorruption campaign (Kuo 2019).

In 2018 Chengdu received a new direction from Xi Jinping when he announced on a visit to Sichuan that "it is necessary to highlight the characteristics of park cities and take ecological values into consideration." He proposed to support Chengdu's development of this new urban model. The term used was *gongyuan chengshi*, public park city. This was a clear departure from the garden city (*tianyuan chengshi*) terminology used in the 2008 plan. City planners in Chengdu embraced the new park city concept and set about developing what it might mean in theory and in practice. They published a book, *Park City: Theoretical Exploration of New Urban Construction Models*, and issued the Chengdu Beautiful Livable Park City Plan (2018–35) (Chengdu Planning and Resources Bureau 2020). In 2019 Chengdu held the first Park City Forum and released the Park City Chengdu Consensus 2019.[8] While planners and policymakers are still working on the precise content of Xi's park city, it is clear that in Chengdu at least, parks and gardens have taken on a new prominence in city building.

In South Gate, a high quality of visual public order is relatively easy to maintain. The extensive scale of the area's urbanization project meant that most of the old village buildings were demolished at the time of urbanization. The neighborhood is characterized by wide, tree-lined avenues flanked by modern residential complexes, with shops on the ground floors of some street-facing units. There is, however, a notable visual difference between the commercial apartment complexes and the resettlement estates for former villagers. Most of the latter consist of five- and six-story, sometimes rundown, walk-up buildings surrounded by walls. The commercial apartment complexes are in clusters of much taller buildings of fifteen stories or more, with elevators; in fact they are often referred to as "elevator buildings" (*dianti lou*) to signify their technological and commercial superiority. (Benevolence Garden, the hybrid resettlement-commercial estate, includes only elevator buildings.) Professional property management companies, many of which are subsidiaries of the development companies that built the apartment complexes, charge residents a monthly maintenance fee based on the size of their apartment to keep the grounds immaculately manicured. Many of the commercial complexes feature outdoor pools and underground parking. In short, they conform to the strict aesthetic regime described by Pow (2009) in the case of Shanghai's pristine middle-class gated communities.

Maintenance of the grounds of the resettlement estates is much laxer. Cars are parked aboveground, and residents hang their laundry, plant vegetables, and raise chickens in the common spaces. All the resettlement estate apartments are occupied by former residents of South Gate village, to whom they were allocated as part of their compensation package. Some rent rooms or whole apartments to newcomers, mainly migrants from rural areas, who do most of the vegetable and chicken cultivation. Initially, the South Gate community leadership (the former village head and villagers' committee) hired a professional property management company to tend the grounds of the resettlement estates, but the former villagers objected to paying the monthly fee because they had not been given their property ownership certificates. In the end, the community organized its own resettlement estate management system, paying a few residents in each complex to act as property managers. This creative approach to problem-solving and developing the capacity for self-government was an important factor in South Gate's status as a model transitional rural-to-urban community.

The other visual markers of South Gate's transitional nature are the open fields requisitioned by the city government upon urbanization, which remained undeveloped in 2019. Some have been auctioned off for commercial projects; others are earmarked for public infrastructure. Although they cover about a quarter of the total area of the two communities, they are not immediately noticeable as they are generally hidden by long walls, behind which is a patchwork of small, intensively cultivated garden plots where residents grow vegetables, turning the fields into informal community gardens. Gardeners manage their own space, sometimes erecting small sheds for tools and compost. There is mutual respect for the boundaries of each plot, and apparently little theft of produce.

A few gardeners are former South Gate farmers, but the majority appear to be recent arrivals, rural migrants from elsewhere and the elderly parents of residents on the commercial estates looking for a productive hobby. Many are former farmers. An elderly woman selling vegetables on the street outside of a commercial apartment complex was from a rural area in another part of Sichuan. She claimed that she lived with her daughter in the complex and grew and sold the vegetables "for fun." Another elderly woman busy chopping up greens in a field made the same claim. She was a Chengdu urbanite who had bought an apartment in South Gate for her retirement, and her busy tour and travel schedule meant that she often had to chop up much of her harvest for compost. Indeed, when Jessica Wilczak asked a group of retired women in North Gate community if they cultivated vegetables in the fields, they denied it vigorously, telling her they no longer needed to grow their own. Native former peasants conspicuously stated that they did not cultivate the fields, although some expressed a nostalgic envy of those who did, pointing out that the plots had been part of their former village land.

Signs in the fields forbid the burning of vegetable matter, suggesting that the *shequ* tolerates these temporary gardens as long as certain rules are respected. At the same time it is clear that these gardens will eventually be eradicated and are considered eyesores rather than resources. The new North Gate community center directly faces one such unofficially cultivated field. In early 2019 a decorative wall was erected along the edge of the field facing the center and lined with a long strip of closely trimmed sod and patches of shrubs and flowers. The field behind it, which remains unchanged, is thus hidden from view. One of the residents explained that the new wall was built for the leaders' visits. Official visits often determine the final outcome of a neighborhood's bid for elevation to model community status (Pan 2011: 171), but this status also sets the conditions for future visits. North Gate, as a model community, is a frequent stop for party members from across the city and the country. The informally tended fields are considered unsightly and no part of a model community.

Within the grounds of both the North and South Gate community centers, a much smaller formal community garden has been created for each community. In the community-building fever that began to sweep Chengdu in 2017, community gardens were a prominent feature signaling both a collective spirit and environmental consciousness. South and North Gate's gardens were described as a link to their agricultural past. In practice, though, they are maintained by one or two people hired by the community center rather than by collective labor, which would have provided a link to both past ideals and the contemporary community-building drive. A standard part of the tour of the North Gate community center includes a visit to its small community garden, which, as the secretary proudly announced, provides food for the community canteen (see next section). While this is occasionally true, the tiny garden, maintained by an elderly former villager, cannot even supply enough material for a single group meal at the canteen. More often the caretaker simply hands out the produce from the garden to friends and community center staff. South Gate's new community garden consisted of tidy rows of produce, each labeled with the name of the residential resettlement or commercial estate charged with maintaining it. The idea was that residents of the different apartment complexes would come together to cultivate the crops. Again, though, a general lack of interest in this initiative means that the vegetables are eaten by center staff rather than community members. Now many of these beds have been demolished to make way for a small building, where community volunteers occasionally sell potted plants. A sign on the front of the building proclaims that it is an environmental education center for schoolchildren.

Double Promotion and Rectification in Shenzhen

At the end of September 2015, Shenzhen's Longhua District launched a six-month "special rectification campaign" to promote better urban governance and improve "orderly management of the urban appearance and environment" (*shirong huanjing guanli zhixu*). In a revival of typical Maoist-style mobilization, as emphasized by the term "rectification" (*zhengzhi*), subdistrict (*jiedao*) cadres were pictured cleaning up a tract of waste ground while volunteers rode bicycles holding flags and banners and shouting through loudspeakers about this "double promotion." In Shenzhen double promotion (*shuang tisheng*) refers to economic and ecological improvement on the one hand, and improved government services and governance capacity on the other. The double promotion of urban appearance and environmental management is intended to "rectify all kinds of urban *chaos* (*luan*), improve the city's appearance and environment, and steadily promote the construction of a civilized city."[9]

This was part of Shenzhen's tremendous effort to regain its "civilized city" (*wenming chengshi*) status, which it had lost in 2013.[10] China's city governments voluntarily apply to be assessed for evaluation by the national Spiritual Civilization Development Steering Commission in the hope of being awarded the title of "civilized city."[11] The commission also promotes civic morality in urban communities (*shequ*) (Heberer and Göbel 2013: 64). Such civilizing campaigns (*wenming huodong*) are integral to community-building attempts to make up the spiritual and moral shortfall in society, and they create a sense of community by promoting volunteering and proper "civilized behavior" (Heberer 2009; Nguyen 2013) (see chapters 4 and 5 for more on volunteering). The title "civilized city" "refers to the city with a higher overall quality of citizens and a higher degree of urban civilization in a moderately well-off society (*xiaokang shehui*)."[12]

Shenzhen's urbanized villages were primary targets of this campaign, although the process of problematizing villages-in-the-city had begun ten years earlier.[13] Urbanized villages in Shenzhen were presented as "urban malignant tumors" (*chengshi duliu*) characterized by a "dirty, chaotic and inferior" environment (*zang, luan, cha*) (Chung 2009; Du 2020). There is a clear connection between urban renovation projects and increased governmental responsibility for the provision of public goods. Before redevelopment began, the village's public goods had been partly financed by Pine Mansion's shareholding companies and the local lineage foundation, but now, with the transfer of land use rights from collectives to the state, they are almost entirely covered by the government (see chapter 2). This change is not so much the result of a more stable and equitable mode of budgetary allocation as it is of the government raising the level of its provision of such urban infrastructure only when and where collectives agree to engage in a proposed urban development program. Since the start of Pine Mansion's redevelopment project in 2011, visible change has appeared: roads are in better shape; the quality of public transport has increased, with bus shelters and no honking signs erected at regular intervals along the road that services the newly built residential towers; police and street cleaners have increased in number; and the frequency of garbage collection has gone up. This greater governmental intervention constitutes an investment in infrastructure to attract real-estate developers who will get a better price for their housing as a result, and will pay the government use rights.

It is not surprising then that while many native villagers locate the change brought about by urbanization in the pensions and health coverage that they now receive, both former village and current urban community (*shequ*) leaders tend to adhere to the civilizing discourse: the urbanization started with the redevelopment of the village. When asked about urbanization (*chengshihua*) they refer to the urban redevelopment project itself or to the change in *shequ* management. This is due both to the improved delivery of urban public goods that accompanies the redevelopment and to the strengthening and rationalization of management, which they compare to the prior "chaos" (*luan or hunluan*). For instance, one shareholding company (and residents' committee) leader linked the redevelopment to the improvement of the road network. He characterized the urban village renovation (*gaizao*) policy as a major aspect of the government's work, which, he declared, is turning the area around Pine Mansion into Shenzhen's backyard (*bieyuan*). This seemed to give Pine Man-

Figure 3.1. The new residential towers, Pine Mansion, Shenzhen. © Anne-Christine Trémon.

sion's peripheral location a positive connotation: *bieyuan* is a literary term for the external courtyard of an official residence. However, both local and migrant inhabitants appreciate the effort being made to create a "proper" urban environment. Mrs. Zeng, a long-term migrant resident, noted that "since they have done the *xiaoqu* [the new residential complex] the environment has improved. They've repaired the roads and given the houses a facelift."

The temporal coincidence of the redevelopment programs and the municipal financing of infrastructure is perhaps best illustrated by the experiment with a new garbage collection system using underground containers. Burying the garbage not only hides it from view but also eliminates the foul odor that spreads through the streets, particularly in hot weather. These environmentally friendly, deeply buried containers were tested out in two of Pine Mansion's neighborhoods singled out as model villages. The containers were installed in August 2016, just after the collective that managed that part of Pine Mansion's land had signed phase II of the community's redevelopment contract with the developer (see chapter 2). The underground garbage-collection stations are equipped with a locking device and a GPS alarm that alerts the private garbage company on contract to the government to empty the tanks when the volume reaches a certain level. A newspaper article explained that installing the containers underground integrates them fully "into the urban green landscape, enhancing the image of the urban environment."[14]

In preparation for the visit of a high-ranking municipal official, the facades of these two neighborhoods' buildings were uniformly clad with black-painted panels and stylishly calligraphed inscriptions. The official was quoted in the media and the subdistrict party report, and by Pine Mansioners saying that this was one of Shenzhen's first villages-in-the-city that did not stink (*wenbudao chouwei de chengzhongcun*). Visual order is here related to the fear of the "contaminated city" (McFarlane 2008: 419) and the notion that offensive odors are not only unseemly but also unhygienic, as in the now obsolete theory of miasma that causally linked disease propagation with exposure to bad smells. I (Anne-Christine) was unsure about the system's environmental friendliness, which was flaunted in media and party reports. The garbage trucks are rather large compared to the lighter ones that collect garbage elsewhere. This partly accounts for why the system has not been implemented everywhere, as the streets in the former village area are too narrow for the bigger trucks. There is also another explanation for the system's implementation in only some parts of Pine Mansion. The main reason can be derived from the temporal coincidence between turning the neighborhood into a model village and negotiations on the next phase of the redevelopment project: to persuade the native villagers and developers to sign such deals, the government selectively pours money into infrastructure, such as these underground garbage containers, to make the place more appealing. The media coverage of this small-scale experiment was also meant to incentivize other *shequ* to invest in improved garbage disposal solutions.

Local leaders, although proud of their model community, were somewhat ironic about this "face project" (Steinmüller 2013). It was mainly a matter of appearance. They let slip some comments about setting up environmentally friendly garbage collection in Pine Mansion that were much less optimistic than the media and party reports, based on their view of their own native community's "backwardness": a young employee at the Chengguan office remarked that "Pine Mansion is just beginning to urbanize. It may be hard to hear, but here they're all peasants, born peasants. 'No matter what, I throw everything in the trash can'—there's no way to sort the garbage, so this [policy on sorting garbage] is not being promoted." He and his employer had been on a business trip to Zhejiang and found that it worked there: "Households have two sorts of bags, but these are

Figure 3.2. Street cleaners, Pine Mansion, Shenzhen. © Anne-Christine Trémon.

provided by the government, so it works," they explained. Still, they justified their pessimism with the explanation that because of its rural origins, Pine Mansion was not ready for such a new policy, and therefore there was no point in attempting to promote it.[15]

Some were even skeptical about the garbage-burying system itself. One employee at the Wangge office (see next section on grid governance) observed when his boss temporarily left the room that the underground system remedies the smell but does not eliminate the many piles of garbage that continue to be left beside the roads: "Just walk around, and you'll see them." His superior, Mr. Liu, was much more prone to stick to the official discourse about burying the garbage to eliminate the smell. Still, I could only agree with a non-native survey respondent and her female friends, who said that the environment has considerably improved over the past years. Large amounts of garbage used to be dumped directly on the street rather than in bags at designated spots, with some even thrown out of windows. Now there is a fine for such behavior, so the improvement is due to the system of control (*jiandu tizhi*), they explained. Another element almost everybody agreed on is that street cleanliness has improved. In 2018 street cleaners could be seen everywhere throughout the day. This was also the case in Xi'an.

Xi'an's Campaigns and Street Cleaners

The Xi'an Urban Landscaping Act (*Xi'an shi chengshi lühua tiaoli*) came into effect on 1 June 2014.[16] It stated that urban green space—parks, school and university sports grounds, the banks of rivers and lakes, and all green space on state-owned land—should be seen as a providing service to the public and overseen by local government with zero tolerance for illicit use, rent, or exchange. For example, Clause 27 of the act says that no individual or governmental organization should modify the purpose of urban green space, and any modification in the form of use, rent, or exchange must receive municipal government approval and be accompanied by a plan to reimburse the cost of creating new green space to compensate for its loss.

In recent years this greening campaign has converged with a project launched in 2006 promoting the city: Xi'an's "lighting-up project" (*dianliang gongcheng*) is an effort to beautify the ancient city wall, the Drum Tower and the Bell Tower in the city center, and the skyscrapers in the surrounding districts.[17] For example, roadside trees are required to be illuminated with patterns or Chinese characters representing things such as happiness, family, harmony, etc. Often flowers planted next to bridges and overpasses are spotlighted, and parks and public squares are illuminated.

Conforming to the 2014 Landscaping Act, the subdistrict (*jiedao*) contracted out the greening of the space surrounding River Hamlet to landscape companies that sent workers to trim the trees and bushes and remove fallen leaves and branches.[18] They were also expected to hang strings of lights and celebratory ornaments on the trees for the municipal beautification project. The landscape workers were predominantly males over age fifty, who had moved to Xi'an from rural areas in Shaanxi and neighboring provinces. Contractors paid them 4,000 RMB per month on average. They worked in groups, moving from site to site and project to project, often traveling to the current site in a small van with their tools, working for a few hours and leaving. Some were able to ride a motorbike to work with their tools strapped to the back seat because they lived nearby, and still others took buses. Little training is required for landscaping work; in fact most of the landscape workers had previously been farmers, but farming was no longer economically viable, the invested money and labor exceeding the value of the harvest.

Only days after his inauguration as the new mayor in 2016, Wang Yongkang launched a citywide campaign to collect dropped cigarette butts, which media and policy texts dubbed the Cigarette Butt

Revolution (*yantou geming*). Wang himself collected cigarette butts along the Xi'an city wall, a tourist attraction, creating a news story and propaganda for the campaign. The slogan "No cigarette butts on the ground, a more beautiful Xi'an" (*yantou bu luodi, xi'an geng meili*) appeared in newspapers and on street walls and banners throughout the city in an uncanny echo of socialist- and collectivist-era propaganda. The slogan was adopted by the city's district and subdistrict governments and the community offices.

During the 2019 period of fieldwork in River Hamlet, a survey respondent vividly recalled how the campaign, when it had just been launched and was at its height, had shaped her daily life: "We walked along the streets with our heads down, looking not at our phones but at the ground for any possible cigarette butts." The subdistrict office organized volunteers wearing red armbands to oversee the urban community (*shequ*), policing residents and visitors to make sure they threw their butts into the bins provided. Even though the Cigarette Butt Revolution campaign had waned by 2019, its impact on the appearance of the streets and neighborhoods was seen and felt by residents as they went about their daily lives.

The campaign lasted for three years, the entire term of Wang's mayorship. In April 2017, the Xi'an Municipal Management Committee (*chengshi guanli weiyuanhui*) published a policy titled "Xi'an Cigarette Butt Revolution and its Implementation."[19] The policy stated that each cigarette butt found on the ground would result in the deduction of a tenth of a point from the set number of points allocated for this purpose to each community, street, and district. The Xi'an Municipal Management Committee's official website published the names of the top and bottom three communities every month. District government officials would be questioned by the designated oversight committee as to why cigarette butts were still found in their administrative zones. In May 2015, during the pilot phase of this citywide policy, more than twenty government officials, including the party secretary and the deputy chief of Lianhu District, were under investigation for this. The municipal government of Xi'an carried out random checks for cigarette butts and other litter, which could result in a fine. The obligation to maintain a litter-free environment required each *shequ* to collect a certain number of cigarette butts. Schoolchildren searched street after street to complete their assigned quotas. A system for reporting people littering was set up in many communities. While the citizens appreciated the litter-free public space, they felt that the policy put excessive pressure on ordinary people.

In 2018 a street cleaner in River Hamlet had 900 RMB deducted from her monthly wage of 2,600 RMB because cigarette butts had been found on the 200-meter length of the busy street she was responsible for cleaning. Such intensive punishment of street cleaners sparked opinions among citizens who did not agree with making them responsible for the wrongdoings of random people in the public space. Already on a rather low wage, the street cleaners were forced not only to clean up after others but also to anticipate who on the street might drop litter and go chasing after them. Subdistrict bureaus set a strict rule imposing a fine of 1 RMB per butt found in the area designated to each cleaner. This could mount up to a large fine, and it attracted citizens' criticism.[20] News of the extortionary fines first broke in River Hamlet. Online and media criticism caused the district leaders to soften their approach, and they replaced the system of imposed fines with educational campaigns about the importance of cleaner roads to improve the city's image.

Nevertheless, the burden of cleaning the city roads and public space still falls disproportionately on the street cleaners, whose poor wages and working conditions already make their lives precarious. While this exploitation of the labor force results in a clean environment that citizens enjoy, the cleaners' very low wages and unstable employment conditions exclude them from obtaining urban citizenship and thus keep them on the margins of society. The usual wage is 2,000–4,000 RMB per month, and there is a wide variety of employers. Some work for Metro Line 3 on temporary contracts, wearing the metro uniform. They work in the underground areas, mainly cleaning surfaces, toilets, and stairs. Despite their more comfortable air-conditioned and sheltered working environment, their working day is often very rushed and stressful, with bursts of intensity at peak times. They are strictly managed and are required to clock in and out of their shifts. Their performance is regularly evaluated, and is overseen by the many surveillance cameras that prevent them from collecting and reselling recyclables to boost their income.

Street cleaners are also employed by the district government via contracts managed by middlemen. In a uniform with *Huanwei* (environmental sanitation) printed on the vest, they work in shifts on different road sections, cleaning the street and emptying the garbage bins grouped at intervals along the two-kilometer-long main street. While their working environment is harsh and challenging, their movement is fairly free, and they are less affected by traffic peaks than those working for the metro; additionally, although their wages are the same or lower, they are able to collect recyclables such as plastic bottles at the end of their shift to sell privately.

Many such informal recyclables collectors had operated throughout River Hamlet prior to its demolition. There were no garbage bins in the alleyways, which are crowded with restaurants and other businesses. People did not bother to put their everyday garbage into the bins on the main street, and open piles of garbage littered the pavement. Collectors pushed their three-wheeled carts through the alleys, picking up cardboard boxes, for instance, from convenience stores and shipping and distribution points.

Finally, street cleaners work for communities and businesses, often part-time. Most of these are responsible for the care of children or elderly family members when not working, and such part-time employment suits their need for flexibility. As middle-class residents in Xi'an have grown more comfortable with a service economy that hires street cleaners at low wages, it has also become common for them to book cleaners for their urban apartments on a weekly basis.

Visual Appearance: The Chengguan

The Chengguan is an urban management force that operates in almost every city in mainland China. Depending on the structure of the governance of an urbanized village, it may be incorporated within the *shequ* office or independent of it; in all cases it is subordinate to the office bearing the same name at each level of the municipal hierarchy. There is a Chengguan in Pine Mansion and South Gate; in River Hamlet, however, where the governance structure is still in flux, it does not exist at the local level. The Chengguan offices are charged with enforcing a wide range of local ordinances and regulations. Their main mandate is to regulate the streets and public spaces, but they also enforce city sanitation. They generally hire local *hukou*-holding men as a form of parapolice responsible for controlling street vendors, hawkers, shoe shiners, and illegal cab drivers. Misconduct by these informally hired and poorly trained Chengguan law-enforcement officers has triggered many protests in China in recent years, and they have been increasingly criticized ever since some employed bullying tactics that resulted in injuries and even deaths (Swider 2015). New administrative laws promulgated in 2017 and 2021 seek to reduce the violence and scandals by professionalizing the Chengguan force, improving their recruitment and training, clarifying the use of force, and heightening their accountability.²¹ The outbreak of the coronavirus pandemic has also prompted a change in their attitude toward street vendors following the central authorities' call for increased tolerance in the aftermath of the lockdown to fight rising unemployment (Zhou 2020).

While some cities have City Appearance (*chengshi shirong*) offices that are separate from the Chengguan, in our cases the Chengguan offices hold both mandates, revealing a continuum between the maintenance of order in public spaces, with a focus on street vendors, and the broader policy of transforming urbanized villages into proper "civilized" neighborhoods. The approach of these offices at different levels in the municipal hierarchy ranges from zero tolerance to a certain amount of leniency; in Pine Mansion and River Hamlet long-term leniency abruptly gave way to zero tolerance, while in South Gate the reverse has been the case.

Zero Tolerance in Pine Mansion

The extreme importance of the *shequ*'s external appearance was very clearly stated by staff of the Chengguan unit on the sixth floor of the community center (*shequ zhongxin*). The head of the Chengguan, a man in his fifties, and his assistant, in his thirties, are both Chens of the local lineage, born and raised in Pine Mansion. Asked what has changed since urbanization and Pine Mansion's incorporation into Shenzhen, the head started by mentioning the asphalt roads that have recently replaced the broken cement roads. He continued: "In addition to the roads, it is the community's appearance [he is an exception among native villagers as he uses the term *shequ* rather than *cun*, "village"]. Originally there were only tile-roofed houses here. Redevelopment (*jiugai*) has turned them into this type of commercial housing, and now these renovation projects are continuing."

Asked what the Chengguan is mainly responsible for, he answered "The appearance of the village (*cun rong cun mao*), hygiene, and urban facilities. All those sewers, roads, road hygiene, road maintenance, sewer maintenance, these are our responsibilities."²² Information about infrastructure and equipment in need of repair is sent to the office from the Wangge (see next section). The head of the Chengguan referred to this as the digitalization of urban management (*shuzihua Chengguan*): for example, if a Wangge team member finds a road damaged or a broken flowerpot, they take a photograph and send it in. "We have to process this within a certain time, for instance a day. ... We're responsible for its rectification on receiving this information, and we direct the tasks [depending on whether it's] water pipes, roads, billboards that have fallen off …"

One of the Chengguan's head obsessions and main purposes for the next few years is tidying up the water pipes and electricity cables that "make some villages look like spiderwebs" and "form a canopy over the buildings," he described with a sigh. These can no longer be seen in the model villages. Pine Mansion's Chengguan has already improved the situation considerably compared to the urban villages in the nearby city of Dongguan, or even in neighboring villages in Shenzhen, his assistant said. "In the past you could see wires hanging out of restaurant windows and factory walls completely covered with handbills. These can no longer be seen here." He added "There are no more untidy job postings or messy street vendors [*luan zhangtie luan bai mai*]." The two Chengguan staff repeated these statements several times.

The crackdown on "untidy" paper postings taped to the walls of factories and shopfronts advertising jobs can be explained by the community-building policy goal of promoting community culture. To facilitate the implementation of national "socialist spiritual civilization" programs, community spaces and resources such as billboards, plaques and columns are to be used to propagate a "healthy" and "wholesome" culture (Nguyen 2013). Moreover, eliminating job postings signals that manual laborers are no longer welcome: the jobs that used to be advertised were mostly for industrial workers in Pine Mansion's factories.

The Chengguan's measures to improve the urban appearance of the village are quite drastic. Pipes and wires are cut off or bundled. Digitalized city management helps to locate and remove postings immediately, and if they include a telephone number, the phone line is cut off pending payment of a fine. Street vendors are pursued and fined, and their vending carts are confiscated. The head boasted that the Chengguan is even stricter in Pine Mansion than in the urban villages in Shenzhen's core districts. Indeed, in other urbanized villages in Shenzhen there is a more relaxed approach to street vending, partly following the reaction to the bullying mentioned above. By practicing zero tolerance, Pine Mansion's community leaders conspicuously distinguish their redeveloping and gentrifying village from Shenzhen's inner-city urbanized villages, which have a very bad reputation.

Eviction by Shutting Off Utilities in River Hamlet

Since 2018, River Hamlet has been under the direct jurisdiction of the Gaoxin High Tech District Branch of Xi'an City's Management

Comprehensive Administration Law Enforcement Bureau, locally known as Gaoxin Chengguan. According to the bureau's official website, its main responsibilities include the appearance of the city (*shirong*), landscaping, parks and squares, construction waste, household waste, billboards, and outdoor lighting, with secondary responsibility for roads, bridges, tunnels, heating and gas, illicit construction, digital governance, and miscellaneous work in support of the party.[23]

River Hamlet's local residents had direct experience of the Chengguan's operations during the demolition in 2018–19.[24] The Gaoxin District Chengguan set up a station in River Hamlet prior to the demolition and hired squads of private security men in black uniforms. The Chengguan played an instrumental role in expelling not only illegal street vendors but also migrant vendors from their shops and native villagers from their houses. At the end of October, heavy trucks drove down the main business street with loudspeakers blasting out the message: "City announcement: all original villagers are evicted from illegal buildings and must vacate them, and all nonlocals must close their shops and move out." By early November heavy demolition vehicles were knocking down shops and houses. Security guards formed a wall protecting the operation as villagers and nonlocals cried, shouted, and protested.

In January 2019, two months after the demolition began, many of River Hamlet's villagers were still refusing to accept a relocation deal and leave their houses. Those who signed the developers' deal received cash compensation, and their names were posted on notices displayed throughout River Hamlet. The demolished buildings on the main commercial street and some demolished houses further into the village created an eerie atmosphere. Hardly any of the migrants remained in their shops except for a handful wanting to sell what they had left before returning to their hometowns for the lunar new year.

Local, mainly middle-aged and elderly villagers sometimes gathered in front of the debris to talk. They were cold at home because, unlike the urban apartments, the village houses had no central heating. The elderly were worried about the cold nights and consulted with one another about how to go about obtaining a lease on an apartment owned by friends or relatives that they could move to while awaiting relocation. They feared that the government (probably the subdistrict government), which had once attempted to cut off the electricity, would do this again, putting their heaters and electric blankets out of action and making it impossible to warm their houses and themselves. This was illegal, one woman reminded the crowd. Indeed, in 2012 the Supreme Court of China enacted a regulation outlawing violence in demolition practice, including cutting off electricity and water supplies, forcing people to persuade others in their kin group to relocate voluntarily, destroying physical structures without prior agreement, and violent action by the police and security forces.[25] Yet the use of such violence is still widespread in China. In River Hamlet the electricity continued to flow for the time being. As their despair grew, more villagers signed the deal on offer as the weather got colder and they lost hope of a better proposition in the coming days or weeks.

To disrupt the remaining villagers' resistance, in January, Xi'an's coldest month, the subdistrict stopped the sewerage service to River Hamlet's village houses. The smell of human feces was appalling. The villagers had to decide between staying in this noxious living environment and moving out. Once they left, the bulldozers moved in on the houses immediately. The odor drove away several more households. The subdistrict's withdrawal of the sewerage service had met its aim of forcing the villagers out of their houses and establishing a new social order.

Managed Disorder in South Gate

The community centers are the most obvious physical manifestation of Chengdu's new community governance and development project and were microcosms of the visual and social order that the community leadership and staff sought to produce in the *shequ* at large. The community center in North Gate was completed in 2017, when the community was separated from South Gate, and the South Gate community center was renovated from mid-2018 to early 2019. Both centers are similar in their overall functionality and, based on Jessica Wilczak's visits to a dozen other community centers in Chengdu, represent what appears to be an emerging template for such centers in this city.[26] They provide office space for community staff delivering services for citizens, meeting rooms and classrooms for cultural and educational activities, next to these two buildings a canteen sells low-priced lunches, and there is also an outdoor teahouse. Each center has a large outdoor stage for community events and performances. Volunteers wearing bright blue vests patrol the area during the day, keeping it clean. At the inauguration of the newly renovated South Gate community center during the Chinese New Year festivities at the beginning of 2019, the party secretary gave a brief but patronizing speech. Jessica Wilczak's field notes describe the scene that evening:

I returned at 6:30 when the celebrations started. There were about 500 people there, again largely older people and small children. The stage was brightly lit, with a promotional video for South Gate community playing on the screen behind the stage. There was a seniors' band of traditional Chinese instruments, and a choir singing revolutionary songs. The young female Party Secretary for South Gate community stood up and said a few words but was surprisingly brief and spoke from her position in the audience. She pointed out all the community center's beautiful new public facilities [*gonggong sheshi*], and asked "Everyone is going to take care of the facilities, right? [*hao bu hao*]." "Ok [*hao*]," came a few calls from the audience. "So if I see you out here letting your little kids pee or poo [anywhere except in the toilets]," she continued, "I'll give you a talking-to [*hui gei ni shangke*]."[27]

There are public toilets available in the community centers themselves, as well as a newly built freestanding public toilet in both North Gate and South Gate, installed as part of Xi Jinping's Toilet Revolution (Shen, Song, and Zhu 2019). The party secretary's tone was that of a teacher speaking to young children, and the phrase she used to warn the residents literally means "I'll teach you a lesson," although it has less ominous overtones than it does in English. The interaction suggested that the new public facilities were in some way a classroom for producing clean, well-behaved urban citizens. Later in 2019, South Gate community hired an environmental organization to carry out an environmental educational activity, pitched mainly at a white-collar audience, that sent families on an ecological treasure hunt for recyclable trash in the community.

Unlike in Shenzhen, the Chengguan do not have representatives at the North and South Gate community centers, although there is a police representative at each center to handle population registration and minor public security issues. Chengdu's Chengguan patrol members are headquartered in one brigade office in each city district and carry out tasks determined by subdistrict (*jiedao*) urban management committees. The Chengguan do not often appear on the *shequ*'s streets. Moreover, relationships between the Chengguan and the street vendors in the community did not seem particularly antagonistic. After the wet market, in its final position opposite the South Gate community center, was demolished and the sellers had moved to the ground floor of a resettlement estate (see chapter 2), the lack of space in these small shops led them to spread out onto the sidewalk in front of their shops, as is common practice in Chengdu. One day all the produce was back inside the shops. A shop owner explained that a visit from "leaders" (upper-level government officials) was expected, and the *shequ* had asked them to move their wares inside. Chengguan officers were speaking to shopkeepers who had not yet moved their wares inside, but they did not appear aggressive or antagonistic. The next day the shopkeepers simply moved their produce out onto the sidewalk again.

Clearly a certain amount of visual disorder is tolerated in North and South Gate communities as part of their transition to urban status, although such disorder is not allowed at certain times, such as leaders' visits, and in certain spaces, such as the resettlement estates and open fields. It is a system of managed disorder, developed in the interests of maintaining social harmony and accepted as part of a teleological system in which the disorder of the rural will gradually be attenuated.

Grid Governance: The Wangge in Urbanized Villages

Since 2015 grid governance has become a priority in many Chinese cities, and this has intensified with the Covid-19 outbreak (Zhu, Zhu, and Jin 2021). With the aim of achieving social stability and keeping the party's leadership unquestioned, grid governance (*Wangge hua zhili*) or management (*Wangge hua guanli*) puts particular emphasis on the enhancement of neighborhood governance. Although the Third Plenum of the 18th Party Congress formally identified grid governance as "an innovative social management method" for improving governance efficiency, coordination, and capacity, it is basically an extension of the existing bureaucratic system (Mittelstaedt 2022: 4) and an intensification of community-building at the grassroots level, fostered by digitalization.[28]

As shown below, its main mode of intervention is the collection of information. Therefore, it proved very useful during the Covid-19 pandemic to track Covid cases and implement the lockdown. The grid governance scheme brings municipal administration, public security, and social service management together in a comprehensive governance network that links urban communities (*shequ*) to subdistrict and district governments via a shared online database. Each *shequ* is divided into a number of spatial grids, and information is gathered about each area represented on the grid for the effective monitoring of certain groups of residents. The targeted groups vary according to the composition of each *shequ*'s population and governance priorities, but they are generally groups deemed likely to be involved in conflict and thus a potential source of social instability (Tang 2020). Indeed, while it is meant to improve the efficiency of local governance and public service provision, the main goal of grid management is to help prevent large-scale social unrest and build social stability by resolving neighborhood conflicts, preventing them from escalating. It thereby serves the community-building policy aim of building self-governing communities, where little interference from higher levels is needed. This requires targeting "problematic" sections of the population, such as migrant laborers (Nguyen 2013: 221). Grid management is a form of graduated governance that adjusts its mode of intervention to its target populations.

Surveilling Migrants in Pine Mansion

In the years following legal urbanization, Pine Mansion's workstation (*gongzuozhan*, the predecessor to the community center) made an inventory of the buildings in the village following Shenzhen's 2001 introduction of municipal government policy on unauthorized housing in urban villages. Penalties were to be imposed on households with buildings over four stories high and over 480 square meters of floor space (Wang et al. 2009: 962). The native villagers were required to sign a government contract granting them the use of the public land on which their house stood and to pay a land-use fee if they owned more than one building. After paying the relevant penalties and fees, village households could register their property with the housing authority and claim their property ownership certificates. Bach (2010: 437) comments that "this fiction of registration more than anything gives the villages a sense of spatial exception outside of state control." The wish to evade control applies to both rural migrants, many of whom are not registered with the police station (*paichusuo*), and the landlords, many of whom do not register their tenants with the local police. In 2005 the city authorities reached the pessimistic conclusion that "the timely monitoring of the move-in and move-out of tenants is impossible" (Shenzhen Municipal Government 2005: 24, cited in Bach 2010: 437).

The Wangge, or community grid management center, was established in Shenzhen's urban villages to address this problem. Pine Mansion's Wangge headquarters opened in 2017. Its head, Mr. Liu, is a good-humored man with a round smiling face who originates from Huizhou, a city to the northeast of Shenzhen. Along with a few new community center employees, he is one of the rare nonlocal cadres. Although he is neither local nor a lineage member, the fact that he speaks Hakka smooths his relations with the local Chen leadership. However, his outsider status probably accounts for why

Liu was the first person I heard referring to Pine Mansion not as a village or a *shequ* but as a village-in-the-city, *chenzhongcun*. The main criterion he mentioned for using this label was its "high population mobility" (*renkou liudong da*). He also explained that managing a *chenzhongcun* is a complex task because it contains a wide variety of buildings. He drew a contrast with what he referred to as garden neighborhoods, i.e., commercial housing complexes, which are much better managed "because the population is more stable, and the real-estate company does the management." At the time of interview there were only three commercial housing complexes in the subdistrict and one in Pine Mansion under construction. Liu stated: "People in these residential complexes are more mature (*chengshu* [in the sense of evolved, civilized]), and the public facilities are good, so they are easier to manage. *Chenzhongcun* are hard to manage—actually they are impossible to manage (*guan bu dao*) unless you tear them down completely and build an entirely new residential district."[29]

The Wangge is the result of a fusion between the municipal police department in charge of *hukou* matters and Shenzhen's floating population and house rental management office. It was officially named the Wangge only in 2017. Pine Mansion's Wangge has 70 employees, who wear blue uniforms that resemble those of police officers. They are on temporary contracts and are paid on the basis of their performance, which is assessed by a points system that rates their work following criteria corresponding to the Wangge's mandates (information gathering, conflict resolution) and their professional attitude.[30] Each employee is in charge of one territorial unit, or *ge*. The 72 units are identified by a number with 14 digits. Several large maps of the *shequ* were hanging in the head's office, showing its boundaries and the boundaries between the areas of three main residents' committees and between the 72 *ge*. A table detailed the number per unit of "ordinary buildings" (houses and shops) and "special buildings" (administrative, factory, school, etc.); the number of apartments (39,684 in total, 551 on average per unit); and the size of the population (54,666, with an average of 759 people per *ge*).[31] Each building has a code number, which, the head of the Wangge explained, is useful for when a building is demolished, as its number is simply erased from the database. The name, photograph, and contact number of each building owner, all of whom are native villagers, is displayed on a small plaque on the building next to the identification number, together with the name, photograph, and contact number of the Wangge employee in charge of the unit and of an officer of the police station.

Wangge employees collect information about their unit. The Wangge's first function is to surveil and regulate the small commercial (as opposed to the large industrial) real-estate market, including housing rentals as well as shops, small factories, and all spaces under three hundred square meters, and to prevent and help with resolving real-estate-related conflicts. Its second function is the collection, uploading, and actualization of data on the residing population—number of children per family, disputes, incidents, and crimes—in the subdistrict Wangge's database. The Wangge office provides much of this information to the police station, which authorizes residence permits. This facilitates checking the backgrounds of nonlocal residents and ascertaining that people applying for a residency permit do not have a criminal record.

The office works in close collaboration with the Chengguan (with which it shares an electronic platform), meeting to discuss current issues every Monday. Liu, the head of the Wangge, described the Chengguan as in charge of matters out of doors while he is responsible for indoor matters. However, Wangge employees are expected to upload information about all sorts of utilities problems in the community. I often saw Wangge employees pausing on the street to take notes on their cell phones, geolocalizing a pile of uncollected waste at the roadside, for instance, after which the Chengguan's law implementation team (*zhifa dui*) takes action.

In housing matters, one of the Wangge's main roles is to carry out an annual survey of house rentals. Its report on rental prices serves as a basis for the calculation of tax on property income. Property income tax, which was roughly 6 percent in 2018, is paid voluntarily, but is mandatory if a homeowner wants a property or rental certificate to be issued—and a certificate is required to register a child at a school.[32] Disputes between tenants and owners are mainly linked to school places. One of the main sources of conflict is tenants needing a contract to secure a school place, and landlords refusing to provide one because they want to avoid paying tax. Moreover, each residential address is only eligible for one school place, renewable only every six years (the time it takes to complete primary school); this is a huge problem, not only because of the population's mobility but also because landlords often fail to inform new tenants that the school place will not be available for X number of years, or the landlords provide friends in need of a school place with a fake tenancy contract, depriving the official tenant of their legal school place.

Wangge employees have a strong incentive to collect as much information as possible every day because their salary is based on performance, which is assessed every month. This accounts for the frequency with which they knock on the door of every household to collect information. The head of the Wangge contrasted Pine Mansion with other places that have fewer migrant workers. Native Pine Mansioners are not visited because, as Liu explained (addressing me as if I were a Pine Mansion native), "we know you're not going to move."

Preventing Social Disturbance in South Gate

In contrast to Shenzhen's Wangge system, the community-level Wangge in Chengdu does not have separate headquarters but is managed from the community centers.[33] It is a more diffuse and personalized network of social management that assigns volunteers, generally party members, to resolve grassroots problems, thus preventing the escalation of community disputes to the point of requiring police intervention or the involvement of higher government. In June 2014, Chengdu's Municipal Party Committee signaled the beginning of the city's efforts to build its own grid governance system with the publication of "Opinions on Accelerating the Construction of Grid Service Management Supported by Informatization" (Han 2015). In 2016 the local media reported that the number of Wangge staff in Chengdu exceeded 390,000 and handled 3.5 million issues, including conflict resolution, livelihood matters, and public security hazards (Liu 2016).

In North Gate, a large billboard listed the secretary and head of the residents' committee (*zhuren*) as the nominal heads of the Wangge system. Below this, a branching chart broke the *shequ* down into increasingly small subcategories, with residential estates at the second level, groups of buildings within each residential estate at the third level, and individual buildings on each estate at the fourth level. The names of the party members responsible for each level was listed with their personal phone numbers. Theoretically, the Wangge member responsible for one's building is the first person to contact in the case of any dispute with neighbors or the property management company. "Theoretically," because many of the middle-class residents of the commercial estates were unaware of the functions of the Wangge, and even of the existence of the community center. However, observable efforts were underway to increase the profile of the Wangge and the party. In the fall of 2019 on the higher-end commercial estate where Jessica Wilczak lived, hammer-and-sickle stickers appeared on the personal mailboxes of all party members living in the complex. Based on the number of stickers, about 5 percent of residents appeared to be party members. While Jessica was not visited at home by Wangge volunteers, one of her neighbors, a middle-aged professional, introduced herself in the elevator as the local party contact. She was very friendly and urged her to get in touch with her if she had any problems. As in the neighborhoods described by Tang (2020), the North and South Gate communities' grid governance strategy relies on mobilizing party members to strengthen the grassroots management of middle-class enclaves.

Grid governance appeared to operate more sporadically among former villagers, who felt personally tied to the party secretary, a former villager himself, either appealing directly to him or a member of his family or drawing on previous village institutions for the resolution of problems. For example, during the urbanization process, a dispute resolution office was set up at the community center to deal with resettlement and compensation issues. The office was still in place in the summer of 2019, when Jessica left, and former villagers continued to turn to Aunt Fang, the older female cadre who ran it, for help settling disputes with neighbors or family. Aunt Fang described a recent case that she had resolved for an elderly former villager's two sons, who were fighting over who would inherit their father's apartment. She had suggested that the elder son should inherit the apartment on the condition that he pay a sum of money to his younger brother, which, she said, was accepted by all parties.

Not all groups of residents are left to the management of party volunteers: *shequ* staff are enlisted to deal with more sensitive groups. The grid governance network in North and South Gate communities consists of not only resident volunteers but also community center staff, whose work includes Wangge responsibilities among other tasks. When asked about her role in the Wangge, a South Gate community staff member claimed that her primary task was to manage the nonlocal population (*wailai renkou*). The party secretary and her staff call on nonlocal *hukou* holders to ascertain that they are living at the registered address and that the number of household members they had reported is accurate. The staff member recalled waiting until ten o'clock one night for a Tibetan family to return home.

The South Gate party secretary, Mrs. Gu, complained that community staff had no legal authority over the population. Moreover, although a police representative worked at the South Gate community registering nonlocal domestic residents, the police and the community center appeared to operate separately.[34] Party Secretary Gu recalled calling in the police to deal with a domestic dispute and being told that this was a matter for the *shequ*; however, she and her staff did not feel they had the legal authority to intervene in the matter.³⁵

Disputes between newcomers and native residents in Pine Mansion are dealt with by the Wangge because they generally concern tenancy issues, while disputes between native villagers are dealt with by the community center, where a native Chen heads the dispute resolution office. Similarly, in South Gate there is considerable pressure on *shequ* leaders to prevent social disturbances requiring official police or subdistrict government intervention. Lacking both financial resources and the North Gate party secretary's personal authority as a former villager, the South Gate party secretary was forced to improvise. In 2018 she negotiated with the estates' (*xiaoqu*) property management companies and businesses in the community to raise funds to hire security guards and purchase a small electric golf cart for their night patrols. The vehicle displayed the names and logos of the property management companies and businesses that had supported the project. Rather than rely on former village institutions and figureheads, as the dispute resolution officer in North Gate community did, the South Gate leader experimented with the new grassroots self-management and self-funding model advocated by the city.

Infrastructural Governance

China's villages-in-the-city (*chengzhongcun*), or urbanized villages, are particularly interesting sites for observing how civilized cities are established as part of the aim of creating a "moderately well-off society" (*xiaokang shehui*). Villages are expected to merge into the modern city, and their native inhabitants, deemed uncivilized and backward, are expected to become modern, civilized urbanites. In an effort to eliminate the remains of the rural villages-in-the-city, infrastructural governance, or the use of infrastructures as a governing technique, actively shapes a homogenous, civilized urban landscape. Infrastructure is used as a governing technique when local leaders hide undesirable elements such as litter, piles of garbage, and unofficially cultivated fields from view to please potential buyers and visiting officials; when authorities decide to cut off sewerage and electricity services to compel native residents to accept relocation and compensation or to drive out unwanted, unregistered migrants; and when the grid employees collect detailed information on non-natives to track and subject them to minute surveillance. Infrastructural public goods are both an end and a means.

Emerging from this chapter is a strong sense of variability and flexibility in the spatial but also temporal implementation of policy on building communities and shaping the civilized city. In terms of space, different assemblages of the same basic units emerge in all three cases, with the Chengguan and Wangge's importance varying according to local housing conditions and the composition of the population, and the community centers (*shequ zhongxin*) enjoying varying levels of importance and autonomy. In conformity with the ideology that associates modernization and civilization with urbanization, these infrastructural improvements reward the citizens and communities who come closest to this ideal; those deemed far from it fall under close surveillance and are susceptible to correction.

Timing is dependent on conjunctural policies decided from above, with sudden bursts of activity when a campaign requires mobilization. It is also dependent on the process of urbanization and on the inhabitants' maturity in an evolutionary view of this process. While top-down approaches clearly prevail in deciding what and who should be subject to measures, the governance of urbanized villages also depends on estimations of when local conditions are ripe. Finding the right moment to act, therefore, appears crucial. This is particularly true for local leaders who, while echoing higher-level government discourse, can be opportunistic in the way they pay lip service to the setting up of model communities.

Graduated governance consists of adjusting the timing of local governance to the stage reached by urbanized villages in the evolutionary process of urbanization, and it translates spatially into the emphasis on differing target populations living in different parts of the *shequ*. Accordingly, even the attention paid to providing cleanliness and order in public space varies temporally and spatially. The next chapter explores how similar microtechniques of governance are gradually deployed across the population in the process of building solidary communities.

Notes

1. As Sangren (1987) notes, civilization opposes chaos just as order opposes disorder, with the first opposition encompassing the latter in a system of structured value that is relative and hierarchical; this set of basic assumptions about reality serves to legitimize Chinese patterns of social order and political authority (1987: 133). Ritual activity rests on and reproduces these assumptions. On early Chinese notions of ritual as a never-ending attempt to create order in a fractured world rather than based on the premise of an inherently harmonious world, see also Puett (2008).

2. See Unger (1984) on the changes in workpoint remuneration systems from tasks rates (1961–65) to the Dazhai method (1966–79).
3. This chapter's approach, however, is not purely Foucauldian, in that it pays attention to institutional actors and ideology, which Foucault (2000) does not consider important in the study of power.
4. Ministry of Civil Affairs, Opinions on Promoting the Construction of Urban Communities in the Country, 19 November 2000, available at http://www.reformdata.org/2000/1119/21297.shtml.
5. As outlined in 2000 by the Ministry of Civil Affairs (MoCA), which set up a Division for Grassroots Authority and Community-Building (*jiceng zhengquan yu shequ jianshe si*).
6. Building "green communities" (*luse shequ*) is a policy variant of community-building that has emerged as a central feature of urban governance reform in China (Boland and Zhu 2009).
7. Jessica Wilczak, *First Interim Research Report*, 21 November 2018. The remainder of this section is based on this and on her *Final Report*, 30 July 2019.
8. "Park City Chengdu Consensus 2019 Released," *Chengdu ribao*, 23 April 2019, http://scnews.newssc.org/system/20190423/000959834.html.
9. Shenzhen Longhua District, "Guanhu Accelerates Double Promotion," 16 December 2015, http://www.szlhq.gov.cn, accessed 8 August 2019.
10. This happened when its mayor, Xu Zongheng, was placed under investigation and subsequently dismissed for corruption. Shenzhen has since been working hard to regain its lost civilized city status. In March 2013, it became the first city to implement a civility law that imposes fines for "uncivilized" public behavior (Cartier 2013).
11. The Chinese name of the commission is *Zhongyang jingshen wenming jianshe zhidao weiyuanhui*. On "civilization," see Dynon 2008; on the national civilized city title, see Cartier 2013.
12. Zhongguo wenming [Chinese civilization] website, 14 September 2017, http://www.wenming.cn/wmcs/wenmingchengshi_jujiao/201709/t20170914_4422911.shtml, accessed 16 October 2018.
13. Starting in 2004, urban villages in Shenzhen's inner-city districts were denounced in a series of media reports as hotbeds of unlawful activity, including prostitution, gambling, drug trafficking, and illegal building (Chung 2009).
14. *Nanfang Ribao* (*Southern Daily*), 2016. Exact reference not given for anonymization purposes.
15. Separate urban waste collection and recycling targets were introduced in the twelfth Five-Year Plan (2011–15) in 2011 (Bondes 2019: 57). However, Shanghai's 2019 Municipal Solid Waste Act was the first systematic municipal regulation on waste in China. Until then, city governments had launched temporary campaigns that tended to cease with the term of the leaders who instigated them.
16. Xi'an Landscape Act, https://baike.baidu.com/reference/16828759/e409Y56AOBp6Nh B9qCU5SM9IHgUKz1kK-SDR55moGvOn7VWaS_sJi1C5znMJPKoNPAj9lIn_3gl17T_qtdKdz0vVc3XeU4JuSw.
17. "Lighting-Up Project in Xi'an," Sina.com.cn, 1 October 2006, http://news.sina.com.cn/c/2006-10-01/105310152675s.shtml.
18. Unless stated otherwise, this section is based on Wang Bo, *Final Report*, 31 October 2019.
19. "One Cigarette Butt, One Yuan Fine: On Xi'an's Cigarette Butts Revolution," People.cn, 24 July 2018, http://society.people.com.cn/n1/2018/0724/c1008-30166027.html.
20. Xinhua News, 2018, http://www.xinhuanet.com/politics/2018-07/24/c_1123166722.htm.
21. On 30 March 2017 the Ministry of Housing and Rural-Urban Integration promulgated the "Urban Management Law Enforcement Measures," which stipulated that urban

management employees shall belong to the administrative law enforcement category of civil servants, be recruited through the civil service examination, and receive formal training; temporary employees in the urban management department will be fully dismissed. In 2021, the new version of the "Administrative Punishment Law" clarified that the state will promote the establishment of a comprehensive administrative law enforcement system in the field of urban management and centralize the power of administrative punishment.

22. Anne-Christine Trémon, interview with the Chengguan, 27 March 2018. The Chengguan head and his assistant both belong to Pine Mansion's dominant Chen lineage. They must have been appointed for political reasons, namely their ability to negotiate with the heads of the shareholding companies, who belong to the same village. Indeed, in addition to supervising "urban appearance" (*shirong*), they also play a part in upgrading Pine Mansion's industries (see chapter 2).
23. Xi'an Gaoxin district website, http://www.xdz.gov.cn/info/16436/128318.htm, accessed 26 August 2020.
24. This section is based on Wang Bo's *Final Report,* 31 October 2019.
25. The Supreme Court of China's Decisions on State-Owned Land-Grabbing and Demolitions, http://www.court.gov.cn/shenpan-xiangqing-4033.html, accessed 26 August 2020.
26. Unless otherwise stated, this section is based on Jessica Wilczak's *Final Report,* 30 July 2019.
27. Jessica Wilczak, *Fieldnotes,* 19 January 2019, cited in *Final Report.*
28. In 2013, based on the results of local experiments mainly carried out in Beijing, the Third Plenum of the 18th Party Congress advocated its implementation at the local level.
29. Interview by Anne-Christine Trémon, 2 April 2018.
30. Mittelstadt provides a comparison of Wangge employees' work performance evaluation systems in several cities (2021: 15).
31. A few of the *ge* in the redevelopment area had very small populations in 2018, as the newly constructed residential towers were not yet inhabited. Those with the largest populations of over nine hundred include factories with dormitories.
32. The Wangge does not collect the taxes. It provides property certificates after checking tax payment with the tax administration. The voluntary character of property tax may change, as in early November 2022, as Shenzhen was nominated a pilot area for China's property tax reform.
33. Section based on Jessica Wilczak's *Final Report,* 30 July 2019.
34. Foreign nonlocal residents had to register at the subdistrict police office.
35. Interview by Jessica Wilczak, 23 July 2018.

— Chapter 4 —

Building Moral Communities

> Local urban government in China should "implement the spirit of the CCP's 2017 Nineteenth National Congress," "creating strong links between the Party, grassroots civil servants and citizens by encouraging them to join in common activities … stimulating ethical and caring attitudes toward others across all sections of society, [promoting] residents' participation in community governance and development [*shequ zhili yu fazhan*], [and] mobilizing the resources of all parties to maximize the use of manpower and material resources [*renli wuli*]."[1]

All of the items on this list issued by Shenzhen's Municipal Party Propaganda Committee come under the heading "community-building" (*shequ jianshe*). Community-building implies that "a conscious effort has to be made to cultivate community (*shequ*) consciousness so that individuals can return to a state of social solidarity despite the individualizing pressures created by marketization" (Xu 2008: 639).

Urbanized villages are primary targets of this policy, which appeals to citizens' desire to improve their own "quality" (*suzhi*) and to their moral values of caring for others. *Suzhi* refers to a mix of cultural and educational, economic, and moral qualities and can be applied to both individuals and whole populations; high *suzhi* broadly indicates that one is well-educated, law-abiding, and in stable employment. By governing themselves and caring for each other, "citizens of 'quality' relieve China's governmental authorities of a considerable burden" (Bray 2006: 545).[2] The widespread focus on *suzhi* in China and its close relationship to the promotion of community self-governance has led to debate among anthropologists about the extent to which it can be interpreted as part of a trend toward neoliberalization. Some consider it part of a new government technique for shaping self-governing individuals in the context of relaxing state control. Others stress its affinity with ethical Confucian traditions of the moral self that extend much further back in Chinese history, to well before the global diffusion of neoliberalism (Kipnis 2007: 2008).

This chapter examines public goods and services—mainly senior care, cultural entertainment, and pedagogic activities—the provision of which relies on party members and ordinary citizens' ethical commitment to work and volunteering and builds on, while further contributing to their shaping, the gender and generational dimensions of class relations between natives and newcomers in urban villages. The chapter also considers the underlying, more abstract notion of *gongyi*, the public good or public interest (see introduction). Studying the linkages between claims to be acting for the public good (Brandtstädter 2013: 14) and actual practice in public goods provision, it discloses some of the ethical principles to which citizens refer when talking about these matters and carrying out community-building projects and policies. During the collectivist era, Confucian ethics combined with Maoist ethics (Madsen 1984), lending *gongyi* the meaning of the greater public interest to which private interests must be sacrificed. Over the past two decades, along with other concepts such as "compassionate people" (*aixin renshi*), the term has become increasingly fashionable and has taken on a more charitable and philanthropic meaning as an ethical orientation toward others in need, more than to the larger collective to which one belongs (Thireau 2013),[3] although the notion of *gongyi* still bears both connotations.

Community-building involves what Nikolas Rose calls an "ethopolitics" that "concerns itself with the *self-techniques necessary for responsible self-government* and *the relations between one's obligation to oneself and one's obligations to others*" (1999: 188, emphasis in original). *Gongyi*-driven community-building activities such as those carried out by NGOs and trade unionists in Italy, which Andrea Muehlebach characterizes as moral neoliberalism, rest on both self- and other-oriented ethical attitudes (Muehlebach 2012).

In 2004 the CCP's Central Organization Department issued a document on community party-building, stating its goal "to lead the community residents' committees and support community self-governance" (Ngeow 2011: 221).[4] This rhetoric of self-governance (*zizhi*) figures largely in central and local policy related to community-building. Reading the new focus on communities as an exercise in Foucauldian governmentality, David Bray argues that it is a project to increase the overall quality (*suzhi*) of the population so that it becomes fit to govern itself. Communities are tasked with raising the educational and moral standards of their individual members, particularly in sections of the population that are seen as problematic (2006: 544).

Luigi Tomba (2014) refines this argument, claiming that the state exercises different governmental strategies with different groups in different localities. Middle-class people in stable employment living in commercial estates that have replaced state housing in former urban units (*danwei*) rarely come into contact with their residents' committees, focusing rather on the activities of the homeowners' committees in their own gated residential complexes. In former *danwei* dominated by blue-collar workers laid off by the former state-owned factories, on the other hand, weaker social groups are subject to more direct forms of pastoral intervention and welfare allocation via the residents' committees.[5] Tomba (2014) thus identifies a two-tiered, class-based governance system in Chinese cities, with *laisser-faire* practices and moralizing discourse among middle-class gated communities and a socialist moral economy for poorer communities.

In urban villages, however, the governance of even middle-class residential complexes (*xiaoqu*) is more hands-on and less *laisser-faire* than it may seem. This partly reflects the extension of party-strengthening policies (Wright 2010; Pieke 2012) and the return of an even more authoritarian top-down governing style under Xi Jinping. It is also due to the specific characteristics linking urban villages to their rural past. In the 1990s, the first new *shequ* were built on the institutional foundations of the existing residents' committees (*jumin weiyuanhui*). However, urban villages are considered in need of close governance, and therefore urban communities in former rural villages are not built on the foundation of residents' (formerly village) committees but governed from community centers—or to give them their full title, Party-Services-to-the-Masses Community Centers (*shequ dangqun fuwu zhongxin*). In spite of the rhetoric of self-governance that rests on the presentation of these community centers as grassroots organizations, they are only nominally so. Following the principle of *guanban fenli*, the separation of government and management, they are tasked with handling grassroots affairs and executing (*ban*) orders from the higher administrative levels that supervise and govern (*guan*). In practice, residents tend to view community workers as part of the party-state, and indeed community centers function as parastatal organizations whose key functionaries are party members appointed by subdistrict and district offices (Audin 2015).[6] Even though some appointees may be native villagers, state and party supervision is close.

Community-center employees aim to build solidarity on a community scale. They exercise a form of graduated governance and moralized provision of care by co-opting sections of the *shequ*'s population and encouraging some people to care for others. Solidarity is generated in the service of aging natives based on gender, generational, and class divisions between old and new urban villagers via the exploitation of female migrant labor laid off from blue-collar jobs and the volunteering of younger women aspiring to middle-class status and self-improvement. Governance is moral and affective, in that community-building projects persuade community members to participate, mainly through volunteering, and teach them how to behave as good citizens. They draw on traditional Confucian moral virtues by connecting with people's desire for self-improvement (raising their "quality") and sense of altruism.

Community-building in urban villages is neoliberal in the Foucauldian sense of governmentality (Rose 1999; Rose and Miller 2010), but also in the sense of political economy, which is central to Foucault's thinking on neoliberalism, but has been downplayed by the governmentality school. As several scholars have noted, the primary aim of contemporary community-building policies is to improve the efficiency of government and reduce its costs by devolving social welfare functions to the *shequ* (Bray 2005: 192; Heberer and Göbel 2011: 4). This is also achieved, as this chapter shows, by introducing competitive funding-allocation mechanisms and utilizing low-cost and unpaid labor. The community centers are understaffed and rely on their staff and residents volunteering to perform public welfare (Hoffman 2013: 844; Audin 2017). Furthermore, "mobilizing the resources of all parties," as quoted at the start of this chapter, means encouraging commoning. This involves leaning as much as possible on the resources available among the governed population by making use of common village-funded resources and drawing on local history to secure funding.

I start by further exploring how affective governance is practiced in community-building using microgovernance techniques of the type described in the previous chapter: Mao-style mobilization campaigns and more quotidian incentives such as point-scoring systems. The emphasis is on community-center workers and citizens volunteering to care for others with the aim of self-improvement, closely monitored by state and party institutions. I next turn to a primary feature of affective community-building in urban villages and urban China in general: community residents caring for seniors. In all three locations, new forms of senior care outside the family are being offered in cost-saving public-private partnerships that use female migrant labor, while community centers also organize events for mainly native senior citizens using mainly newcomer female residents' voluntary services. The notion that native citizens should be rewarded for their contribution to urban development also underlies the system of competitive project-based funding, where money is granted to communities able to capitalize on the affective dimensions of nostalgia for the rural past and traditional Confucian values.

Volunteering in Serving the Masses and at Charitable Events

Urban communities (*shequ*) were intended to replace the work units (*danwei*) that had formed the backbone of not only the economy but also urban social life (Read 2000; Derleth and Koldyk 2004; Wong and Poon 2005; Zhang and Yan 2014; Audin 2015). They were the Communist Party's base units, reflecting the Leninist principle of organizing the party on the basis of production and government bodies. In the 1990s, Grassroots Party organizations were demoted by both the dismantling of the urban work units (*danwei*) and the heightened importance afforded to elected residents' committees.[7] The shift toward greater emphasis on the party's role in community-building is a response to this sidelining.

Committed to serving the people, the Chinese Communist Party has always stressed the importance of its grassroots units. These are the basic blocks of the organization's edifice: close to the people, they are in the best position to mobilize the masses and ensure social stability. The party puts forward its concern for society (*shehui guanhuai*) and has made great efforts to become a welfare-oriented and service-guided organization (Ngeow 2011: 218). To this purpose, party members become "twenty-four-hour" members, carrying out party duties both at work and at home, rather than "eight-hour" members limited to daytime work in their work units (Li 2008: 26). Previously discreet and even secret, membership now requires visibility. Clearly identifiable, party members are expected to set an example and act as model citizens.

In recent years party members have increasingly had to participate in the volunteer-based events that are central to community-building and on which most charitable and cultural activities organized as part of community-building in urban villages rely. Such events are meant to turn the *shequ* into a space beyond the workplace, where one can participate in socially significant activity. Volunteering is a tool of affective governance, not only in the sense that it relies on citizens' affective commitment but also because it directs citizens toward working in the public interest—in this respect it is strongly continuous with mobilization techniques and the socialist morality of self-sacrifice instituted in the collectivist era (Madsen 1984). However, not only is there a new emphasis on self-improvement and raising one's quality (Hoffman 2013), but its modalities have changed: volunteering is made possible by the class and gender inequalities in present-day China. Volunteers' class positioning varies with the social properties of their urban communities, but in all cases they are mainly middle-class women, for whom this unpaid labor is additional to work performed at home.

Shenzhen: Volunteering by Migrants and Social Workers

In the promotional video released for its fortieth anniversary, Shenzhen boasts that it is "a city of immigrants … with 1.35 million registered volunteers."[8] The points-based system for accessing local *hukou* includes contributions such as participation in charitable activities, i.e., donating to the local community, giving blood, and voluntary work.[9]

On a Sunday morning I discovered a small crowd in Pine Mansion's main square next to the community center. Blue tents had popped up on the basketball ground and were shading children having haircuts and elderly people having their blood pressure checked by volunteers (figure 4.1). Leaflets on one of the tables called the event the *Jushan jiayuan ri* and translated this into English as Homestead Beneficence Day. Two female social workers based at the community center were supervising the volunteers. "It is a request from above," one of them explained, referring to the Longhua District Authority. The event is organized by the district's Organization, Propaganda, and Civil Departments.[10] From March 2018 onward a Beneficence Day was to be held on the last Sunday of every month in all fifty-seven *shequ* in Longhua District as part of the district's philosophy and policy of community-building (*shequ yingzao*). The second social worker, Mrs. Yu, was more talkative (she agreed to meet me for an interview a few days later): "[The district authority's] philosophy is community-building; this is the starting point. Its purpose is to encourage this community's residents to form a model of mutual assistance." This echoes how the main goal of Beneficence Day is presented on Shenzhen's Care Action Organizing Committee web-

Figure 4.1. Beneficence Day in Pine Mansion, Shenzhen. © Anne-Christine Trémon.

site: namely to "establish a welfare service (*gongyi fuwu*) system for community mutual assistance."[11] What is not stated on the website but was mentioned by both social workers is that it follows a model developed in Taiwan and Hong Kong.

A central component of Beneficence Day is the charity fair, *yimai*. On sale are schoolchildren's calligraphy, handmade artificial flowers, and snacks such as sweet potatoes baked by the social workers. Free health and beauty services are also available. Prices are by donation; some donate without buying anything. The sum collected is partly donated to poor mountain areas (*pinkun shanqu*) and partly used for the community. The leaflet states that a series of fundraising activities has been developed under different names: Help the Seriously Ill, Love and Help Education, Meals for the Elderly, and Warm Bundle. Every three months a round of fundraising is held in support of one of these, and the sum collected is used on the next quarter's project. The social workers are also planning to invite people to bring books, toys, and clothing to be given to the *shequ*'s neediest households.

The beneficiaries are all migrants, non-native men and women of all ages. There are two kinds of volunteers, although all are women. The first is social workers employed by the community center; wearing the same red jackets as the volunteers, they explain that volunteering is part of their job: "It's mandatory, something you must do," said Mrs. Yu. The community center has only sixty employees, which works out at one per one thousand inhabitants. Community volunteering helps to make up for the center's shortage of manpower with supplementary unpaid labor, and the center's social workers are also expected to donate a certain amount of free labor when they organize weekend events such as Beneficence Day. The second kind of volunteer is a member of the local volunteer teams: the volunteers' association (see below) and the school volunteers who stand at the school entrance to make sure students enter and leave the building in an orderly fashion. The community-center volunteers provide services such as medical examinations, which mainly consist of checking blood pressure, while the school volunteers provide free haircuts and makeup sessions and look after the donation box in the middle of the basketball field. They explained that when they are free they can pick one of the three available shifts and simply show up. There is more pressure on the members of the volunteers' association, who register for specific activities, and if they fail to turn up they are pushed back to the end of the waiting list for volunteering assignments.

Mrs. Gong is a slender, gentle woman originating from a village near Shantou in the northeast of Guangdong Province.[12] She and her husband moved to Shenzhen shortly after they married in 2003; her husband opened a shop, and they have been living in Pine Mansion ever since. She began volunteering when her children started at Zhenneng Primary School. Like her, most of the volunteers came to volunteering through the school. She joined the group, which operated informally for several years before registering as a volunteer association in 2016. Although it is a nongovernmental organization, she said, "the activities we do are basically for the government." The community center regularly calls them in to help with activities, and other organizations such as the All-China Women's Federation involve them on International Women's Day. Every *shequ* in Shenzhen now has its own team of volunteers. The Pine Mansion group has seventy to eighty registered volunteers, who are mostly migrant women.

Mrs. Gong described their activities as "in the public interest" (*gongyi xing de*), defining *gongyi* as "getting together to organize activities and volunteer when you have time." She characterized their group as one of like-minded people, with native villagers making up only ten or perhaps less of the seventy or so in the group. Most of the volunteers work full- or part-time while raising their children. They spread news about upcoming events via a WeChat group and by word of mouth. The school volunteers are organized separately, but there is an overlap in membership, which is very fluid. Most volunteer as a way of making friends. "For us immigrant workers (*wailai wugongde*) it is better to have more friends," she said. Mrs. Gong quoted a popular saying among Chinese who leave their hometown for work: *Ren zai waidi, duo ge pengyou, duo tiao lu quite*: when you're away from home, the more people you know around you, the more potential backup you'll have in a difficult situation.

The migrant volunteers participate in a range of charitable activities with solidary goals, including a birthday party for the elderly organized every year by the community center and, on a more regular basis, medical checkups for the elderly. In both instances it is mainly native former villagers who benefit. The volunteers provide free labor for the community, helping with activities such as environmental protection (picking up garbage in the streets) and parent-child activities (the same, but together with their children). The volunteers' association also stages its own fundraising activities, such as organizing mini marathons, and the volunteers organize recreational activities for themselves that ratify their urban status, such as Sunday morning jogs and riding the new tramway.

High Morale on Shaky Ground in Xi'an

Community party-building is partly about reviving the party's role as the vanguard of harmonious society. In Xi'an, Communist Party members are singled out as role models for their communities, with plaques of honor on their doors rendering them visible and identifiable.[13] Party-building includes publicly displaying party members' contact details for the benefit of anyone who might want to file a complaint. The community party branches also use social media platforms to disseminate party policy to members. They provide support with relocation of the displaced during the redevelopment of the village and with the resolution of disputes over compensation for their houses. Selected party members are tasked with collecting opinions in the community and communicating them to administrative bodies at a higher level. One subdistrict office worker was upset to have been selected to "go and study" (*qu xuexi*) the needs of the residents. She was in her early thirties and pregnant with her second child. She found the task far more demanding than she had imagined, and confided that she had thought it would be a mere formality.

Those working at the community center were even more outspoken about the difficulty of community-building work. The community workers were at the front line when River Hamlet's residents were experiencing severe distress due to the demolition. They faced an increased workload: the community center had initially been created to provide social services to workers at River Hamlet's military garment factory (see chapter 1), and it organized pensions and retirement funds for the employees until the factory shut down. However, the demand for social work has increased over the past decades with the urbanization of the city's many villages. Although the subdistrict administration has nominally assumed much of the former villages' power and added new functions, including the distribution of minimal social benefits (*dibao*) and poverty alleviation funds for qualifying applicants and monitoring the population via registration, checks, and security measures, in fact the community office performs most of these tasks. Most importantly, as many of the original villagers were relocated and took on urban *hukou*, they had to transfer their healthcare and other benefits from the village committee to the municipality at this office.

The community workers' emphasis on their work ethic can be understood as an effort to boost morale when the ground on which the office stands is literally shaking and they are not being paid on time. When demolition began in River Hamlet in November 2018, shockwaves from the demolition of nearby buildings, although faint, could be felt in the community center building's fabric. Yet the office seemed quiet and orderly. Mrs. Fang was answering phone calls with exemplary customer-service skills, despite not having received her modest salary for the past three months and not knowing when she would receive the overdue payment. She was twenty-eight and from a nearby neighborhood, and she had quit her job as an elementary school teacher after marrying to avoid the long daily commute. She passed the Civil Service Examination and secured a job in River Hamlet, which allowed her to begin planning to start a family. Six others working at the community center had similar backgrounds and stories.

Mrs. Fang had been a community office worker for two years, filing benefit claims and handling numerous new requests. She said the missed salary payments were insignificant compared to the frustration at work about the difference between what was expected and what she and her coworkers could manage, such as with the elderly home-care program (see next section). She remarked, "The local office just gives orders, and it's the community center that deals with the people and their needs." Acting as intermediary between the residents and the lowest branch of government, community offices have both permanent civil servants and temporary staff. The salary for the temporary jobs is often too low for college graduates majoring in social work or sociology, who have higher expectations in terms of income and stability. Some community centers with abundant resources and close ties to the city government offer better salaries and job security, but these are hard to land. Community office positions in most communities across Xi'an are not greatly sought after by college-educated job seekers. They are filled by people like Mrs. Fang, who prioritize being close to home and in a desirable school catchment area, although they have trouble making ends meet in the context of rising living costs and salary arrears.

Community workers also have to manage the tension between their disposition to serve the people, on the one hand, and the daily frustration created by their limited resources and vast obligations on the other. The party secretary and head of the *shequ*, Mr. Tu, explained that before it had closed, the state-run factory used to contribute to community funds. He called this act of giving money back to the community *fanbu*, which means to support one's parents in their old age, to show filial piety, to repay, to return a favor. In the absence of the factory's donations, the community was unable to offer residents a full range of services. Party Secretary Tu also openly criticized the separation of government and management, for it devolves too many tasks to the grassroots management bodies, the community centers. Under the logic of this separation, the community office has to apply for specific funding for specific purposes, competing for project-based funding and keeping him and his staff under pressure. He said that even though the community center was not allocated resources by the city and did not even have enough money to pay their staff, they had to "keep up their morale and march on."

According to Mr. Tu, it was their passion for providing services to the public and their love for their profession as social workers that made it possible for him and others to continue their daily work entering health-insurance data, distributing charity funds and pensions, and offering cultural performance events. After all, they were working to support those in the most need, and if they did not do it, who would? He added that the district and subdistrict offices just gave the orders, and it was the community center that dealt with the people. Confirming the importance of work at the community level, the High-Tech District's absorption of the original village in 2018 increased the community center's workload hugely while the subdistrict office was closed during the demolition in November and December that year.

Outsourcing and Volunteering in Chengdu

In 2019 there were only fifteen or sixteen permanent staff providing information about administrative issues and dispute resolution services at the South and North Gate community centers. Each center also has a canteen and a popular outdoor teahouse, both run directly by the *shequ*.[14] Apart from these, there is a social organization providing cultural classes for children and adults, a commercial teahouse run by a tea master teaching long-spout tea-pouring techniques, a massage clinic occasionally hosting a blind masseur offering residents massage at a reduced price, and a training center for young adults with intellectual disabilities. Like other Chinese cities, Chengdu has recently had a drive to outsource service provision to private social enterprises (Zhao 2012). A member of staff at one of Chengdu's oldest social enterprises, established around 2009, shared her thoughts on why purchasing services was becoming so popular. The main reason, she said, was that the government wants to control costs. A contract with a third-party organization rather than with permanent staff avoids the burden of having to pay for social benefits (*fuli*) and makes it possible to plan how much they will spend each year in advance.[15]

Jessica Wilczak participated in a volunteer training session for the Traditional Culture Festival organized by one such third-party social organization in North Gate community. The volunteers were all women, most retired but still very active native villagers in their fifties and sixties. There was also a group of stay-at-home mothers from other areas of the city who had heard of the volunteer opportunity via an online network. Teacher Fang opened the meeting with a speech about traditional Chinese values, and specifically the relationship between husband and wife. "When a husband gets home," Fang explained, "even if he's tired after work, he should go into the kitchen and ask if his wife needs any help making dinner. The wife, in turn, should prepare some fruit for him, massage his neck and shoulders, and ask how his day has been." One of the younger women objected at this point, saying "*He* should give *me* a massage!" The teacher backtracked and said that the point is that each should take care of the other. After this, a tall, middle-aged teacher gave an etiquette lesson, explaining how to stand with the hands folded, right over left, in front of the belly, elbows out, with a small smile; how to greet guests with a thirty-degree bow; how to shake hands only with the top part of your hand; and how to hand an object to someone with both hands as a mark of respect. This lesson in comportment, aimed directly at improving one's quality (*suzhi*), seemed to be taken more seriously than the lesson on marital relations, and everyone stood up to copy the teacher's gestures.

Furthermore, across Chengdu, party-building (*dangjian*) is a key part of the new community governance strategy. Party members are expected to be the vanguard of community-building. The head of the North Gate residents' committee, Mr. Xu, told Jessica a personal story to explain his understanding of community-building. One day he was at the convenience store, and a child ahead of him at the counter was trying to pay for some candy. The child didn't have enough money, so Xu himself made up the shortfall. After he left the store he passed the child and the child's grandmother. "That's the man who paid for my candy," exclaimed the child. Xu imagined how such gestures, small to the doer, would spread throughout the community, inspiring others and initiating a virtuous cycle of altruism and goodwill. Indeed, this is exactly what is expected of party members in the vanguard of the community-building project. But in a separate conversation, Xu admitted that his work at the community center was taking a personal toll. On weekends, government officials cannot travel more than two hours' distance from their jurisdiction, and during the week they must remain within thirty minutes of it, ready to respond to any emergency. He often receives calls in the middle of the night. "You can't imagine how difficult it is!" he exclaimed.[16]

In April 2018 Chengdu issued its Citywide Party-Building Leading Urban and Rural Community Development and Governance Concentrated Action Plan, and implemented an online volunteer registration service for party members, who, with community-center staff, are expected to volunteer their services in the community. North Gate community is seen as a model of both party-building and community governance in Chengdu. A young twentysomething member of staff at the community center was in charge of party-building activities. She was not a community resident, but had been sent there by the local office where she had previously worked. She herself was a Party member, and described with pride the current rigorous system for joining the Party. She explained that after a person submits their application their behavior is monitored for a year, and they have to study for and pass a number of tests. She emphasized that she had not been allowed to join for two and a half years after submitting her application. Among the Party-building activities she organized were classes, training, and visits. She explained it as a way of upgrading one's personal quality (*suzhi*): "Not all Party members are of the same quality," she said, "so they need to be trained."[17]

The Action Plan was accompanied by a big push to attract and publicize party members and non-members as volunteers at the community, district, and city levels. Volunteering is one of the main tenets of the city's governance strategy. The number of volunteers is used as a proxy for the success of the new community governance policy. The South Gate community party secretary, Mrs. Gu, made attracting volunteers her signature project. She set up a system of points with local businesses with which volunteers could receive a discount on goods and services in proportion to the number of hours they had put into volunteering. Staff compiled a list of several hundred volunteers, most of whom, they admitted, were not regularly active, with only a handful actually showing up. The volunteers performed tasks such tidying the community-center reading room, receiving visitors at a desk by the entrance, helping out during community events, and monitoring the public space around the center for litter or misuse. Most were retired women or stay-at-home mothers, with a mixture of both locals and nonlocals and varying income levels.

The volunteers in Chengdu were different from those in Shenzhen in several ways. First, the South Gate volunteers included some resettled residents. One of these, a retired woman from the rural outskirts of Chengdu who had recently been allocated an apartment in a nearby community after her land was requisitioned, claimed that she was volunteering simply because she had nothing to do all day.[18] Second, a culture festival in North Gate community attracted volunteers from across the city who were part of a WeChat volunteer network. All but one of these were women, and most were stay-at-home mothers, whereas in Pine Mansion most women work outside the home. One woman expressed her gratitude for the opportunity to volunteer and learn about these cultural events; otherwise, she said, she would just stay at home "getting stupider and stupider." A third, much smaller category of volunteers consisted of petty criminals doing community service. A young man who had hacked computers and a middle-aged man convicted of real-estate fraud were two such reluctant "volunteers" at the teahouse in the renovated South Gate community center. A common feature across all three categories, as also among Shenzhen's volunteers, is the widespread sense that volunteering is a means of improving one's personal quality and citizenship.

Caring for Seniors

Two common elements in our three urban villages are the aging native population and the fact that many have children who have moved away to urban districts downtown. This is particularly the case in River Hamlet, where elderly former villagers have clung to their rural *hukou* and native locality. In Shenzhen this is only partially true, as shares in the collectives can only be transmitted to the younger generation on the death of the former generation, retaining young people in the village. However, many original villagers, even those who had moved to Hong Kong, have returned to the village to live out their old age, the former village functioning as a retirement locality. In North and South Gate the situation is mixed, but the native villagers are clearly older on average than the new residents. In China, caring for seniors in the family home in the name of filial piety (*xiao*) is heavily favored over putting them into facilities for the elderly. This is explicit government policy in line with the resurgence of state-sponsored Confucianism, and is probably intended to reduce the state's burden of caring for seniors in an aging population (Yang 2016; Feng 2017). At the same time, accelerated urbanization and demographic pressures, amplified by the now-abandoned one-child policy, undermine norms of family care and lead to reinterpretations of filial piety, at the same time as the ability to pay for the high cost of professional care in institutions is becoming a social privilege (Zhan and Montgomery 2003; Zhan, Feng, and Luo 2008; Chen 2016). In addition, the economic slowdown has turned the seniors care service sector into a new growth engine, in which real estate and insurance companies have invested, with policy support from the State Council's "Opinions Regarding Speeding Up the Development of Seniors Care Service Sector," issued in 2013 (Strauss and Xu 2018).[19]

In the three urban villages, people talk shamefacedly about putting elderly relatives into care facilities and accuse adult children doing this of ingratitude, lack of family values, and "disregard of five thousand years of Confucian values" (*weibei le wuqian nian de rujia chuantong*).[20] Yet in a situation where many elderly native villagers have been left behind by their children in the former villages, community-building focuses strongly on their care. "Caring for the seniors" campaigns display filial piety toward the elderly generation. Although the community centers favor care solutions that allow seniors to remain at home (*jujia yanglao*), supporting this by offering free blood-pressure tests and consultations with medical professionals as well as basic home services including food and medical checks, care centers for the elderly are a growing phenomenon in China, including in villages-in-the-city. Free access to these services and centers is highly uneven, however, determined by people's level of income and local citizenship.

Senior-Care Centers and Seniors' Activity Centers as Cover-Ups in River Hamlet

In the eyes of two subdistrict female employees, Mrs. Hu and Mrs. Lin, who were in their early and mid-thirties and had been brought up in middle-class urban families, some businesses, especially the River Hamlet seniors' activity centers and seniors' university, are "villagers' affairs" (*cunliren de shi*).[21] They are spaces dedicated to social and entertainment activities for the elderly, such as group dance, calligraphy, flower arranging, and singing. Subdistrict employees neither manage their funding and expenses nor oversee the type of activities they offer. Mrs. Hu and Mrs. Lin had heard about the dance groups and the competitions that used to be hosted annually in River Hamlet (see next chapter, "Rivalry over Dance Space") but never attended them.

The newly established community (*shequ*) office knew more about the ins and outs of the village but was mainly concerned with the new urbanites living in the gated communities. The district government expects the community office to provide an elderly home-care program serviced by community volunteers, care workers, and family members. However, such a program requires steady and substantial funding, which was not available to Mrs. Fang and her coworkers. When upper-level officials or university partners whose students carry out social-work internships visited, they staged a performance by recruiting some elderly residents and arranging for them to hold their activities at the community office for a few days.

Care for the elderly native villagers of River Hamlet before its redevelopment was financed by the village collectives. One of the village committees (corresponding to Production Team No. 1) focused on activities for seniors in the project repurposing the former temple complex and public square that it administered not far from its headquarters (see map 1.7). The tiny temple was dedicated to the ancestors of this former natural village's predominant lineage. The three right and left wings of the temple that one passes between to reach the altar hall at the end of the complex had been redeveloped as a village clinic, a seniors' activity center, and a seniors' university. The temple's entrance was decorated with several metal plates containing inscriptions such as "Happy seniors' *shequ*" in recognition of the care for seniors provided by the community—actually the former village collectives. The room occupied by the seniors' university was not, however, used as a classroom for courses for seniors, as the name suggests: instead it was a meeting point for elderly, mostly female, former villagers. Calligraphy courses were offered for their grandchildren, because while they were being taken care of, their grandparents could concentrate on practicing their dance routines in the square.

The label "seniors' activity center" was also a cover for other types of activity, with gambling parlors branding themselves as such. While these purported to be nonprofit centers for the elderly, offering activities including card games, pool, and karaoke, in reality they were commercial parlors that encouraged them to spend their money on such entertainments, and they also offered gambling for people of all ages in back rooms equipped with karaoke systems and pool tables. These migrant-owned gambling businesses were obviously thriving and redistributing some of the new wealth of the rentier native villagers. Their disguise as senior centers gave the hidden gambling rooms in the back immunity from the law. The sheer number of senior centers—ten along the two-kilometer street—falsely advertised the *shequ*'s community-building success.

Most native River Hamlet seniors live with their families, supporting themselves mainly with rent collected from migrants. They are fortunate to have a reliable source of income; although this changed with the demolition of their old buildings, many had accumulated savings over a decade of renting out rooms or houses. By contrast, many senior migrants have to work; prior to the demolition, many had lived with their shop-owner children in the living quarters at the back of their small shops. The majority of the rural migrants who initially arrived to run the shops in River Hamlet's central street in the years following the urban reform had been doing well financially and were able to afford to house their parents in urban apartments. Making money was easy for those who opened small shops early on in the urbanization of River Hamlet. Mrs. Cheng, who ran a jewelry shop for ten years (see chapter 1), also rented the space above her shop and moved in. In 2009, when she married a local man, she and her husband bought an apartment nearby, and she was able to move her parents to Xi'an permanently. Their business provided a solid base, allowing them to care for their elderly parents, and they benefited from the childcare the parents provided. However, as houses prices grew by 400–500 percent compared to 2009, it became harder for newcomers to emulate their success. Many recent migrants working in the service economy struggle to establish a foothold in their new environment. For them, caring for their elderly parents is unattainable, as they are unable to purchase an urban apartment in which to live with them.

Before the village started urbanizing, the state-designated work unit (*danwei*) provided care for the elderly exclusively reserved for its members, that is, for the few residents of River Hamlet who already had urban *hukou* benefits. These workers were employed by state-owned factories in the 1960s through the 1980s. Many such retired workers still live in the single-family dormitories, or *tongzi lou*, with four dormitories to a floor sharing one bathroom. With the rise of the market economy and the dismantling of the *danwei* they must now pay more for drugs and healthcare out of a fixed pension that has not increased with the cost of living. Only the few pensioners in their eighties receive 8,000 RMB a month due to their long service in the socialist manufacturing sector. Most are in their sixties and seventies and live in the dormitories, which now belong to the municipality, on a monthly pension of just 300 yuan. Seniors pay a symbolic rent of about 100 RMB per year; one of them, Mrs. Huang, aged 66, could not remember when she had last paid this.

Factory *danwei* have become rarities, and people in their fifties have left the single-family dormitories in which they grew up. Unlike the previous generation of workers, who have received state care throughout their lives, those who can have to pay for commercial care. In fact, although state-provided care is still desirable, and many people apply for a government job because it will provide a good pension and senior care in the future, most people seek private senior care.

One private care provider, the Feng Care Center, which escaped demolition because it is situated in the part of River Hamlet that had already been redeveloped (map 1.7), offers care for the elderly for a premium fee in contravention of Xi'an municipal government policy, which does not issue licenses to private centers. Many such businesses skirt the rules by claiming to be social corporations. The Feng Care Center, established in 2004, justifies its social corporation status by collaborating with a Japanese research foundation that regularly sends interns to work there, and by offering internships for college students, particularly those majoring in social work. Most of the residents are 70 to 80 years old and are ranked as independently able, or dependent. The monthly cost ranges from 1,800 to 2,800 RMB depending on each resident's health and psychological condition. Their adult children usually pay six-monthly or annually, and although they are encouraged to visit every week, they do so rarely, except on national holidays and birthdays. Almost all the elderly residents are from Xi'an. Sending one's older parents off to live in any care center is not a popular or even accepted practice in Xi'an, but some seniors are saving to move to such a center later in their lives: one of them exclaimed, "I'm taking control of my own old age by paying for care services and even a funeral service if I can—that's the kind of freedom I want!"[22]

Nurturing Life:
Senior Care in South and North Gate Community Centers

Care for the elderly receives more attention from Chengdu municipal authorities than it does in Xi'an, perhaps because Chengdu's senior population is bigger than the national average.[23] The municipal government has made the community the focal scale at which senior care is provisioned. In 2016 it rolled out a three-year action plan for the construction of community nursing homes (*shequ yanglaoyuan*), actually mainly daycare facilities, which are less expensive than nursing homes offering beds. The aim was for "community care to be the core, and home care to be the support (*yi shequ wei hexin, jujia yanglao wei yituo*)."[24] The plan included a one-off subsidy for the construction of elderly daycare facilities, and the concrete impact was almost immediately evident: most communities in Chengdu now have some kind of facility for seniors, most commonly as part of a larger community center and sometimes as a stand-alone building. In North and South Gate, the daycare centers all seem well-used and fill a simple need for free socializing space for seniors in the community.[25]

Offering events and activities for seniors at their daycare center during the day while they live in their own homes at night has become the model encouraged by the municipal government. The centers are only loosely programmed: most often they function as mahjong and tea rooms, sometimes with a basic health clinic or even a canteen attached, as in the case of North Gate community, which provides regular inexpensive meals for community members. Although their goals seem rudimentary, many of the events staffed by volunteers at the community center already include a senior care component.

The community centers rely on their effective volunteer programs. The services provided at the North and South Gate community centers both rely on and support a range of paid and unpaid care work. Volunteers, mostly middle-aged female native villagers and rural migrants, maintain cleanliness and order while wearing volunteer vests, circulating through the building, cleaning up trash in the square, and putting away books in the reading room. Two main groups of volunteers were present at the North Gate community event offering health advice for seniors living at home: middle-aged women, most of whom belonged to the dance group, and younger women

Figure 4.2. North Gate's community center and canteen, Chengdu. © Jessica Wilczak.

from outside the community. Their common goal was to facilitate the elderly's participation in community events held for their benefit. They registered attendees, handed out meal tickets, and provided information. The professionals in traditional Chinese medicine and from holistic clinics who had been invited to speak mainly offered home remedies and exercise tips rather than actual medicine. Most elderly people enjoy this type of event for the atmosphere, the free food, and the attention they receive from the volunteers.

The North Gate community center is predominantly populated by elderly villagers who spend most of their day there, eating their breakfast in the canteen before engaging in mahjong and knitting until it is time for lunch, which they also take in the canteen. Apart from the teahouse, the most popular area in the center is the mahjong parlor. Many go home for a nap after lunch and return in the afternoon—it is a very short walk as the center is at the edge of the resettlement estates. The community center also offers a simple medical clinic for blood pressure and other basic checkups, which is not permanently staffed, and a blind masseur charges a reduced fee because the space is provided to him for free. Access to this socialization space, although it is far from elaborate, boosts the seniors' quality of life, and they have praised the party secretary for creating it. While government officials are partly responsible for enabling this space for the elderly, it is the work of the volunteers and the agency of the seniors themselves that makes their care at the community center possible.

Welfare Benefits as a Countergift in Pine Mansion

Although its overall population is generally young, Pine Mansion's native population is visibly aging, largely because it was formerly an emigrant village (*qiaoxiang*). Overseas emigrants and those who left to work in a city have returned to live out their years in the village. Since Shenzhen has opened up new opportunities closer to home, middle-aged people tend to live and work downtown, leaving their elderly parents in the former village and visiting them once a month and on public holidays. In 1994 a home for the elderly (*laoren yiyuan*) was built in Pine Mansion with contributions from the diaspora (Trémon 2022). In 2004 the building was torn down and replaced by the taller Zhenneng building, named after the Chen lineage's founding ancestor. Its ground floor is still used as a community center for the elderly, and the natives still call it the *laoren yiyuan*. However, it is now formally run by the officially registered and state-sanctioned Association for Elderly People (*laoren xiehui*), and although it still receives substantial subsidies from shareholding companies, it is also increasingly funded by the district administration. Pine Mansion's elderly native villagers spend their mornings and afternoons there, chatting and playing mahjong. Caring for the elderly is a central precept of the local lineage's moral economy. The large shareholding company gives each of the community's senior residents 1,000 RMB in a red envelope on New Year's Day, and 500 RMB on several other public holidays and on the days when ancestral rituals are performed. This home for the elderly is for both native *hukou* holders and non-*hukou* holders who have returned from Hong Kong and elsewhere, some of whom have very little by way of savings and no pension. They receive monetary assistance from fellow Chen villagers but are not eligible for the state's new schemes for elderly people described below.

All retired native villagers receive a pension from the shareholding companies and benefit from subsidized elderly care that their adult children, who often work in downtown Shenzhen, cannot provide. Most care workers employed by younger native villagers to care for their aging parents are younger seniors themselves. They describe their work as dirty and demeaning, but they have no choice. Their adult children do not live in the village, unlike many non-*hukou*-holding seniors who live in the village together with their children and care for their grandchildren as dependents on their children's income.[26] The care workers, or "nannies" (*baomu*), employed by the native villagers are all female migrants originating from nearby provinces, many from Guangxi, who used to work for Hong Kong–run factories but were laid off when they reached fifty, the official retirement age. They were subsequently hired as *baomu* by a private recruitment agency.

The elderly-care industry has been expanding in Shenzhen. The districts' livelihood microprojects (*minwei shishi*) and charity organization (*Cishanhui*), both run by the Civil Affairs Department (*minzheng bu*), oversee care for the elderly as a partnership that is managed publicly but run privately (*gongbanminying*). They grant funding to selected projects set up by subdistrict governments and run by private enterprises that tender for them. One of the first pilot projects, initiated in 2017 in the subdistrict containing Pine Mansion, is a daycare center run by the Kindhearted Home Company that won the tender organized by the local office. Funding from the district's charity organization covers subsidized activities, and the subdistrict provides the company with free space for staff offices and for leisure activities such as ping-pong. The facilities are theoretically open to *hukou* and non-*hukou* holders alike.

Its most advertised and visible activity is the daily delivery of midday lunches for the elderly. The company coordinates with elderly people's associations (*laoren xiehui*) in each *shequ*; in Pine Mansion, lunchboxes are delivered to the home for the elderly just before noon.[27] *Hukou* holders' lunches are subsidized by nine yuan, and non-*hukou* holders who earn points by volunteering at charity events connected to the project can exchange these for food stamps to buy basic products such as flour and cooking oil at the charity shop at the Kindhearted Home center.

The company manager, an educated man in his thirties originating from a rural village in Guangdong Province, stated that public goods should be free but defined the term *gongyi* as both welfare (*fuli*) and countergift. He explained that prioritizing *hukou* holders is only normal, standard policy, but interestingly, he seemed aware of the potential paradox and legitimized the subsidy in moral terms. He added that although "these native people's families have money," the benefits they receive "are a kind of gift from the government in return (*huikui*) for their contributions to the local economy."[28] He added afterward that from his own and the government's point of view, these are welfare benefits (*fuli*) for *hukou* holders. A village moral economy to which the notion of the countergift is central (Yang 1994; Yan 1996; Kipnis 1996) here bolsters the *hukou*-based system of welfare allocation. Chapter 5 discusses how territorial entitlements remain the backbone of the state public goods regime, a view that is, though challenged by alternative visions of "the right to the city," strongly adhered to by ordinary citizens.

Competitive Funding of Neo-Confucian Projects

The status of community centers is hybrid. They are presented as grassroots organizations because they are located at the lowest administrative echelon and, in theory at least, work in close collaboration with the residents' committees. However, their staff is appointed from above, and as chapter 1 has shown, most government funding allocated to the new urban communities has been redirected to the community centers and away from the elected residents' committees.[29] Community centers are therefore management bodies rather than grassroots civic organizations (Howell 2016). They are supposed to be self-governing, but this is mainly to encourage them to devise their own means of funding their activities. Despite being responsible for a wide range of tasks, *shequ* are famously underfunded.

Community leaders and staff are thus in an ambiguous position and face a double bind: they are not officially a part of government, but they are expected to enact the government's community-building policies by using often insufficient funds that they have to compete for. Much of their funding is distributed by the districts' Civil Affairs Department (*Minzheng Bu*)—formerly the district's Social Security Department—via project-based competitive allocation. Most of the overhead costs for salaries and office space are covered by the district, but they are kept to a minimum. This forces community leaders to be creative with community resources such as land and facilities, using them as springboards in their applications for complementary funding—this is because part of their budget for any project must be locally sourced in cash or kind. This competitive project-based funding system operated at all three of our case-study sites. Here I compare the strikingly similar systems applied in Pine Mansion and in Chengdu.

Confucian Project at Pine Mansion's Lineage Temple

Until a few years ago, Pine Mansion's public goods were partly financed by the collectives and lineage foundation. Now most, and particularly those directly related to urban renovation, are financed by the government. The Chen head of the Chengguan stated that "basically all [the funding] comes from the government, except that related to the village" (*shuyu cunnei*, literally "part of the village," meaning activities sponsored by the shareholding companies and the lineage foundation).

Mrs. Yu, the social worker I met on Beneficence Day, stated that "investment in welfare" (or in charities—she used the term *gongyi*) had started just before she began working in Pine Mansion in 2016.[30] In recent years, she explained, "projects have slowly started to come into the *shequ*," allowing social workers to reach "more and different populations," implying that they benefit migrant workers more than previously. "In the past, there were far fewer services for the residents, but in recent years the *shequ* has started to offer more diverse services, welfare services (*gongyi fuwu*)." The funding is limited, particularly for social work primarily concerned with non-native villagers' welfare, and is subject to project-based competitive bidding in which different communities compete for titles such as the Most Civilized or the Most Compassionate *Shequ*.[31]

One example of such a project is the Sunshine Lunch (*yangguang wucan*) program launched in 2014 by the Pine Mansion community center's social workers. The rationale for the project, according to the social worker Mrs. Yu, was that primary school students "buy snacks from the convenience store [and then] have nowhere to go, so all they can do is wander around the community." The underlying idea was, as always, the fight against disorder, *luan*. While a survey counted about two thousand school-aged children among Pine Mansion's nonregistered population, the program was restricted to only twenty from "needier families in the community, such as single parents or sick people, parents who are both working, and those who live far from the school." Parents submitted their applications, and the children were selected following interviews and home visits (*jiafang*) that "allowed cross-checking the family's situation with information given by volunteer parents and other data."[32]

While project-based charitable programs allow identification of the most urgent problems from the bottom up, Mrs. Yu emphasized that such projects run for a limited time and receive little funding, and therefore can have only a limited effect on needs and problems. In the context of competition for scarce budgetary resources, projects are selected according to what Mrs. Yu called "priority criteria." She did not specify what the criteria were, but it appears that only projects aimed at the most urgent matters—that is, threats to the local social order and security—stand a chance of being funded. Mrs. Yu explained that they had to select the children rigorously because of a lack of space—they had no dedicated space, so children had lunch in an office at the community center—and of money. When I met her, the Sunshine Lunch program had been terminated.[33] It had operated for three years, during which the social workers had applied six times—each time seeking initial approval and backing from the Women's Federation, the subdistrict office, and then the district's

Social Civil Affairs Bureau—to different departments, which had granted funding for different periods. The funds allocated by the district are limited in scope, as each community center is responsible for its own projects and must apply for separate funding for each one from different departments; moreover, funding applications are time-limited, as the various departments provide funding for only one term.

Although it looks complex and burdensome, Mrs. Yu emphasized that the budget allocation system has been streamlined since she started as a social worker in 2016. She believes that smaller problems as well as the most urgent ones now have an increased likelihood of being awarded funding. There are more sources of funding and greater funding capacity under Shenzhen's new livelihoods project (*minsheng xiangmu*), which respond to the Chinese central government's greater emphasis on livelihood policy. Project descriptions are stored in the Shenzhen Household Network (*Shenzhen Jiayuan Wang*) database, which social workers can consult to select projects they consider suitable for their community rather than having to design and draft each new project application. Its project-based logic has intensified: the system has become increasingly based on competition for funds among urban communities and between different departments in each community.

However, the funding remains conditional on urban renovation. The beneficiaries are generally communities that already partly fulfill the criteria for "rectification"—i.e., redevelopment. The head of the subdistrict Party Working Committee and head of the subdistrict office, Bei Jibiao, declared that they will make full use of the funding for the livelihoods program "to carry out consolidation and upgrading in areas where the rectification is complete"—that is, in areas that have agreed to take part in redevelopment projects. Pine Mansion has benefited from this favorable context more than other communities in the subdistrict because it is listed as one of the subdistrict's key priorities. Mrs. Yu boasted that Pine Mansion had had more social work projects in 2016 than any other community in the subdistrict, with five running in the same year.

It is not just the stage reached in urban development that determines funding priorities. In this competitive context, community-center staff have to devise ways of distinguishing their project by its local characteristics. They exploit past village history and village-funded social goods to fulfill the requirement for creating a sense of belonging to the community and the self-funding criteria. Thus the Pine Mansion community center was granted money for its Zhenneng Project, named after the founding ancestor of the local lineage. This was a set of interconnected projects aimed at capitalizing on the village's local history and utilizing the Pine Mansion Chen's self-financed newly renovated ancestral temple. In 2014 the council of the Chen Lineage Foundation launched a fundraising campaign for the renovation of the ancestral temple to bring it up to the standard of the residential towers being built. The renovation plan was announced in an open letter posted in the temple square next to the usual donations board on 13 October, the day of ancestral worship, which that year involved a particularly large and lavish celebration because it was not only the Chen founding ancestor's birthday but also the centennial anniversary of the village's primary school, which is named after him. The temple had not been renovated since 1925, and its condition had deteriorated under the Cultural Revolution. The open letter calling for contributions invoked the prestige and "face" (*mianzi*) of the entire community.

A renovated temple next door would add value to the future apartments; unsurprisingly, therefore, the real-estate developer contributed a large donation, which is listed beside the donations from Pine Mansioners and their relatives in Hong Kong on a plaque inside the temple.[34] The temple is not only mainly the concern of the native villagers; it is also a place for ancestor worship, which is frowned upon by the party-state and therefore is not seen as having any place in community-building. The Confucian framing of the Zhenneng project legitimized the temple's renovation, and in return the renovated temple became a local material and cultural resource—an asset for driving real estate prices up and for attracting government funding.

The project funded other charitable activities, such as afterschool classes for both native and non-native schoolchildren, organized by the social workers and supervised by volunteers. These took place in the tiny Confucian hall that opened up in an old village house that, as part of the temple complex, escaped demolition. The project included an academy (*shuyuan*) inside the renovated temple, with lineage elders and invited academics offering lectures specializing in *guoxue*, "national studies" or the study of traditional Chinese culture. The term *guoxue* refers to scholarly studies of the historic roots of what is considered Chinese rather than foreign (Makeham, 2011); *guoxue* is sufficiently vague and Chinese cultural values are varied enough to legitimize almost any local project, including lineage revival.[35] Confucianism features centrally in national studies, and while the craze for national studies and the neo-Confucian revival started in the 1990s, it has received a significant boost in state propaganda after

Xi Jinping took power. Xi's era is marked by the reactivation of socialist values alongside the Confucian family values. The glorification of rural frugality and hard work best illustrates this mix.

Again, the project received funding for only a year, and all of its activities had ceased by 2018, most probably because they were conceived of as temporary and linked to the temple renovation. Other types of activities such as the creation of an "ecological farm"—basically, teaching children how to plant and cultivate to inculcate the values of rural frugality and hard work—were held in 2019, but these stopped because of Covid. However, as a result of this renovation, Pine Mansion was labeled "a livable community construction unit and a double-promotion key renovation area"[36] and "a live sample of community construction in the district," a model to be followed by other communities.

From Shareholder Collectives to Self-Funding Communities in South Gate

In April 2018, the Chengdu Municipal Party Committee announced that it would be investing 1.5 billion RMB in community-building projects and issued a number of policy directives to follow up its September 2017 decision to further develop grassroots self-governance capabilities and improve the quality of public goods and services.[37] These directives included purchasing, nurturing, and developing services from social enterprises; improving the recruitment, training, and advancement of community workers; improving the quality of property-management services in residential complexes; promoting the establishment of homeowners' committees and extending the reach of party organizations in residential complexes; and changing the set of performance indicators for local government officials so that their duties would no longer include attracting investment, instead allowing them to focus on providing public goods and services (Yan 2018).

North and South Gate community centers receive 80,000 RMB each year for office costs (*bangong fei*), but the South Gate party secretary said that this does not cover the building's heating and electricity costs, particularly since its renovation and expansion project.[38] They also receive "activities fees" (*huodong fei*) of 300,000 RMB per year for organizing community-center activities. If they need more money, communities (*shequ*) must apply to upper levels of government for special project funding. The South Gate party secretary Gu has been active and successful in applying for funds. It was she who applied for money for the community-center renovations that were being carried out while Jessica was there.

Mr. Wang, the celebrated and popular North Gate party secretary, has held this position since the separation and creation of North Gate community in 2017. Prior to his promotion he was a community worker in South Gate community for about ten years. He adamantly maintains that communities should be entrepreneurial and financially independent of government. In his view, the addition of the word "development" has been the most important element of Chengdu's "community development and governance policy." Communities should not be "waiting, dependent, and demanding" (*bu deng, kao, yao*) in their relations with government but rather sustainable.[39] He listed three sources of income: money for overheads, i.e., office and activity fees, provided by the district; project funds (*xiangmu zijin*), for which communities must apply; and community funds (*shequ zijin*, money from third-party donors). He also mentioned a fourth source of funding: community economic income (*shequ jingji shouyi*). He made an interesting distinction between public income (*gonggong shouyi*) and the former collective economy (*yuanlai de jiti jingji*):

> The former collective economy was a collective organization with members, shareholders (*gudong*); the residents, or villagers, were the shareholders, and they received dividends at the end of the year. However there are no shareholders in the community. If there are native shareholders—and the native residents account for only a fifth [of all residents]—then the other four-fifths think they cannot enjoy the public benefits of the community—that's how it is. There's another thing: the original type of collective economy was basically dividends distributed in cash to members of collective organizations. But now, with the development of this community and of society, even if some form of collective economy still exists I consider that directly distributing cash is unscientific (*bu kexue de*)—all of this is unscientific. Because now it is necessary to allow the citizens and residents of the community to achieve a transformation, and to participate in community development and governance (*shequ fazhan zhili*).

This strong impulse to distinguish the community economy from the collective economy implies a distinction between village commons and state-encouraged commoning of public goods. Wang sees the community economy as the successor to the collective economy. In his eyes it is a new, more evolved ("scientific," in the evolutionary rhetoric) form of collective economy, in that rather than a shareholder economy it is a stakeholder economy. The shareholding system is "unscientific," he argues, because not everyone in the community is a former villager. Its backwardness is emphasized by Wang's dismissive reference to the distribution of dividends in cash, which conjures the image of a traditional, face-to-face peasant community (since all transactions in Chinese cities are now carried out digitally), and also of tax evasion and corruption. Instead, Wang claims, collective income should be used to provide public benefits to all stakeholders.

Mr. Xu, the head of the residents' committee, works very closely with Party Secretary Wang. He is a strong supporter of the project-based allocation of funds. "Why should the government give us money," he asked, "if we don't have something specific to spend it on?"[40] Unsurprisingly, as North Gate is one of Chengdu's model communities and therefore a primary funding beneficiary, both Wang and Xu were very publicly supportive of the entrepreneurial turn in Chengdu's community governance policies.

Partly because there is a strongly felt imperative to build community in an affective sense, and partly because activity fees (*huodong fei*) form a large part of the fixed non-project-based *shequ* budget, cultural activities dominate the daily work of the community center. Tours of the North Gate community center are also vital to the daily rhythm of the place. The party secretary and/or heads of the residents' committees conduct tours for high-profile guests while community-center staff show lower-profile guests around. During Jessica's time in the field, visitors included residents' committee and party members from other recently urbanized villages in Chengdu, community leaders from other cities in China, city- and district-level leaders from Chengdu, a UNESCO delegation, and a group of Communist Party members from Azerbaijan. South Gate community also began to host tours once its community center renovation was completed, although these were not nearly as frequent or high-profile as those in North Gate.

In both communities the activities can be separated into three main categories: celebrations and performances at Chinese New Year and during National Week; classes for children and adults covering a wide selection of *guoxue*-related offerings including calligraphy, history, Confucian morality, and tea-making classes; and special-purpose charity and educational events such as temporary markets for goods from poor areas in Sichuan and taking care of the urban environment by sorting waste. In addition, there are self-organized residents' groups such as the night-jogging group, senior choirs and bands, and a dance group for middle-aged women.

One third-party social organization managed most of the North Gate community center events. It had a special national-studies (*guoxue tang*) classroom to the side of the main community center entrance with a large plaque bearing the name of the organization, which was started in 2018 and had five permanent staff members. It was part of the city government's new community development and governance policy, related specifically to the mandates to both contract out services to social organizations and incubate social enterprises. The staff had all met through the *Guoxue Yuan*, the National Studies Academy, through which they had offered some classes at North Gate. Wang Shuji was only partly satisfied with these classes as he felt they were not tailored to the needs of Qingyuan residents. He suggested to the organization that he would be willing to hire it as an independent entity rather than as part of the *Guoxue Yuan*. The five staff members formed a new social organization, and North Gate community provided them with a space and a contract for service provision.

The new social enterprise specialized in *guoxue* classes, including calligraphy, painting, history, and Confucian morality; it also branched out with other classes such as the adult English-language classes taught by Jessica. Some of the classes were taught by the permanent staff, others by volunteers and paid teachers that the staff contacted via their personal networks. In addition to organizing classes, the company arranged events, including a Traditional Culture Festival and the National Day celebrations, and handled the community center tours when the *shequ* workers and leaders were busy. The woman in charge was Teacher Zhu, an educated, middle-aged woman who had previously worked in hospitality and hotel management. Another staff member, Mr. Fang, in his thirties, who taught Confucian morality classes and offered Confucian family counseling, said rather evasively that he had done "many things" before joining the company. He had a much more entrepreneurial orientation than Teacher Zhu.

In the spring of 2019 the residents' committee voted not to continue its contract, and the organization left North Gate community. In its place North Gate set up what it called a Culture Palace (*wenhua gong*) on the floor above the administrative offices. This is basically a space offered to local education and training companies to present classes for residents at a low or discounted price. This was not the end of the social organization, however: they had already expanded to other *shequ*, including South Gate and several similar recently urbanized communities in the northeastern part of Chengdu.

The Moralized Provision of Public Goods

Since the early 2000s, the prominence of urban communities, or *shequ*, as the key units for maintaining social stability in the context of China's rapid social and economic transformation has continued to grow in central and local policymaking. Grassroots party organizations such as these are expected to play a key role in ensuring social stability. In all three urban villages the community centers are understaffed and rely on volunteering: unpaid labor provided by their own staff and other *shequ* residents. Community leaders and staff seek to deliver public goods at the lowest possible cost to meet the goal of increasing the level of public goods provision in the context of budgetary scarcity.

The governing apparatus itself partly relies on grassroots volunteer labor. Local party members, especially those working at the community centers, are expected to set the standard with their exemplary behavior. The shift toward offloading fiscal responsibility to lower governmental levels and the amount of administrative work involved in the urbanization of villages mean that already-overworked staff are volunteering many hours a week. They are supposed to organize and execute government policies at the local level by implementing projects in response to the latest policy orientation and campaigns, and for this they have little choice but to rely on citizen volunteers. Volunteering is both the goal of and the instrument for reaching the ideal of inclusive and socially stable urban communities: the volunteers are trained to behave as good urban citizens, and their volunteering activities mainly consist of caring for fellow community residents. In Shenzhen, although not in Chengdu, the *hukou* points system is a driver of volunteer participation, even though volunteering rarely earns migrants urban citizenship. However, both settings show them acting as moral citizens.

Furthermore, the gendered interpretation of the injunction to improve oneself is a common feature of all three cases. The moralized governance of public goods provision is therefore graduated, in that it implicitly targets specific sections of the population: mainly lower-middle-class women who aspire to social mobility for themselves and their children and have internalized the injunction to improve themselves. As is often the case, women are seen as best qualified for the care tasks central to community-building projects: serving food, cutting hair, checking blood pressure, supervising children's homework, and teaching calligraphy. Local government has the intention of creating inclusivity, but in fact the charitable events mainly cater for migrants, and activities for native villagers such as seniors' birthday parties and medical checks are largely performed by outsider volunteers. In this way senior care provision is graduated along gender and generation lines and shapes class relations, in that volunteer labor benefits elderly native residents and their adult children who have left their urban villages.

This allows municipalities to provide senior care in such a way that it resolves both the moral dilemma arising from the Confucian emphasis on filial piety and respect for the senior generation and the necessity for an efficient and productive labor force for economic growth. Local moral reciprocity values resonate with the state-organized prioritization of native seniors. In Xi'an's River Hamlet, reciprocity is more a matter of nostalgia for the socialist past, when the factory *danwei* made donations to the larger community. It is most explicit in Pine Mansion, where giving back to the natives legitimizes the government-contracted private senior care company's free services and lunches for local elderly former villagers, and less so in South and North Gate, where there is more emphasis on equality between native villagers and newcomers, although in fact resettled native villagers in Chengdu, particularly seniors, benefit most from the many services offered at the community centers.

In a context of budgetary scarcity, volunteering is encouraged by the state, as is a form of commoning at community level. Indeed the *shequ*, as grassroots management bodies, have to partly rely on local internal resources, the presence and use of which are preconditions for obtaining government funds for projects complying with its mandated policies. Such resources are drawn from urbanized villages' pasts—both their former collective economy in the form of real-estate rents and collectively funded community goods such as temples. In short, community-building in urban villages capitalizes on their past, reframing it in terms of Confucianism while aiming to develop them into "proper," modern, urban communities populated by law-abiding, self-governing, high-quality (*suzhi*) citizens. The former rural collective economy is to be replaced by a modernized public economy deemed more scientific, in that it takes different stakeholders' interests into account and thus functions in the public interest.

While community-building is a form of cultural governance—soft power exercised by the party-state seeking to legitimize its authoritarian rule by leaning on nationalist discourse and consensual cultural symbols from the past (Perry 2013)—at the local scale of the urban community or *shequ* this governance is strongly moralized, in that references to Confucian teachings and values are intended to shape citizens' comportment in such a way as to save higher-level government intervention and budgets. To this extent, community-building testifies to the existence of a moral neoliberalism in China, a notion to which the concluding chapter returns. First, however, chapter 5 explores the latest trend in community-building: the creation of "livable communities."

Notes

1. Shenzhen Caring Action Office Network, "Beneficence Day," 3 May 2018, http://www.szguanai.com/content/2018-05/03/content_21006404.htm. The article describes Beneficence Day (which will be presented below). The Shenzhen Caring Action Office is run by the Municipal Party Propaganda Committee.
2. The Communist Party of China (CPC) has repeatedly claimed that China is "not ready" for democracy because the "quality" of its population is, on the whole, poor (Yu 2009, cited in Nguyen 2013).
3. Particularly since the earthquake in Sichuan in 2008. On *Gongyi Zhongguo* (Charitable China), a popular TV show, candidates compete to obtain money for philanthropic projects to help the poor, the elderly and people living with disabilities.
4. Central Organization Department, Opinions by the Party Central Organization Department on further strengthening and improving street (subdistrict) and community party-building work, 4 October 2004, available at https://www.fosu.edu.cn/jwjcc/党纪党规/规范性文件/1190.html
5. This reflects the fact that residents' committees were established to provide services to people outside of the work unit (*danwei*) system and were—and still are—thus primarily responsible for people of lower social status.
6. *Jiedao* subdistricts ("street offices") and *qu* districts form part of the state's formal urban apparatus. Their primary tasks often involve implementing upper-level state policies on subjects such as urban administration and managing the floating population (see chapter 3).
7. Following the 1989 Law Governing the Organization of Residents' Committees.
8. Shenzhen People's Government Information Office, "Shenzhen China," 7 February 2018, https://www.youtube.com/watch?v=5eiSBYHqX20.
9. See "Pine Mansion" in chapter 1 and "Hopes of Accessing *Hukou*" in chapter 5.
10. In the Longhua civil administration headquarters these departments are clustered together on the same floor, and some actually overlap, with the same organization bearing different names.
11. The committee is run by the Shenzhen Spiritual Civilization Construction Committee.
12. Interview by Anne-Christine Trémon, 29 March 2018.
13. This section is based on Wang Bo's unpublished paper, "High Morale on Shaky Ground," 3 October 2019.
14. On the canteen, see chapter 3, and on the teahouse, see chapter 5.
15. Interview by Jessica Wilczak, 21 August 2019.
16. Interview by Jessica Wilczak, 29 June 2019.
17. Jessica Wilczak, *Fieldnotes*, 24 July 2019, cited in *Final Report*, 30 July 2019.
18. Interview by Jessica Wilczak, 23 July 2018.
19. State Council, document 35, 13 September 2013, http://www.gov.cn/zwgk/2013-09/13/content_2487704.htm.
20. Wang Bo, *Final Report*, 31 October 2019.

21. Wang Bo, "High Morale on Shaky Ground," unpublished paper, 3 October 2019.
22. Wang Bo, interview, 5 March 2018, and Wang Bo, *Final Report*, 31 October 2019.
23. In 2018 people over sixty years old accounted for about 21.34 percent of the city's population of 14.76 million; https://sichuan.scol.com.cn/cddt/201910/57352712.html. In 2018 people over sixty constituted 17.9 percent of the total population in China. *Xinhuanet*, 9 February 2019, http://www.xinhuanet.com/english/2019-02/09/c_137808376.htm.
24. Chengdu city three-year action plan for the construction of community nursing homes 2016–2018, https://baike.baidu.com/item/成都市社区养老院建设三年行动计划（2016—2018年）/19444592?
25. This section is based on Jessica Wilczak's *Final Report*, 30 July 2019.
26. On pensions, see chapter 1, "Powerful Shareholding Companies in Pine Mansion, Shenzhen."
27. The company also monitors a database of registered elderly people to keep track of health data such as blood pressure, illnesses, etc.
28. Interview by Anne-Christine Trémon, 28 March 2018.
29. Residents' committees have also become more bureaucratized, turned into administrative agencies (Audin 2015; Wu 2018).
30. Shenzhen's Municipal Civil Affairs Bureau has made social work central to community construction. Each center must employ at least six staff, among whom 60 percent must be licensed social workers. These are hired from nongovernmental social work agencies by the district government (Tang and Sun 2017).
31. See Shenzhen Care Network, http://www.szguanai.com/node_103713.htm.
32. Interview by Anne-Christine Trémon, 4 April 2018.
33. However, the situation was resolved by the Shenzhen Bureau of Education's decision to keep public schools open all day from 1 April 2019. Until then, only private schools were open at lunchtime, and public-school students whose parents had the means to pay for lunchtime care would use private care institutions. After a fire broke out at one of the private daycare centers in 2017, all such centers' business licenses were withdrawn, although I observed that some continued to operate without a license.
34. This was the first village call for funding that was little circulated overseas and to which few overseas Chens contributed; the reasons for this shift are explored in Trémon 2022.
35. In the 1990s the government launched a new "patriotic education" campaign focused on the Confucian classics and encouraged the construction of Confucius institutes abroad and Confucian academies across the country to bolster its legitimacy after the Tiananmen Square incident (Zhao 1998). Note, however, that the Neo-Confucian revival in China is also bottom-up, resulting from grassroots citizens' initiatives (Dutournier and Ji 2009; Billioud and Thoraval 2014). On *guoxue* and lineage revival, see Payette 2016.
36. On the double promotion campaign in Shenzhen, see chapter 3, and on livable communities, see chapter 5.
37. These were issued under the umbrella of the 1 + 6 + N policy system, where 1 refers to the original thirty-point document issued in September 2017, 6 refers to the six major supporting documents, and N refers to an uncounted number of supporting documents to guide concrete projects.
38. Interview by Jessica Wilczak, 23 July 2018.
39. Interview by Jessica Wilczak, 17 January 2019.
40. Cited in Jessica Wilczak's *Final Report*, 30 July 2019. The remainder of this section is based on this report.

— Chapter 5 —

SEGREGATED PUBLIC SPACE AND THE RIGHT TO THE CITY

With urbanization, native villagers have been faced with a flow of strangers into their former village space, a phenomenon to which they have contributed by renting apartments to migrants. Native villagers also face increased intervention from higher administrative bodies, as, once urbanized, they are fully subordinated to the authority of the state and lose their village institutions' prior relative autonomy. The state is asserting its power by shaping urban space via redevelopment projects to integrate the villages into overall city planning. The state also makes its presence felt visually, by carving out new public spaces for political propaganda and for citizens' altruistic volunteering at charitable events, but also for citizens to engage in leisure activities and to create a feeling of belonging in the *shequ*, the urban community.

Since the reform era, Chinese public space has shifted from the monumental representation of socialist ideologies to a wide array of political as well as recreational and commercial spaces (Gaubatz 2008: 73–75). Municipal government urban planners have fostered the creation of plazas and pedestrian areas to accommodate commercial development as well as parks and squares to satisfy the fast-growing population's recreational and socializing needs.

This chapter shows how public space is created as part of building "livable communities" (*yiju shequ*). The concept of livability has been in circulation for about fifty years among urban planning experts across the globe (McArthur and Robin 2019). A malleable term, livability has been used to push for policies focusing on social services, aesthetics, safety, and environmental issues (Ley 1990; Pacione 1990). This understanding of livability has been reinforced by a host of international indicators and ranking systems.[1] Livability services city branding and is driven by a consumption-oriented vision of urban life in the effort to attract global capital; in the Asian context, Singapore is a premium example of a state touting livability to meet this goal (Teo 2014). However, livability is also a form of response to the idea of the "right to the city," initially voiced by Henri Lefebvre (1996 [1968]).[2] While the right to the city has become a rallying cry for many urban social movements, it has also gained traction with NGOs and international organizations (Mayer 2009; Costes 2010). A recent UN Habitat policy paper, "Right to the City and Cities for All" (United Nations 2017), defines "livable cities" as cities that are inclusive (pro-poor, gender, youth, and aging), welcoming to migrants, and safe, and which protect their heritage.

China's grassroots livability policies, shaped by preexisting community-building (*shequ jianshe*) policies, reflect the shift in central-government rhetoric toward people-oriented development since the early 2000s. This shift was roughly contemporaneous with a push for economic upgrading via a move from an industry-heavy to a service-based economy across a number of Chinese cities. Such local efforts to upgrade have resulted in what has been called a "talent war" among Chinese cities to attract educated white-collar workers (see chapter 1; Shen and Li 2020). Livability is considered a key tool in this war: cities compete for talent via preferential *hukou* policies and policies aimed at improving the quality of life.

This emphasis on the well-being of urban dwellers means that public space features centrally in livability projects. However, in urbanized villages where native villagers coexist with new residents, the shaping of public space also aims to integrate the migrants and create a new, more inclusive sense of belonging to the *shequ*, or urban community. The construction of urban public space in former rural villages is not easy, because the limited space available for public use often overlies former village public space, juxtaposing urban public space onto former rural public space. Despite the Chinese state's modernist approach, the planning of this space is therefore contingent (having to deal with existing conditions) rather than total, to borrow James Holston's (1989) terms. While this recombinant urbanization (Kipnis 2016) has not replaced village sociality entirely with urban sociality, it has resulted in variegated forms of sociality.

Amanda Huron (2017) argues that the cohabitation of strangers constitutes an obstacle to commoning. Indeed the prevalence of superficial "traffic" relations, i.e., minimal contact between city dwellers (Wirth 1938; Hannerz 1980), is often noted as a characteristic of cities. However, while urbanized Chinese villages are on the one hand quintessentially urban as places that bring strangers together, on the other they are places where native villagers, tied by dense networks of face-to-face communality, have to deal with the arrival of massive inflows of strangers. The potential for conflict is therefore heightened, while the preexisting commonality that Ostrom emphasizes as a condition for successful commons-building, namely that its members "share a past, and expect to share a future" (2015: 88), is severely weakened.

The process of creating public space in urban villages is graduated. Livable Community policy explicitly prioritizes the more advanced urban communities, which it targets with Livable City (*yiju chengshi*) projects. Redevelopment projects generate splintered urbanism on the city scale, as they prioritize urban villages deemed more "mature"—that is, more advanced in the urbanization process—and often capitalize on existing village-level public infrastructure and services.[3] The creation of public space also generates splintered urbanism at the urban village scale, and the uses of public space reproduce existing divisions between social classes.

The availability of space is often limited. Although urban villages manifest a low degree of residential segregation (Hao 2015), and despite the state's wish to integrate city inhabitants into solidary, self-governing urban communities and foster their sense of belonging in their locality, social segregation remains strong. Indeed, the limited public space available generates rivalry among residents over access rights. Referring to urban commons as a city's "atmospherics"—its spheres of sociality and connectedness within networks—Borch and Kornberger (2015: 6) claim that unlike common-pool resources, urban commons are not rivalrous. In cities, one person's consumption of a park or shopping mall not only does not decrease but actually increases their value for others, as when crowds come together for people to enjoy the presence of others or to observe what others are purchasing. Note that, *stricto sensu*, this open access combined with nonrivalry makes "sociality" a public good rather than a common-pool resource in economists' typologies. However, the absence of rivalry in urban settings is highly contestable, as this chapter shows.

To what extent is the new urban public space actually public? This chapter plays with several meanings of the term "public" in relation to space. First, public spaces emerge "with the differentiation of a nominally representative state on the one side and civil society and the market on the other," implying a separation from the household as the private sphere of social reproduction (Low and Smith 2006: 6). Public plazas and squares particularly embody the conception of public space as a site for the collective expression of citizenship (Low 2000; Low and Smith 2006; Miller 2007; Lazar 2014). It is hard to apply Habermasian notions of the public sphere in China's case (see Huang 1993; Madsen 1993; Rankin 1993). The Chinese state's provision of public squares and parks serves governmental purposes; from a Foucauldian point of view, public spaces are, par excellence, a site for the exercise of governmentality and the shaping of disciplined subjects, but they are also "representational spaces," sites for the reassertion of state sovereign power (Lefebvre 1991 [1974]; Oakes 2019).

Second, "the public" refers to a form of typically urban sociality in that it consists of people who are virtually strangers whose impersonal interaction in public space is often considered a typically urban characteristic (Wirth 1938; Sennett 1977; Hannerz 1980). A third notion of "public" has a better bearing on the situations encountered in the field, namely the public as a group of people uniting around a shared issue or interest (Dewey 1991 [1927]). This notion allows for grounding the public in physical space and viewing public spaces as sites of a diverse range of citizenship practices (Smith 1996; Mitchell 2003; Lazar 2014; Woodman and Guo 2020; Low 2017). In China, emerging publics can be citizens claiming civil rights through legal action (Brandtstädter 2013), or equally, ordinary citizens claiming their right to access space, forming a public through their simple, quotidian, often collective practices in public space (Farquhar 2009; Thireau 2020). Local residents' everyday uses of public spaces demonstrate a variety of purposes, motivations, and understandings that can lay the foundation for the formation of counterpublics.[4] For migrant incomers, being able to use public space is a recognition of their right to the city as new urbanites (Mitchell 2003; Harvey 2012).

In a final sense, "public" refers to a state-provided public good, publicly managed and accessible to all. As public spaces are increasingly neoliberalized and turned into profit-generating sites, the question of who they benefit makes them spatial representations of ongoing redefinitions of citizenship and the state (Staeheli and Mitchell 2008; Loughran 2014).

This chapter first examines the various livable city projects enacted in Shenzhen, Xi'an, and Chengdu. The Shenzhen municipality is the most explicit about the prioritization of already-developed communities. The "let some people get rich first" logic is transposed from the national to the city level. While the creation of public space for communal use features centrally in livable city projects, there is limited availability of truly state-provided public space. Next, ethnographic observation of the actual uses of public spaces highlights their strongly segregated character. As village public space is reshaped as urban public space, native villagers tend to maintain certain communal activities that they carried out in such spaces before urbanization. Actually, migrants appear to use public space more frequently than natives. Because their rented apartments have limited living space, they need it far more for their childcare and personal well-being activities; however, they are often relegated to the margins of spaces monopolized by native villagers. In the third section I explore the differential, class-based understanding of the right to the city among non-native urban village residents, and the sense of future possibilities and entitlement that leads them to seek to change their *hukou* and claim their right to the city. While low-skilled migrant workers express their right to the city based on their contribution to building it, middle-class, non-*hukou*-holding residents espouse the municipal authorities' vision of the right to the city, in which an individual's deservingness depends on their self-responsibility and ability to contribute financially to the urban public goods regime.

Creating Livable Communities in Limited Space

Community officials in Chinese cities are being enlisted to enact municipally issued livable-city policy. Because of the broadness of the term, local community responses are varied. A general characteristic of livable communities is that their basic urban infrastructure—sanitation, sewerage, garbage treatment, transportation—should function well, and they should also include improved public services and cultural and sports facilities. The livability policies for urban villages are more specifically concerned with integrating native and non-native residents into solidary urban communities. The creation of public space is a key instrument for achieving this goal, but success strongly depends on the presence of preexisting communal village space.

Public spaces are not new to urbanized villagers. The introduction of the *hukou* under Mao reduced their ability to sell agricultural produce at urban markets and strongly restricted their potential for moving to the city, contributing to local retrenchment.[5] Although village life was mainly based on interactions between familiar members connected through kinship and neighborhood ties (Fei 1939; Yang 1959), there was another form of public life in the small village committees and cultivation groups, and at the administrative village level, in the village assembly (*cunwei dahui*), which had returned to the fore in the reform era. Although the policy of building livable cities presents the creation of public space as an ex-nihilo government action, it depends heavily on preexisting former-village public space and on the timing of redevelopment projects. Thus public space in urbanized villages takes various official and unofficial forms.

Building an Integrative Public Square in Pine Mansion

Shenzhen's livable communities (*yiju shequ*) policy has accompanied its "double promotion" (chapter 3) of economic and ecological improvement together with improved government services and governance capacity. In 2012 Shenzhen's municipal government issued its Work Plan for the Construction of Livable Communities in Shenzhen, with an emphasis on a "comfortable life, a beautiful environment, complete functionality, and a sense of happiness for the people" (*xinfu gan*).[6]

Reflecting Shenzhen's history, the plan recognizes a gap between the districts that originally lay within and outside of the special economic zone, and how, in the outlying districts where Pine Mansion is located, urban communities had not been planned, infrastructure was lacking, and "the quality of services and level of grassroots cultural institutions need to be improved." Shenzhen aimed to reach the status of "advanced city and model city for the construction of livable cities in the country and Guangdong Province" by 2020. This goal was scheduled in three steps, each with quantified targets for the percentage of communities that achieve livable status: in the short term (2012–13), funds and resources "should be used first to support communities with better basic conditions to build livable communities," while secondarily fostering the development of communities "with ordinary or poor basic conditions"; in the middle term (2014–15), established livable communities should be used as models to "accelerate the construction of communities with certain basic conditions"; and finally 2015–20 involved "increase[d] investment in communities with poor conditions."[7]

Pine Mansion was addressed in the second step. In 2015, the subdistrict government invested 700,000 RMB in the construction of what it calls a "'street heart park" (*jiexin gongyuan*), i.e., a park "integrating leisure and greening." Evolutionary rhetoric is used to

Figure 5.1. Public square in Pine Mansion urban village, Shenzhen. © Anne-Christine Trémon.

describe the change in a *Southern Daily* article: "Taking advantage of the opportunity to create a livable community … wasteland overgrown with weeds and littered with garbage has become a street heart park."[8] The "park" (actually a small square) is situated on the far side of the pond that faces the ancestral temple (*citang*). It stands next to the community office and the main shareholding company's headquarters and is bordered by *diaolou*, tower buildings built in the late nineteenth and early twentieth centuries by merchants and returned overseas Chinese, the village's most prosperous members, to display their wealth. These *diaolou* have been moved from their original sites among the low-rise houses with tiled roofs to clear space for the construction of high-rise buildings.

Presenting the square as if created out of chaos and dirt, the *Southern Daily* makes no reference to the former village space it has actually replaced. The article hints at Pine Mansion's long history but does not mention the ancestral temple, the main reason why this village square lies there. There is little greening, but the village's renovated public square includes a children's playground and fitness equipment, a concrete stage for communal and propaganda activities, and a brand-new basketball court, replacing the old one. Until 2016 the basketball ground was fenced and kept locked for the use of only the native-villager basketball players. After the government funded the renovation, the fence was removed, and the area was opened to all. Now children and adults play and exercise there during the day.

While the concept of the livable community is rather vague, it denotes a wish to combine urban renovation with migrant integration: "In Pine Mansion, where migrant workers form the majority of the population, the demand for leisure [facilities] was particularly urgent."[9] Pine Mansion's migrants had not awaited governmental intervention, however: since the early 2010s couples had strolled in the evenings around the stalls offering cheap clothes and counterfeit items for sale, young factory workers had clustered around the pool tables on the sidewalks provided by internet cafés, and children had played and adults had danced on whatever tract of space was available. Now, apart from the playing and the dancing, most of this activity is gone as a result of the industrial and migrant population upgrading policies described in chapters 2 and 3.

Cleanliness, acceptable leisure, and governmental presence together form what is understood as a livable community and a civilized city. The creation of China's livable communities largely amounts to creating neatly demarcated public spaces, earmarked for leisure, that everyone knows have been paid for by the government. When asked whether Pine Mansion's public square was open to all, most responded that it was, because the government had paid for it. The government makes its demiurgic intervention visible by using it to advertise its policies with slogans and informative posters. However, nobody in Pine Mansion uses the term "street heart park"; they call it "[the place] near the ancestral temple" (*citang nabian*). When I referred to it as a public square (*guangchang*), several people expressed the opinion that it certainly could not qualify as a square due to its small size, and one exclaimed, "It's certainly not a public square—it's a basketball court!"

The pond between the temple and the square confers the impression of a wide-open space, but the usable space is much smaller than it appears. Many migrants complained about the small size of the park and lamented the lack of space for leisure activities. Most of the green spaces around Pine Mansion are owned by a private golf course company and inaccessible to ordinary citizens. Within the community the density of the buildings leaves very little space for leisure. Besides the temple square I counted only three tiny spaces at crossroads and one small playground with government-provided play and fitness equipment. The temple square is by far the largest space. It was the only point of reference for Mrs. Bei, who had just arrived from Henan Province to live in the village with her daughter and son-in-law. She had trouble orienting herself because, unlike the village she had come from, "the buildings are so close together you can hardly see the sun."[10] Confirming the diagnosis of splintered urbanism resulting from the concentration of efforts on the temple square and the lack of space elsewhere, Mrs. Yu, the social worker, noted that the fact that activities are only organized in the temple square excludes a large proportion of the urban community's residents due to their numbers and the distance many have to walk to get there.

The native villagers are proud of the upgraded square, mentioning it frequently as one of the major changes to the village that urbanization has brought. When asked, they state that there should be no discrimination between themselves and newcomers—whom they refer to as outsiders, *waidiren*—in the use of public facilities. The fact that the government paid for the remaking of the public square and installed the basketball court probably plays a role here. The space is indeed public, in the sense that diverse people use it for a variety of activities and interact with one another there. However, the dividing line that sharply differentiates native villagers from migrants in the community is visible in their use of this public space, where a temporal division can be observed between natives and outsiders, as shown next.

Dearth of Public Space in River Hamlet

In July 2020 the Xi'an Municipal Development and Reform Committee published the Livable and Happy Community-Building Plan 2020–21.[11] With this policy the municipal government aimed to implement measurable goals and concrete promises at the community level. The plan sees the ideal livable community as one providing public services, including transport, schools, exercise equipment, bookshops, restaurants, medical centers, seniors' centers, and efficient offices verifying and issuing identification and other civil documents. As it is disseminated down the administrative hierarchy from the municipal to the district, local, and finally community level, the officials of each echelon are expected to replace these broad goals with more measurable goals tailored to local circumstances. A variety of assessment criteria are adopted at the community level because the officials enacting these policies have to consider existing resources, what they can afford, and where extra funding might be obtained.

Each urban district determines how it will distribute its funds among the communities it governs. Generally Xi'an's core and older districts have prioritized improving living conditions, especially for marginalized populations such as retirees, former factory workers, and manual laborers. As one community official commented, "Economic reform was gentler in these older communities due to social stability concerns."[12] By contrast, in Gaoxin High-Tech District, which includes River Hamlet, economic growth has been prioritized over social stability, resulting in very selective approaches targeting only some marginalized groups, such as the former factory workers who had enjoyed a complete set of social and health services in the socialist era. For the rest, a policy of *laisser-faire* prevailed for as long as River Hamlet's informal economy was left to prosper—until the demolition.

The government has made virtually no attempt to finance public facilities. In densely populated River Hamlet, empty land is rare, so public space is both very limited and divided. There are two kinds of public space: first, two of the five former natural villages (see chapter 1 and map 1.7) have squares near the village committee (*cunweihui*) buildings. There is also a tiny green space at the end of a pedestrian overpass and a public square in a private mall in the south of the former village.

One of the former village committee squares is three blocks from River Hamlet's main street, hidden from view by the buildings surrounding it and with a narrow entrance. Walking in, one finds oneself in this tiny square with access to the former village temple complex, which now houses a village clinic, a seniors' center, and a seniors' university. Most migrants who work and live along the main street know of the square but rarely use it. Mrs. Yang from Xianyang, a city west of Xi'an, who arrived with her son to live in River Hamlet three years ago, said that she had passed the square many times but had never entered it, thinking it for native villagers only. Mrs. Zao, who originated from a rural area in the neighboring province, Shanxi, knew of its existence and about the native villagers' dancing and other activities in it as she had kept a vegetable shop next to it for ten years.

The local government has attempted to make the square a more official urban public space by installing a toilet at the side of the square next to the temple and the clinic. Since 2016, under the slogan "Toilet Revolution," city governments have built numerous public toilets in urban spaces (Wang 2020). On the main street a sign indicates their whereabouts. The natives felt that this government installation was depriving them of space they had exclusively enjoyed. Mrs. Wang, enthusiastic about practicing public square dance and socializing with her friends in this tiny square, commented, "It's so filthy to dance right next to a toilet! Can you imagine?" She admitted that the locals did not want the square opened to outsiders to practice dancing in. For natives, the government's installation of a public toilet in the village square was tantamount to taking away what they considered theirs.

Migrants thought hard when asked, "Is there any public space here?" Several ended up identifying just one area, the tiny green space at the end of the overpass. "It's so tiny it's invisible!" exclaimed Mrs. Cheng, who had been making jewelry in River Hamlet for fifteen years (see chapter 1), adding that she was sure that just two parked full-sized cars would fill the entire space. Moreover, the green space was a requirement in the construction of the overpass to satisfy the general condition that there must be a certain amount of green space with every construction of urban infrastructure (Li et al. 2009). Some street vendors set up their food stands on it, at the risk of being fined, and thus this intended public space became a private retail space.

Livable Communities and No-Man's-Land in Chengdu

The livable city rhetoric is also in evidence in Chengdu. The Chengdu Urban Master Plan (2016–35) called for the building of a "high-quality, harmonious and livable city" by 2022.[13] In Chengdu the connection between municipal livable city rhetoric and community-level projects has been particularly strong. The wide-ranging reforms to the city's community governance system that began in 2017 were issued under the title "Opinions on Deepening the Development and Governance of Urban and Rural Communities to Build High-quality, Harmonious, and Livable Communities," explicitly linking grassroots community governance to building a livable city.[14] The document includes thirty separate points with goals as varied as strengthening grassroots party organizations, promoting volunteerism, improving community-service facilities, and unifying architectural design standards.

As part of the livable city project, the city launched the Chengdu's Top 100 Model Communities competition in 2018 to publicize the concept of community development and governance and promote the building of high-quality, harmonious, and livable communities (Li 2019). The newly created North Gate community was one of the top ten communities selected for the city's new governance approach.

There are several types of public space in South and North Gate communities: the communal spaces inside the gated communities; the streets and sidewalks, schools and schoolyards; the community centers; the formal state-run and informal parks; and some bits of open ground. The state-run public schools have strict control of access to their schoolyards, so these spaces are not public in the sense of being accessible to the public.[15]

There are two formal state-run parks in the joint community parks: a small one and a larger one called Elegant Culture Park that was opened in 2019. The latter, a paved area of about one hundred square meters, is at the corner of an intersection by the community's new Riverside Middle School (see map 1.6). The statue of a famous local poet has been erected in the center, and there are benches and exercise equipment around the perimeter. At the corner of the intersection opposite the park is a large billboard listing the twelve core socialist values championed by Xi Jinping: in short, the park is a didactic, regulated, and highly visible space.[16] Mothers from the nearby resettlement estate sometimes gather here to meet and chat with their young children in tow. But the park is generally not well used as it is completely paved and open, offering no respite from the sun. In many Chinese cities, public spaces designed for window-dressing purposes are often tailored for government-sanctioned functions rather than for city dwellers' quotidian uses (Miao 2011).

This is a stark contrast to a less-regulated green space along the river, where a stretch connected by about a kilometer of paths meanders through verdant grass and shade-giving trees. Its many visitors make it lively at all hours of the day: elderly Tai Chi practitioners gather in the morning, children and their caretakers wander through in the day, and young and middle-aged men gather to play basketball in the evening. This green space sees little state management and is less regulated than the formal park with its mandatory signs, waste bins, and benches. It is not even considered a park, a perception that crystallized during the resident survey. One respondent strolling by the river complained that the neighborhood lacked parks. Asked if this space was not a park, she answered no, because the government was not managing it. The term *gongyuan*, "park," contains the word *gong*, "public." Although it is not officially a park, this green space is well attended, because unlike the official public park it lends itself to a variety of purposes.

In fact it is less regulated because the municipal government had loaned it to a nearby real-estate developer over a decade earlier in exchange for help with selling the housing units. After the units were sold, the developer tried to return the responsibility for the land to the government, which refused, informing the company that it was now responsible for its maintenance. The developer has hired a landscaping company to look after the space, but it is clear that the standards of maintenance and control in this park are much more relaxed than those of official city parks. The vegetation is less carefully manicured, and residents engage in a number of unsanctioned activities, including planting vegetables, burning incense and paper money for their ancestors, and even parking their cars (see chapter 2). The wastelands (*huangdi*) in the community, large fields that have been cleared but are still waiting to be developed, are similarly quasi-public spaces used by residents to grow vegetables. Such spaces can be paralleled with commons, in that they escape both market and state regulation. However, they do not fully conform to Ostrom's definition of commons in that they are not subject to any rules defined by the grassroots community.

Otherwise, the impact of previous village social spaces and social life seems to be minimal in shaping the use of public space due to the top-down-directed resettlement of South Gate. The new community-level management officers headquartered at the community centers play a significant role in running spaces intended for the public. These centers offer space for leisure and education both indoors and outside (see next section) and are the main state-sanctioned public spaces in both communities. Although formal state power stops at the subdistrict level and does not reach the community, the community management offices determine how funding is secured from the government and the types of activity for which government grants are sought, such as day and evening classes. Of course these activities are not reserved for former villagers, despite the latter's current dominance in key positions. Although the odd college-educated non-native manages to land a job at the community center, the fact that the community's leadership, including the positions of party secretary and head of the residents' committee, is made up only of former villagers plays a role in their strong feeling of entitlement to certain public spaces and activities, which incomers do not share. The practical uses of the community centers highlight this separation.

Segregated Sociality and Care Practices in Public Spaces

Because of the limited space available, municipal governments refurbish preexisting public squares rather than creating new ones. In all three cases, the native villagers have a sense of legitimate priority in the use of public space, enhanced by the fact that many public sites were formerly village public spaces where communal events were, and in some cases still are, held, and because local management bodies are generally made up of former villagers. Although government-funded public squares are intended for use by all, observation of their use shows the native villagers' clear tendency to assert their priority. Rivalry over the use of public space is therefore strong, although it differs across the three villages, reflecting the class-based relations between established native rentiers and migrant outsiders (Elias and Scotson 1994; Carrier and Kalb 2015). While several studies have pointed out the mistrust and lack of interaction between natives and newcomers, this rivalry worsens the existing de facto segregation (Wang and Messner 2012; Liu 2019; Li and Tong 2020). Wang (2015) mentions one case in Zengcheng city, Guangdong province, where the conflictual situation escalated into street fights.

The most glaring contrast is evident in the intensive way migrant newcomers use public space for livelihood and reproductive activities. Previous chapters have highlighted the uses of public and communal space for street-vending and gardening activities: this section focuses on caring for others. Brenda Chalfin (2014) argues that when performed in public, care practices, deemed to belong to the domestic sphere of reproduction, subvert state understandings of publicness. In urban villages, newcomers appropriate public space—or rather, exercise their right of use on it—and make a claim on the state by forming a social commons "organized around access by users to social resources created by specific kinds of human labor, such as caring for the sick and the elderly, educating children and maintaining households" (Nonini 2006: 166). In the Chinese context, this commoning of public space is encouraged by the state's livability policies. As shown by the way the state equips new public spaces with children's playgrounds, but also public toilets as in some cases examined next, the use of public space for care practices may not be the most valorized among state-sanctioned uses of public space, but it is not necessarily unforeseen by the state (Smart 2018; Zhang, Wu, and Zhong 2018), nor is it considered illegitimate. This underscores the complementary, rather than the opposition, of commons and public goods.

Divided Use of Limited Public Space in Pine Mansion

There still is a sense that Pine Mansion's government-refurbished temple square somehow belongs to the native residents. Not only does the entire space, including the renovated temple, give value to their new apartments, but their power as native owners is also asserted by their hegemonic use of the space—their spatial privilege (Loughran 2014). This is especially true on the ancestor's birthday on the twentieth of the ninth lunar month. The entire space is filled with tables receiving donations and selling firecrackers, an alfresco dining area, billboards listing the donations received, and a stage for musical and dance performances near the temple where the ancestral worship is performed. The participants sit on plastic stools around a hundred tables on the basketball ground to eat the meal cooked on large stoves in a small annex behind the administrative building, where several hundred kilos of meat are spread on plaited mats on the floor. People walk back and forth between the ancestral temple and the kitchen, meeting and exchanging news. Many migrant newcomers know about these activities and come to watch them, as confirmed by the surveys, but they do not know whether they are allowed to participate or what is being celebrated.

Although the community center's social workers make use of the temple square for charitable events, these mainly target migrants (both volunteers and beneficiaries), further underlining the separation between native and migrant residents. The daily temporal division in the use of the temple square also reveals this separation. Although native children are sometimes brought to the square by their grandmothers, the demographic predominance of the migrant population and the fact that many live in small apartments account for the majority occupation of the square by grandparents caring for children. Many are men, elderly migrants who sit chatting for hours while keeping an eye on their grandchildren. They complained about the lack of public toilets. One member of this gathering of "temple square grandfathers" described his daily schedule: cooking breakfast, going down to the square, returning home to cook lunch, going down to the square, having dinner, and often going back to the square again. Every time he or his grandchild needs the toilet, they have to go back to their apartment.

Among the people getting a haircut on Beneficence Day was a man in his fifties from Anhui, who had been living in Pine Mansion for more than ten years. His wife's brother had resigned from his teaching job in the 1990s and moved there to run a small factory. He was doing well, so Mr. Hong and his wife joined him. With the financial crisis in 2008 the factory went bankrupt, but although his brother returned home, they stayed. Hong's son works there, and his grandson is at a private school in Pine Mansion. Hong cares for him after school. He is unemployed, having lost his livelihood when

188 | *From Village Commons to Public Goods*

Figure 5.2. Children playing basketball in Pine Mansion. © Anne-Christine Trémon.

the Chengguan confiscated the cart from which he sold tofu that he made with his wife. Renting a shop floor costs several hundred RMB a month. Now his wife is ill, and his only source of income is his rural old-age pension of sixty to seventy RMB per month. Hong commented on the native residents who make money doing nothing but renting out apartments, stating that "they have more and more money," and that although well-intended, activities such as Beneficence Day would not create substantial change in people's lives.[17]

Migrant outsiders themselves emphasize their separation from native former villagers. They frequently use the word "they" (*tamen*) to refer to them, sometimes without even adding "locals" (*bendiren*). Three women in their fifties who were chatting on a tiny playground in a peripheral neighborhood commented about the temple square: "Those facilities are being used by the natives, so why would we go there?" one of them exclaimed. It is true that in the evenings the basketball courts are used exclusively by native young men. Mrs. Ding, a forty-eight-year-old woman from Jiangxi who has been living in Pine Mansion for eight years and in Shenzhen for twenty, noted that "before, there were not that many people [using the public square] because *they* had locked it up and wouldn't let us in" (*bu gei jin*). She added that it was still mostly used by employees of the community center and the police station after work; that is, by native residents.

Indeed I observed that when these men arrived at around 6:30 to 7:00 each evening, the children and teenagers playing there left. Because it takes up most of the usable public space, a basketball match, which happens almost every day, consigns other users to the edges of the square. Mrs. Tan, a street cleaner in her fifties from Hubei who occasionally brings her two-year-old grandchild to the temple square, stated that *they* (the natives) do "large-scale activities" (*daxing de huodong*), such as basketball.[18] Although in principle everyone has the right to use the main public square, the space used for activities is indeed divided between natives and outsiders in inverse proportion to their numbers. Moreover, while native women dance in the open space between the pond and the temple at night, non-natives, mostly women, also congregate in the evenings to dance and do aerobics on smaller squares and sidewalks elsewhere in the *shequ*.

Mrs. Wang (see chapter 1) was born in 1950 and lives with her second son and her grandson in a house she has built in new Xiangxi neighborhood (see map 1.5). Her eldest son lives in Martinique, and her husband in Hong Kong. Her husband does not return often because he is "not used to living in the village" anymore, she said.[19] She lives like a typical rentier: in the morning she goes out early to exercise, then she takes the bus to the subdistrict, i.e., the former township (*zhen*), for morning tea and dumplings with friends, shops at the market for vegetables and groceries, and then returns to her house to cook for herself and for her son and grandson when they are around. Native villagers like Mrs. Wang display their status by spending money in subdistrict restaurants and shops rather than those in Pine Mansion; they also spend money playing mahjong every afternoon, although the village leaders disapprove of this habit. The number of mahjong parlors in Pine Mansion has visibly grown, despite being illegal and receiving inspections from the anti-pornography and anti-gambling office. Until a few years ago Mrs. Wang bet several thousand yuan, a lot of money, every afternoon. Because her losses were so heavy, she opted for another mahjong parlor, run by a woman from Hunan, where the stakes are lower. She stressed the difference between native residents' and outsiders' stakes: the former "play big." She now regularly plays every afternoon with a circle of five or six friends, all migrant women who have been living in Pine Mansion for years. Newcomers who have lived in the village for a long time have learned the local mahjong rules and generally play by them.

Another in-between private-public space, where the difference between natives and outsiders is felt less, is the large mall built in the north of Pine Mansion in 2016. Inside the mall, leisure is expensive: the film theater and skating rink cater to the children of families living in luxury apartments with access to a golf course and private international schools. They also provide plenty of free or inexpensive outdoor space for skateboarding, sports, and strolling. The nonnative resident Mrs. Ding commented that the mall was about the best place around. She lives close to the mall, and it takes her only ten minutes to walk there from her home. She goes almost every week. The native villager Mrs. Wang took her grandchildren there when they came on a visit from Martinique.

In spite of the emerging native-outsider sociality around gambling, other interaction remains rare. When asked about the relationship between native Pine Mansioners and outsiders, one spontaneous representative of the temple square grandfathers, Mr. He from Hunan, answered, laughing, "I haven't interacted with them—they're like total strangers!" (*moshengren*). He stated that most Pine Mansion natives do not live locally, many living in Hong Kong and even Malaysia. He and his friends at the chess table said that they have nothing to do with their landlords because they hire people to look after the management of their buildings.[20] Elderly newcomers are more knowledgeable about native residents because they spend a lot of time in the temple square observing goings-on in the urban village.

Rivalry over Dance Space in River Hamlet

Mrs. Zhou, aged fifty, a native from a village nearby who married into her husband's family River Hamlet, stopped going to practice public square dancing in November 2018 because she had no heart for dancing or enjoying herself with her home on the verge of being demolished: "When there's a catastrophe, how can you dance?," she asked, in tears.[21] Until the demolition, dancing was the most widespread use of public space. "Public square dancing" was the answer given by 65 of the 163 survey respondents to the question, "What is the most important public activity you take part in within the community?"[22] "Drumming and dancing" (*luogu* and *yangge*) is a popular Shaanxi rural dance routine with rhythmic music and repetitive patterns of steps. Both the men and the women participating often wear brightly colored makeup. In the past, drumming and dancing was an expensive pastime that required the entire village to collect donations for, rehearse for, and organize the performance every year at the spring festival. The performance style is unique to each village, and village dance groups would meet in competition for hours of intensive drumming and dancing. However, these spectacular events are now a distant memory, as there is no longer sufficient public space for them or any association organizing competitions.

Both native and migrant residents shared an interest in the search for space in which to practice public square dancing. The former were holding on to their limited space for this activity, in the village-committee squares. At the narrow entrance gate to River Hamlet's Team 1's village-committee square, a barking dog was chained inside a cage. The intention was clear: stay away or get hurt. In mid-2018, when the rumor of the impending demolition was at its peak, the public toilet was locked and a maintenance sign was affixed to the door. A group of native former villagers was playing cards beside it. One of them had the key to the toilet and opened it only for the use of the group.[23]

Social activities in public spaces besides the old village committee sites were already limited prior to the demolition because all available space on the main street was in commercial use. Jewelry, food, and makeup stalls occupied the sidewalks. As a result, local residents had to venture south to a public square next to a private mall (map 1.7). The square was built on land that had belonged to River Hamlet and had been expropriated by the district government and allocated to one of Xi'an's universities to extend its campus in 1999, and then it was sold to a private real-estate developer in 2016 (see Xu, Yeh, and Wu 2009 on the commercial uses of publicly allocated land). Anticipating a growing market for entertainment and leisure, the developer built a four-story mall with a glass and steel facade but had only managed to lease the top floor to a movie theater. The retail spaces were empty, with "Coming Soon!" signs in their windows. The major reason for this lack of success was the development of a grand new mall called the "District-Level Central Business District" only five hundred meters to the east.

Because of the short distance between the failed mall and River Hamlet's central residential communities, many residents, before they were evicted, would go to this public square every evening. Most were middle-aged or elderly residents, many from rural areas of Shaanxi or neighboring provinces, who had come to River Hamlet to help their adult children care for their children. Both natives and newcomers enjoyed the open space and lack of crowds. In the evenings several groups danced for hours. Makeshift playgrounds with pretend trains, balloons, and roller skates intended to attract customers drew teenagers and grandparents and parents with children. Native residents and outsiders mingled. Thus in the context of this dearth of public space, as in Pine Mansion, the area in front of the private mall had become the main destination for public square dancing, childcare, chatting, and other activities. It appears that where government-led redevelopment has failed, public space has appeared.

Mrs. Jia, from Baoji in Shaanxi Province, moved to River Hamlet to live with her son's family and help with their newborn child. She had arrived a year earlier and found a job in the urban village as a waitress to make some extra cash. Many grandparents in their fifties and sixties had come to River Hamlet to work to financially contribute to their children's families and to care for grandchildren. Others had come to work and save money before returning to a small city or village to join their children's families. Their similarities helped them to make friends in the public square. They watched the young children playing while they chatted about their in-laws, harvests, and agricultural work back home. The high cost of living in the High-Tech Zone was largely evident in the mortgages of their white-collar professional children, whose mothers often complained how unfortunate their daughters and sons were to have to shoulder such a big debt while the River Hamlet natives did nothing but accumulate more wealth.

A group of up to seven migrant women often gathered around the children's playground, a small area that some shop owners had provided with roller skates, a bouncy castle, a miniature train track, and other makeshift facilities, which could be accessed for a small fee. Several public square dance groups, mostly women with a few men, used this square as a rehearsal space. Through surveys Wang Bo learned that these were often grandparents on a visit or parents whose children were at school. They often said, "We're done with childrearing!" They periodically moved between River Hamlet and their natal villages. Some said they had to take care of their crops, while others explained that they felt more comfortable living in their village than in a high-rise apartment. "Less complicated family relationships, more people you know from childhood," Mrs. Jia said. She felt that she fitted in with her small circle of close friends in River Hamlet but never felt truly herself there. She stayed mainly because her son needed her help and felt that it was her responsibility, but she quite enjoyed the relaxing atmosphere and the many things to do there.[24]

Fewer native former villagers came to this square than migrants, mainly because the middle-aged and older ones did not feel that it suited their village lifestyle. They could easily afford to pay to get into the children's playground but found it little use and a waste of money. Instead the women preferred the old village committee sites for their dance rehearsals, and the native village men preferred to gather in a fish and flower market six hundred meters to the north in a neighboring former village. Despite the distance, they found the low-key single-floor shops and small green space more suitable and village-like. The steel and glass mall made them self-conscious about how they were dressed. "*Bu zizai*" (not feeling like oneself) was how Mr. Yin, a fifty-eight-year-old native villager, described it. He went to the market twice a week to chat with friends, including other native villagers and some bird-shop owners. This meeting space gave them the opportunity to keep up their village identity and maintain stable relations throughout the redevelopment's rapid demolition and rebuilding.

After the demolition began in late 2018, some native villagers began to disseminate articles and blog posts they had found online about illegal sales of land by the former village leaders, including the land that was now the public square next to the private mall. The natives' dissatisfaction with their compensation for the demolition of their houses surfaced in their questioning of the legitimacy of this public square. Why had they never been asked about the sale of this land? How was it that the former village leaders were allegedly promoted or given cash compensation after signing off the village's common land? This dissemination of information was stopped by the local subdistrict office, which quickly removed the printed screenshots posted on walls and electricity poles. Forming an oppositional public in this instance, they used public space to voice their dissent, but were quickly muted.

Public Rusticity and Middle-Class Elevation in South Gate

The primary task of integration in North and South Gate communities is focused on the native villagers themselves. The *shequ* leaders make efforts to turn them into proper middle-class urbanites resembling the new inhabitants. Unlike in Pine Mansion, the largest group of outsiders is composed of the largely middle-class residents of the commercial apartment complexes, who distinguish themselves from the natives through their practices of consumption and education in public spaces.

Most of the weekday regulars at the North Gate community center are elderly villagers.[25] The center is at the edge of a large resettlement estate for former villagers, contributing to the sense that it is part of the village space. Murals on the walls depict fields and scenes of rural life, making the rural past an object of consumption for urbanites. The community's designation as a model of community governance has meant that photographs of the murals have appeared in many local newspapers, attracting visitors from across Chengdu. They connect the space to its village roots and suggest a continuity between former rural village sociability and the urban present. Apart from the villagers, the other residents who use the space are stay-at-home mothers, with and without their children. On the weekends some parents bring their children to the center for classes in Chinese culture, although the quality of these classes is not considered high and only households who cannot afford private classes attend. During the week, while their children are at school, some of these mothers attend tea-serving (*gongfu cha*) classes.

Visiting urbanites from other Chengdu neighborhoods often sit in the outdoor teahouse after visiting the murals. It appears to be something of a pastoralist practice, celebrating a nostalgic rural idyll, as evidenced by the number of selfies taken there. Teahouses belong to a distinctively urban tradition of commoner public sociability that was particularly strong in Chengdu in the first half of the twentieth century (Wang 1998), which seems paradoxically reactivated along an urban/rural opposition in the clear division between the rustic outdoor teahouse that occupies a large part of the community center's outdoor space and the refined tea-serving classes held in the indoor tea studio. This separation suggests a dichotomous structuring of public-rustic and private-urban public space that "symbolizes and realizes" different hexis, or bodily dispositions (Bourdieu 1970, 1972: 193). Apart from the often-retired visitors from other neighborhoods, the outdoor teahouse is mainly used by retired native villagers, former peasants, to chat and relax. Meeting at the teahouse is simultaneously a way of asserting their status as new urbanites and of maintaining positive rural identities in spite of the devaluation of the countryside (Bruckermann 2020).

Inside the tea studio, stay-at-home women and some elderly men educate themselves in how to serve tea, which requires adopting specific body postures (especially when it comes to long-spout tea serving). Tea-serving and tea-tasting is an aspect of China's contemporary bourgeois hexis that reflects the practitioner's knowledge, refinement, and respect for tradition. It has become a popular pastime for middle-class urban dwellers and is a social class marker similar to that of wine- or whisky-tasting in Western countries. The tea students do not participate in other activities, such as the dancing, which is dominated by a group of village women who meet in the mornings to practice in front of the community center. They have a changing repertoire of routines and costumes and frequently perform for audiences at the many ceremonies and official tours that take place in the community center. Conversely, the village women do not participate in the tea classes.

This indoor/outdoor, rustic/upper-class division is traversed by Mrs. Li, who teaches the tea-serving classes and is the manager of the indoor teahouse. She is from another rural area on the outskirts of Chengdu and married into South Gate village, making her both an insider and an outsider. She began studying with a tea master several years ago during the relocation process, and described how tea culture has transformed not only her mind but also her body. She wears traditional cotton or hemp gowns in muted colors, ties her hair back simply, and wears minimal makeup. This distinguishes her from the village women who participate in the square dancing with their dyed and permed hair, bright clothing, and heavy makeup. Mrs. Li was clearly nervous about teaching the tea classes, most notably when she was describing the history and origins of various teas, but she had no hesitation about strictly correcting the posture, gestures, and facial expressions of her more educated middle-class students. Indeed, much of the class focuses on the physical act of pouring tea rather than the qualities of the tea itself. For Mrs. Li and her students, serving tea is a tool of social and physical elevation.

The divisions in the usage of public space are further reflected in the differences between the resettlement and the commercial estates. While communal space on the resettlement estates is virtually nonexistent, the quasi-public space in the private and gated communities is largely only accessible to the residents of each apartment complex. Some of the commercial buildings with elevators attempt to reproduce the functions of the community center within their own walls. Apart from installing exercise and playground equipment, one complex has created a meeting room, where elderly middle-class residents meet for choir practice. Another has set up a community classroom in which, with the support of the North Gate community center, Jessica Wilczak taught English evening classes to adults. One of the reasons for organizing these classes, the facilitator from the community center explained, was to reach out to middle-aged, middle-class residents in the community. "Most people have the idea that the community (*shequ*) is just for old people and children," she said. "That's not true anymore. The community is here to serve all residents." This reaching out by the community centers, however, happens outside the centers themselves on the commercial estates.

Hopes of Accessing Urban *Hukou* and the Right to the City

Many working-class newcomers living in River Hamlet and Pine Mansion use public space for childcare. Carrying out care activities in a public space signals a right to urban life that "combines the practical needs of everyday life with a substantive rather than abstract conception of modern citizenship" (Gandy 2006: 388, in reference to Lefebvre 1996 [1968]: 158). This section explores the sense of entitlement behind non-native residents' decisions to claim, or not claim, their right to the city, both in Lefebvre's sense of the actual exercise of one's right to access urban space and in the juridical sense of applying for urban citizenship. The Chinese *hukou* system is fundamentally based on the principle of territorial entitlement: individuals receive welfare benefits in the locality in which they are registered. The responsibility for such welfare provision falls to local government, and there is considerable local variation in terms of both access to local citizenship and the level of public goods provision (chapter 1, Smart and Smart 2001). By denying the migrants who have built China's modern megacities their welfare benefits and many social services in the locality where they live and work, restrictive *hukou* policies effectively devolve the cost of social reproduction upon the migrants and the localities from which they originate (Friedman 2018; Chuang 2020). However, migrant urban-village residents' desire to acquire local *hukou* is not unanimous. Their wish to change their *hukou* depends on their potential for social reproduction back in their home village or town, based mainly on their landholdings. It also depends on their class-based sense of entitlement and their vision of their right to the city. Finally, it is shaped by the policy of the city they live in; this section focuses most on the case of Shenzhen, which has the greatest selectivity in its points system for earning *hukou*.

Hopes of Accessing Hukou

Shen and Li (2020) note that the desire to engage in economic upgrading, coupled with restrictions to city growth, results in a particular dilemma in the Chinese context:

> Ideally speaking, if a city can host an unlimited number of people, economic upgrading can be achieved through the attraction of higher-skilled workers at a faster pace than lower-skilled workers. This would mean that the population of these cities would continue to grow. However, the concerns over "big city disease" has resulted in the motivation to cap the total population of a

city. This means, in order to attract more people, a city must first reduce the total population. Then who should leave? (Shen and Li 2020: 6)

The answer for many cities is to target the so-called "high-end population" (and deter the low end) through a selective *hukou* policy that attracts highly skilled new residents in the effort to upgrade the existing population along with the economy.

Among the 163 responses to the randomized survey carried out in River Hamlet, 69 had local *hukou* and 94 did not. Very few of the latter were contemplating a change in their *hukou* registration from their locality of origin to Xi'an, but it is not worth citing precise numbers because the survey results were strongly biased. The survey was carried out before the shock of the demolition was suddenly imposed upon River Hamlet. What is clear is that many recent migrants who worked in the service economy were struggling to establish a foothold in their new environment and did not consider purchasing an urban apartment and getting urban *hukou* attainable in the foreseeable future. For them, living in River Hamlet was only transitional until they moved back to their rural origins or the closest township or county seat to purchase housing and care for their parents (see Zhan 2018 for a similar case in Beijing). Rather than saving money to buy a spot in the city, they primarily focused on saving to live elsewhere.

The sudden and complete urban transformation of River Hamlet had been kept secret from both natives and migrants, who did not believe that the district would dare to carry out what had been rumored for years. Moreover, there were projects afoot to integrate migrants into urban society through a relaxation of *hukou* policy that had been introduced just months before the demolition, which welcomed high-school-educated migrants and encouraged them to transfer their *hukou* to River Hamlet.

When Wang Bo's fieldwork began in April 2018, every day a dozen or so rural migrants were having their *hukou* relocated at the household registration office (*huji bangongshi*) next door to the River Hamlet subdistrict office, as long as they could prove that they were joining family members with local urban *hukou* or putting down a payment on an urban apartment. But by early 2019 the entire main street of River Hamlet had been demolished, forcing its residents to move out: tenant migrants first, property-owning natives next. Migrants who lost their livelihoods and apartments also lost their chance to transfer their hukou. But as the previous section on temporary stays for the purpose of caregiving has shown, and for reasons that are further explored in the case of Pine Mansion below, many migrants are opting to circulate between city and countryside rather than give up their rural *hukou* (Chen and Fan 2016).

Of the 159 residents who responded to the Chengdu survey, just over half (52.2 percent) claimed to have local *hukou*.[26] Of those with nonlocal *hukou*, less than a quarter (23.6 percent) said they were planning to apply for local *hukou*. Of this minority, 75 percent were under sixty, which did not differ drastically from the proportion of nonlocals who were *not* planning to apply for local *hukou*, of whom 69.7 percent were under sixty. It seems that age was not the biggest determinant of whether or not a nonlocal resident intended to apply for local *hukou*. However, because the surveys were conducted mostly during the day and on weekdays, the working population is underrepresented. It seems likely that a majority of the working population living in the commercial complexes either had a Chengdu *hukou* or were planning to acquire one. Indeed, acquisition of an apartment and that of Chengdu *hukou*, which were already closely linked, have become even more so under the new points system, with home ownership one of the easiest paths to acquiring local *hukou*.

A Chengdu *hukou* is becoming more appealing to middle-class residents across China: the city still has relatively affordable housing compared to Beijing, Shanghai, or Shenzhen, as well as a high standard of living. It is also easier to acquire: one middle-class couple in South Gate who had lived in Beijing for eighteen years without being able to secure a local *hukou* decided to relocate to Chengdu and succeeded in finally obtaining one. The husband was working in Beijing but returned to Chengdu on the weekends to spend time with his wife and son. He claimed to know many others in their situation, the husband working in a tier-one city (*yixian chengshi*) and the wife and child living in a tier-two city (*erxian chengshi*).[27] "In Beijing it's not enough just to buy a house," the husband explained, "you need to have gone to particular universities and have a master's degree or even a doctorate." Requirements are barely looser in Shenzhen, also a tier-one city.

Among the seventy-five non-native and nonlocal *hukou* holders surveyed in Pine Mansion, only forty-seven replied when asked if they wanted to apply for local *hukou*: thirty-six did not, and only eleven did. This is unrelated to their peasant or rural status, which is distributed equally between these forty-seven respondents and does not seem to depend on their length of residency in Pine Mansion, which for most was less than five years. The unwillingness to apply for a change of *hukou* among a high proportion of respondents was confirmed in interviews: most non-native respondents answered that they did not have the means to change their *hukou*, which is only possible for those with money. Even shop owners and white-collar workers in stable employment, who might have the means, stated that they were not willing to transfer their *hukou* unless it would help to get their child into a local public school.[28] Property ownership may be another factor in their decision not to change their hukou; a third (thirteen) of those who answered "no" owned property in their hometown.

When they are successful, *hukou* applicants are asked to give up their land-use rights in their native village. Land is considered a form of social security (Chuang 2020), and the urban/rural dualism in land ownership makes it impossible to have both rural land and an urban *hukou*, hence many migrants' reluctance to transfer their *hukou* despite having the means to do so (Cai 2016; Tyner and Ren 2016). Mrs. Song explained that her son had applied for local *hukou* so that his child can study in the city. But why would she transfer her *hukou*? "That would make no sense, we have hospitals and insurance at home!" She still owns a plot of land in her native village. Mr. He, from Henan, exclaimed that even if it were possible, he would not want to change his *hukou*; his roots are elsewhere, and he and his wife have "no secure source (*zhuoluo*) of living." If his child's business lost money, he would have no place to escape to. Another temple square grandfather in his sixties would probably have the means to transfer his *hukou* because he lives in a three-bedroom apartment, for which his son pays 3,000 RMB per month. His wife has stayed in Shaanxi. "If I make the transfer I will lose my land; [for now] I still have two mu, and they will be valuable (*zhiqian*) in the future," he smilingly explained.[29] However, willingness to change one's *hukou* also seems to depend on age, as most of those who were planning to do so were under forty. Shenzhen's points system favors younger migrants, and in general people in their twenties and thirties were more willing to answer the question about their plans and more optimistic about their life prospects.

Shenzhen's system for converting to Shenzhen *hukou*, officially titled "points system for entering *hukou*" (*jifen ruhu*), was set up in 2012 following guidelines promulgated by Guangdong Province in 2011. The system aims to meet the objectives stated in China's urbanization plan of increasing the size of the registered population while keeping the largest cities' population within a certain size. Applicants score points for a list of factors and can apply if they reach the qualification mark; they are then ranked based on their maximum score and allowed to transfer their *hukou* based on the available *hukou* quota (see chapter 1). As well as latitude regarding the relative weights of the variables in the points system, these quotas allow the governments of large cities such as Shenzhen to grant urban *hukou* to a small and selected number of educated high-income migrants who can contribute to the city's fiscal revenue, helping to fund the city's public services.

Shenzhen's points system for the identification of applicants eligible for local *hukou* is ideologically justified in its aim of "enhancing migrant workers' sense of belonging, making migrant workers hopeful, hardworking, more law-abiding, and more caring about the city."[30] The city authorities are preoccupied with regulating and stabilizing the floating population, and they see the points system as an incentive for migrant workers to register and plan their future in terms of place of work and residence. Thus not only does the *hukou* regime itself play a pivotal role in population management and resource allocation through "a series of governmental technologies" based on classification and calculation (Wang and Liu 2018), but the points system is also an instrument for governing the population by making it self-governing.[31]

Not only are applicants selected by the points-based channel according to their potential future contribution to the city budget, but they are also selected on the basis of the contribution already made, creating an incentive to make long-term plans. This is evident in the weight given to home ownership and participation in the social security program (Zhang 2012). The longer an applicant has owned property and contributed to the social security program, the more points they accrue. In 2018, home ownership accounted for about a fifth of the points needed for qualification, and points for participation in the social security program nearly a third. The amount of capital invested and/or tax paid also rates significantly; age and marital status less so. One further major category for earning points is the quality (*suzhi*) of the applicant, which is appraised in terms of educational credentials (type of degree or professional certificate); awards for outstanding performance at work; participation in charity activities (e.g., donations made to local communities), and volunteering at events advertising the city, or with the MRT, the city's public transportation network, or at the increasing number of volunteer-based activities that are supposed to foster migrants' integration into the city, such as those supporting charities. Five points can be earned for 250 hours of voluntary service, and two points by donating blood.[32] The threshold for eligibility is generally 100 points, but the real threshold (locally called "pure points," *chun jifen*) varies every year according to the available quota. Temporary residents are ranked each year by their total number of points, but Shenzhen, which had over 10 million migrants, granted just 10,000 *hukou* in 2018, with only those scoring above 304 points obtaining Shenzhen *hukou* that year.

Two Rights to the City: State-Sanctioned, and Based on the Commons

All resident permit-holders (i.e., including *hukou* and non-*hukou* holders) are put into the points-based management scheme that can lead to urban *hukou* and also regulates applications for a school place. Following the 2014 Urbanization Plan, and now the 2021 Plan, all cities with a *hukou*-holding population above five million have adopted points systems, but here I focus only on Shenzhen, which has experimented with these systems already since 2010 with respect to *hukou* and since 2014 with respect to the allocation of school places (see chapter 2).

Not only does changing one's household registration require a huge investment in paid and unpaid labor to earn the number of points needed, but this is also the case when it comes to accessing a key public good such as a place at a public school. The case of Mrs. Gong suggests that the points-based system generates the opposite of a sense of belonging, and that although migrants may feel the injunction to plan their future, yearly adjustments to the points policy create a moving target that can also produce the opposite effect. Mrs. Gong (see chapter 4) is representative of the younger female migrant volunteers, aspiring middle-class incomers who consider it their duty to raise their own quality and that of their children through education, and to contribute to shaping the civilized city through volunteering. She stated, "Maybe some people feel that there can be benefits from volunteering, adding points for getting hukou, because for instance when you do fifteen hundred hours you get thirty points, but it also really does offer something; it encourages us."

When we met, Mrs. Gong had just realized that she would not be able to get her son into the local public middle school the following year. Asked if she felt like part of Pine Mansion after all her years spent there, she answered that most of the time she felt like she belonged (*guishugan*): "As long as there aren't any problems in life. But … when you're facing a very clear problem, eventually you come to feel that you're not a local; there's no way of getting my son into a public school." This was how she introduced the topic. Her two sons were then at the local public primary and middle schools, and in 2018 her youngest son was due to move up to secondary school. When she had originally secured her children's school places, the score (*jifen*) required was not as high as it had become: "Our insurance score [*she-*

bao jifen] was just sufficient. Afterward, … basically we were not able to keep up [*gen bu shangle*]. Many people bought an apartment—they are classified as *diwulei* [grade 5]." Her own score is at the bottom of grade 6 because she does not have social security. Until 2016 a place at a public school could be secured with either social security or a business license, and Mrs. Gong had scored very highly because she had been doing business in Shenzhen for more than ten years. In 2017 the policy was drastically tightened, especially regarding the social insurance requirements, and she now no longer has enough points to get her second son into the public secondary school.[33]

Her position as head of the community's volunteers' association did not help, and her son's teachers could do nothing about it either, although Mrs. Gong confided that she had tried to speak to the head of admissions and to use the connections she had built through volunteering to get her son admitted. She did not consider embarking on collective action such as presenting a petition. She bore no grudge against the system, because she saw the requirements as normal: "Why? Because if it becomes equal for everybody, if there are no requirements, like in our native place [*laojia*] … the teaching quality cannot be upheld. This is a first-tier city, isn't it?" (*yixian chengshi*). By emphasizing Shenzhen's first-tier status, she meant that selectivity is necessary to ensure good-quality education. She considered the system right, justifying it by invoking the principle of length of residency on which it is partly based. She regarded the removal of the social insurance (*shebao*) criterion necessary for the development of society: "There is nothing to be done. Society has to develop." She did not dare to complain that she was the victim of an abrupt and unanticipated change in policy that she had no time to plan for.

While Mrs. Gong did not have the means to buy an apartment in Pine Mansion, she did not complain about those who jump the queue by buying property; here again she implicitly blamed the choice that she and her husband had made at the very beginning to buy a house in their native village rather than saving for property in Shenzhen. She blamed their own traditionalism: "We built a house in the village. We are traditional over there. [You] have to make a house in your home place first, then elsewhere." This points to the difficult dilemma in which many migrant workers are caught, juggling between building a house on land in the home village to keep as a safety net and renouncing all rights in the place of origin by selling the land and investing as much as possible in, for instance, insurance and property that might qualify for points and accelerate their *hukou* transfer.[34] Mrs. Gong even blamed herself for not making the decision to buy insurance earlier, although she probably did not have the means at the time and could not possibly have anticipated the change in policy.

Mrs. Gong not only did not express any sense of injustice but also argued that it is a matter of personal responsibility, with only the individual to blame, if he or she does not comply with the requirements.[35] Parents should consider their children's future in advance to ensure that they receive an education. Otherwise things will be "in a muddle," "turned upside down" (*luantao*). Her most striking argument was about people's territorial rights: asked if she felt there should be a difference in such rights between local and nonlocal *hukou* holders, she answered:

> I feel that, for instance, if all my certificates are in order, fundamentally there is no difference from the locals [*bendi hukou*]. Regarding entering school, the locals certainly have priority over us. Those who have ancestral houses [*zuwu*], those with Shenzhen *hukou*. Why those with ancestral houses, because this place [Shenzhen] has been built by them. Even if some say that outsiders built it, these persons [the locals] will say that it's their territory [*dipan*], right? The outsiders are merely contributors [*gongxianzhe*]. And it is only if you contribute that people here will recognize you.

Her words acutely reveal the ways in which the logic of territorial entitlement to public goods affects the lives of migrant newcomers in urbanizing China, while they may simultaneously use such logic to justify their own exclusion. She alludes to some migrants' argument that they should be entitled to public goods because they have participated in building the city, sounding as if they have read Henri Lefebvre or David Harvey (2012: 78): "The right to use that common must surely then be accorded to all those who have had a part in producing it. This is, of course, the basis for the claim to the right to the city on the part of the collective laborers who have made it."

The temple square grandfathers who have lived in Pine Mansion for many years tend to voice a sense of injustice based on lack of recognition of the labor they contributed to building the city, and they view the charity programs with a certain degree of irony. Mr. He, the most vocal among them, arrived in Shenzhen more than thirty years ago in the 1990s as a carpenter. Not allowed to enter the Shenzhen special economic zone, he settled in a village and worked for a small family factory. He declared, "If we outsiders (*waidiren*) hadn't come, Shenzhen would have been an empty city and the buildings would not have been constructed. … It is more civilized, more advanced, thanks to the peasant migrant workers (*nongmingong*). Beautification [happened] thanks to us."

Yet the fragility of this claim, as Mrs. Gong's self-denial of this right shows, is due to its close proximity to the logic of distribution that is being applied. It is, after all, based on a principle of justice that allocates public goods to those who have inherited or earned the right to benefit from them in a particular territory. The "right to the city" is an empty signifier (Harvey 2012: xv, 87).

Rivalry, Exclusion, and Differences in Entitlement

As McCann notes in the North American context, "Quality of life is now routinely understood as a competitive advantage and defined in terms of consumption opportunities for wealthier and/or more economically valued class fractions who are able to choose the cities in which they live or invest on the basis of specific lifestyle characteristics." Livable city policies, he observes, often result in increasing urban inequality that makes the city *less* livable for many (2008: 37). Natives and outsiders living in Chinese urban villages alike express strong appreciation of state-provided public space. While they do follow state-encouraged best practices as citizens and engage in practices of self-discipline, for instance by participating in charitable events, what they expect from the state is mostly the increased quality of life that public space can provide, allowing them to engage in making friends and caring for their relatives.

Yet available space is limited in urban villages, not only because of the spontaneous urbanization that has led to high density and "kissing buildings" but also due to the prioritization of economic growth in the form of real estate. This results in splintered urbanism at the urban village scale, or the uneven graduated provision of public space, generating rivalry over the use of space. Even where the local state invests in the creation of space for communal activities and leisure, as in Shenzhen, and even more in Chengdu, this is often secondary to the use of space for residential complexes and malls. Public space is often concentrated only in some parts of the urban village, leaving many residents without access. Residents therefore resort to other spaces outside of the state's purview, with new counterpublics tending to form more around the informal use of malls and plots of land awaiting development rather than in the official public squares, where the state asserts its presence. Moreover, because many of these official spaces are provided as substitutes for those of the former villages, native residents exercise priority use rights, relegating others to marginal, improvised public spaces or to the communal spaces on their residential estates, which are also often limited.

While the local state sees the purpose of shaping public space as fostering a sense of belonging to a new urban community, this integration occurs differently across the three villages depending on the class relations between insiders and outsiders. In Pine Mansion and River Hamlet, apart from certain traditional communal village activities, the nature of most activities performed in public does not distinguish native residents from newcomers, whereas in South Gate the class differentiation in the kinds of activity performed is much sharper. However, in all three cases, migrants use public space more than natives do for their daily social reproductive activities, and particularly for childcare.

This latter kind of social exclusion is also the result of decades of graduated provision based on *hukou* policy, reinforcing differences between natives and migrants, whose interactions are most often minimal and limited to relations between tenants and owners, although friendships between long-term non-native and native residents do emerge. Whether or not migrants wish to change their *hukou* greatly depends on the trade-off between what affords them security in the present and their plans for the future. It also depends on their sense of entitlement, which is shaped by not only the Chinese *hukou* system of territorial entitlement but also their social class. While low-skilled migrant workers with poor prospects of changing their *hukou* tend to express a sense of injustice and claim a Lefebvrian right to the city, middle-class non-*hukou*-holding residents have better chances and espouse a different view of the right to the city, one that is promoted by the municipal points system for acquiring *hukou*.

Notes

1. The 2018 release of the Economist Intelligence Unit's annual rankings was accompanied by intensified media coverage of livability and a concurrent rise in the role of the concept in city branding (McArthur and Robin 2019).
2. According to Lefebvre, the right to the city is less a juridical right than a claim to urban life and is an oppositional demand that challenges the claims of the rich and powerful. It means transferring control from capital and the state to urban inhabitants, giving them "renewed centrality" and "enabling the full and complete usage of [the city's] moments and places" (Lefebvre 1996 [1968]: 179).
3. See the introduction to chapter 3 for a definition of splintered urbanism.
4. Warner differentiates counterpublics from oppositional publics in the Habermasian sense: they are the publics formed when "a dominated group aspires to re-create

itself as a public and, in doing so, finds itself in conflict not only with the dominant social group, but also with the norms that constitute the dominant culture as a public" (Warner 2002: 80).
5. William Skinner (1971) modelized a cycle of closure/opening of Chinese villages in relation to dynastic/political cycles. Maoism was characterized by closure.
6. Shenzhen government, Notice on Issuing the Work Plan for the Construction of Livable Communities in Shenzhen, n° 49, 3 May 2012, http://www.sz.gov.cn/zfgb/2012_1/gb786/content/post_4990625.html.
7. See ibid.
8. *Southern Daily*, December 2015, exact reference not provided for reasons of anonymization.
9. See ibid.
10. Interview by Anne-Christine Trémon, 23 March 2018.
11. http://m.cnwest.com/xian/a/2020/07/24/18950251.html.
12. This section is based on Wang Bo's *First Interim Report*, 21 November 2018, *Second Interim Report*, 11 April 2019, and *Final Report*, 31 October 2019.
13. "Consultation on the Chengdu Urban Master Plan, Creating a Harmonious and Livable Living City" Xinhua News Online, 2 February 2017, http://www.xinhuanet.com//fortune/2017-11/02/c_1121895014.htm.
14. *Opinions* available at http://sq.sqyz.info:8087/QTWZ/XX.aspx?BH=1011&PKID=10; see also Li Chunyu, "Chengdu Will Build 'Five Communities.' Let's See Which Are the Five?" *Chengdu News*, 21 September 2017, http://www.gslcec.com/mtbd/2017-09-21/1388.html.
15. Jessica Wilczak, *Final Report*, 30 July 2019.
16. Socialist values such as justice and equality are advertised everywhere in China's booming cities, in newly renovated public squares and on fences hiding construction sites. Along with General Secretary and Chinese president Xi Jinping's motto the "China dream" (*zhongguo meng*), they glorify his "new era."
17. Interview by Anne-Christine Trémon, 25 March 2018.
18. Short interviews with Mrs. Ding and Mrs. Tan, 27 March 2018.
19. Interview by Anne-Christine Trémon, 10 April 2017.
20. Interview by Anne-Christine Trémon, 28 March 2018.
21. Wang Bo, *Survey Report*, 29 March 2019.
22. Ibid.
23. Wang Bo, *Fieldnotes*, 16 November 2018.
24. Wang Bo, *Survey Report*.
25. This section is based on Jessica Wilczak's *Interim Report* and *Final Report*.
26. Jessica Wilczak, *Survey Report*, 19 January 2019.
27. The tier system of city ranking does not represent an official classification. It is unofficial and based on criteria such as population size and real-estate prices, but also on subjective criteria such as the overall quality of the population and business environment. In the media there are frequent reassessments and speculations about which cities deserve to be in the first tier, the consensus being Beijing, Shanghai, Guangzhou, and Shenzhen. Both Chengdu and Xi'an are considered "new tier-one cities," and Chengdu "is a serious candidate for entering the first-tier cities list": "2020 Ranking of New First-Tier Cities," *National Business Daily*, 29 May 2020, http://www.nbd.com.cn/articles/2020-05-29/1440178.html.
28. Guo and Liang (2017) report the same finding in the nearby city of Dongguan.
29. Surveys and short interviews on 25 March and 29 March 2018.
30. https://baike.baidu.com/item/深圳积分入户分值表/18763901?fr=aladdin#2.
31. The objectives and ideological foundations are expressed in "Several Opinions of the Shenzhen Municipal People's Government on Further Strengthening and Perfecting

Population Service Management," http://www.sz.gov.cn/zfgb/2016/gb968/201608/t20160823_4316510.htm
32. http://blog.sina.com.cn/s/blog_1605b61680102wlca.html 2016深圳积分入户查询, 3 May 2016.
33. The case of Mrs. Gong shows that access to social insurance is problematic not only for migrant workers with informal labor contracts (Cheng, Nielsen, and Smyth 2014) but also for petty entrepreneurs such as Mrs. Gong and her husband.
34. However, there are signs that Chinese authorities are contemplating a reform of the system that will allow urban *hukou* holders to keep and inherit land in their places of origin.
35. Parts of her answers, however, were rather ambivalent: "Because I hadn't planned this right, I'm not entitled to complain, but then also it's not as if I hadn't planned things right."

Conclusion
Exclusion and Rivalry, Lasting Inequalities, and Neoliberal Provision

This book has explored the spatially and temporally uneven process of China's urbanization through the lens of its graduated provision of public goods. The provisioning of public goods is a critical social issue in the unmaking of rural villages and the making of new urban communities. The state takes over the responsibility for provision when rural villages are administratively converted into urban communities, or *shequ*. Due to the stigma associated with their mixed population of former peasants and floating migrants—the latter making up the majority—and because these villages were initially excluded from the urban planning surrounding them, the process of statizing social goods is often messier than the vision of a clean break with the past suggests. Urban villages' rural past, inherited from the rural-urban dichotomy of the collectivist era, and their function in housing the huge floating migrant population generate tensions in the provision of public goods that highlight China's broader social and political issues.

In their introduction to a recent volume on infrastructure in the Global South, the anthropologists Nikhil Anand, Hannah Appel, and Akhil Gupta ask the essential questions: "To whom will resources be distributed and from whom will they be withdrawn? What will be public goods and what will be private commodities, and for whom? Which communities will be provisioned with resources for social and physical reproduction and which will not?" (2018: 2). Their use of the future tense makes sense, as they examine the "promises of infrastructure" at a rather discursive level. This book, too, has asked these questions about urban public goods, including urban infrastructure, but has opened them up diachronically and less discursively by looking at the changing paths of their provisioning.

Taking a pragmatic and historicized approach to actual provisioning practices in China's urbanized villages avoids overstating the differences between commons and public goods and shows that public goods can be subject to commoning and clubbing practices. Although their provision is no longer based on the classification of Chinese citizens as rural or urban, lasting legacies of this dichotomy are manifest in the inequalities and tensions that exist in China's urban villages. The concept of graduated provision highlights the contradictions between the authorities' economic and social policy goals, accounting for the ways in which the extension of public goods provision is highly uneven and conditional.

Exclusion and Rivalry

The extensive role of the state and limited role of civil society make China a special case in the growing literature on the urban commons. Considering the state's crucial role in setting the conditions for the functioning of capitalism and the enclosure of the commons, it is arguably understandable that following this line of thought, public goods are not only overlooked but even rejected. It is also true that Marx himself made no attempt to integrate within his theory of capital circulation the fact that when public goods are provided by the state, a significant proportion of capital passes through the state apparatus (Harvey 2017: 17).

Occupy Movement theorists (e.g., Graeber 2014; Pickerill et al. 2015) advocate "commoning" in the reclamation of public city space—space owned and delimited by the state—for self-organized collectives to share according to their own rules. For Dardot and Laval (2014), anti-capitalist revolution will consist of turning all social organizations, including associations and enterprises, into self-governed commons, resulting in a federation of commons based on rights of use that replaces state-backed property rights and therefore requires the abolition of the state itself as a political entity. David Harvey takes a different stance; while he acknowledges "the struggle to appropriate the public spaces and public goods in the city," he points out that "in order to protect the common it is often vital to protect the flow of public goods that underpin the qualities of the common" (2012: 73).

Neglecting public goods to focus exclusively on commons poses several problems. Much of the recent literature tends to focus on the struggles, external to urban commons, against the market and the state—assuming that the creation of a community of users is unproblematic—rather than concentrating on struggles inherent in the definition and shaping of such communities. It also loses sight of the commons' actual workings and at best remains fuzzy in dealing with the practical conditions that allow them to endure (Narotzky 2013). Furthermore, there are no intrinsic reasons why commons should be more just than public goods (Jongh 2021). Equality of access on one scale (a small group of neighbors holding use rights) can entail exclusion on a larger scale (newcomers without such local use rights). Questions of scale and scope inevitably underpin "the uncommons" that constitute the "condition of possibility for the common good and of commons" (Blaser and de la Cadena 2017: 186).

China's rural property rights regime is based on the kind of collective rights of use that Dardot and Laval (2014) favor. For these authors, the instruments required to reach postcapitalist equality are the abolition of the state coupled with the generalization of use rights at the local level. However, Dardot and Laval recognize the limited purview of localized social movements. Local, communal use rights require protection, and a federation of commons requires resource transfers and the redistribution of the fruits of collective labor on various scales.[1] It is doubtful that local civil-society initiatives can connect and impose a radically different order of things without adopting some sort of vertical mode of functioning and institutional mechanisms (Harvey 2012: 84; Kalb 2014; Nonini 2017).

For the time being it must be recognized not only that the Chinese state is not likely to be abolished anytime soon but also that we scholars need to recover a critical stance toward existing empirical situations: "pervasive processes of political economy that channel and constrain the politics of actors within and beyond the state" (Nonini 2017: 36). Such critique has paradoxically been partly lost in the emphasis on commons and alternative forms of governance, which amounts to "normalizing the socio-historical causes of resource scarcity as well as the 'exogenous violence' imposed by the process of capitalist valorization" (Bresnihan and Byrne 2014: 37). Foregrounding citizens' attempts to self-organize in the context of shrinking budgets risks losing sight of necessary critique of the policies that lead to such defunding in the first place. The exclusive preoccupation with commons and commoning is paradoxically forgetful of a critical stance that considers the shortcomings of provisioning in the context of neoliberal policies.

Even more problematic is the ambiguous flirtation with neoliberalism in the literature on the commons and its self-governing ideal (Lazzarato 2009; McShane 2010; Pithouse 2014; Enright and Rossi 2018). The discourse around the commons is deeply informed by the "moral turn" characteristic of neoliberal governmentality (Enright and Rossi 2018: 42). Third-way policies in Western countries often promote forms of local self-governance based on altruistic volunteering and sharing as a new route between the redistributive welfare state and market-driven economic liberalism (ibid.: 41; see also Muehlebach 2012). Similarly, China's community-building policy encourages communities to become self-governing by drawing on their own resources.

The literature on urban commons not only suffers from misplaced idealism in its emphasis on external struggles (Kalb and Mollona 2018) but also is often misguided by public-sector economists' schemata resting on the notion of inherent properties of goods such as rivalry and excludability. For instance, Charlotte Hess (2008), a disciple of Ostrom, locates the difference between urban commons and public goods in the former's inherent vulnerability to enclosure and overuse, although Ostrom saw in commons a solution to these problems. On the other hand, Borch and Kornberger (2015) expand the urban commons, or what they term a city's "atmospherics," to comprise all spaces of urban sociality including shopping malls, underscoring their absence of rivalry, contradicting Ostrom's notions of rivalrous common-pool resources and closed commons.

Rather than considering public goods inherently accessible and available to all (i.e., nonexcludable and nonrivalrous)—intrinsic qualities that public-sector economists have used to justify the governmental provision of public goods—the introduction to this book has argued for a political-economy approach, viewing public goods as goods provided following political decisions. The need for a realist rather than an idealistic perspective (Kalb and Mollona 2018) based on existing empirical situations further arises when considering the full range of occasions when commoning practices occur: white supremacists' self-funding and self-organization of militias to maintain their own idea of order is a form of commons. Public-sector economists overlook one major reason why private actors generally do not build roads wherever they see fit or ensure their own safety by forming militias: it is not because private provision is not optimal but because they are generally not, and indeed should not be, free to do so.

While this focus does not discount commoning practices, it does de-idealize them. Bringing public goods back into the equation requires recognizing that they are not inherently different from commons or club goods; there is no difference in their nature. However, public goods differ from commons in that they are provided by the state or local government. State-provided social goods such as state schools and public parks differ from self-provided neighborhood commons such as coresidents' helping one another with care activities, which is in turn distinct from privately provided, commodified private goods such as shopping malls. Redirecting attention to public goods avoids eschewing the role of the state and takes account of its lasting role as a provider. The Chinese state claims a monopoly on the provision of many public goods, although it may be reluctant to assume responsibility for providing them. Looking at actual processes of provision and distribution opens up a way of looking at the circumstances in which commoning and clubbing logics surface. This book has identified some of the claims made on the state by people's explicit expectations in terms of public goods—for instance, when citizens feel proud that the state has stepped in to create a public space, articulate demands for public toilets, or protest against the privatization of parking fees. Principles of equality, however, are rarely voiced: even though both newcomers and natives recognize that state-provided spaces should be accessible to all, such principles of social justice are disputed by other grassroots principles that foreground natives' priority rights of use and view welfare distribution as a reward for those who have contributed to economic growth (chapters 4 and 5). Redistributive principles are contradicted by reciprocal moralities.

This approach does not mean that the ideational criteria established by economists should be discarded; instead of using them a priori to classify different types of goods, it is more fruitful to use them to assess the situation observed. The distinction that matters relates to modes of provision—communal self-provisioning, state provisioning outside market logics, or clubbing—which are the outcome of political decisions. Furthermore, rather than labeling the intrinsic nature of goods, the notions of exclusion and rivalry help to name some of the social and political problems that underlie situations discovered in the field. Although the Chinese state and its local representatives are nominally committed to equality of access, exclusion and rivalry are widespread.

Exclusion arises when goods are subject to commoning and clubbing practices and to logic. The introduction called attention to the resemblance between these: while commoning aims at defending a good from appropriation by outsiders, whether individuals or the state, clubbing limits the use of public goods and services to those with the ability to pay. Both practices can jeopardize their equal delivery among all potential users. This is one of the major challenges in the transition from a rural village that is accustomed to managing its own common-pool resources to an urban community where the local state steps in. This book identifies some public goods, such as cemeteries and public spaces, that are still commoned, i.e., kept by the former rural community for itself and used for care and sociability. Moreover, in the context of local governments' budgetary scarcity, in a form of state-sanctioned commoning, urban communities (*shequ*), as grassroots management bodies, are encouraged to rely on local internal resources, including volunteering, in the name of community-building.

Furthermore, private developers increasingly provide public goods such as green spaces and parking spaces in residential complexes (*xiaoqu*): here exclusion operates on the basis of ability to pay, a clubbing logic that denies access to many. In the largest Chinese cities, which grant urban citizenship to restricted quotas of the population, club logic prevails in access to public goods such as education and health insurance. Shenzhen represents this trend best among the three case-study cities.

The question of rivalry in the city is mainly spatial. Although one can concede to Borch and Kornberger's (2015) "atmospherics" theory that sociality is highly valued in itself—for instance, a lively crowd participating in a festival is a good thing—this does not contradict the many instances of rivalry. The absence of rivalry in urban settings is highly contestable, since public transport, public space, housing, and schools are often overcrowded, reducing their quality (Harvey 2012: 74; Nonini 2017: 35). More generally, urban space is highly saturated and thus under strong pressure from competing uses, particularly where land is utilized as an investment vehicle (Huron 2017). This saturation of and competition for space can make public goods rival one another, as in Harvey's example of a community garden taking up land that could be used for affordable housing (2012: 102). Conversely, but by the same logic, peripheral space deemed impractical for real-estate projects finds the state and developers passing their responsibilities off onto one another, as in the case of unused land that has become a loosely self-governed quasi-commons in Chengdu's South Gate.

Everywhere else, the state seeks to claim its monopoly of public space by forbidding street vending and job posting and creating new, visibly government-run public squares for propaganda and displaying its attentiveness to citizens' leisure and sociability needs. Yet in China's newly urbanized neighborhoods, the small size of the public squares inherited from rural villages can give rise to tension regarding their use rights, with native villagers tending to monopolize them and reluctant to share them with new arrivals in the city. The continuing legacy of the rural past means that those with local urban citizenship rights are more likely to have access to, and a voice in, decisions about the use of such spaces.

The Enduring Legacy of the Rural-Urban Dichotomy

Although the Chinese state has, with a great fanfare, vowed to abolish the rural-urban dichotomy in access to urban public services, its legacy is strong, particularly in urban villages. In the collective era urban work units (*danwei*) provided a comprehensive array of public goods, including housing, medical care, kindergartens, and shops (Bray 2006), while rural collectives financed their own village-level social goods. Although located in urban territory, villages-in-the-city (*chengzhongcun*) have long been expected to continue to provide their own social welfare services and other public goods such as public security and sanitation, even once they have become both physically and legally urban. Now the *shequ* are charged with delivering key local public services, including public health, culture, sports, and security, while keeping the costs to the minimum and receiving little funding from the government.

It is in urban villages that the continuity between Mao-era village self-governance and economic autonomy in the provisioning of public goods is strongest. Unsurprisingly, therefore, the contradiction between the rhetorical importance accorded to community-building and the dearth of direct funding for building inclusive communities serving all residents is at its starkest in urban villages.

Redevelopment has occurred in different ways and at different speeds across the three cases considered in this book: it began early in the process of urbanizing South Gate in Chengdu, where the local municipal government funded the resettlement of the former villagers, and only later in River Hamlet in Xi'an and Pine Mansion in Shenzhen, where the government saved money by creating partnerships with commercial developers. All three cases have retained some form of collective social organization inherited from the Maoist rural past—i.e., the production groups and brigades, corresponding to "natural villages," which continue to frame sociability between the native villagers and account for their enduring identification with their village. The state of local governments' finances and considerations about what redevelopment projects will yield in terms of state revenue explain the differences in timing of redevelopment.

This timing, combined with local particularities in social organization, accounts for the varying degrees to which former village collectives have continued to exist and play a role in the provision of public goods. In Pine Mansion, powerful village shareholding companies have retained the collective use rights to former agricultural land, the urban use of which yields income that finances villagers' health insurance and pensions, while in South Gate all such land was expropriated by the state early on, the only remaining collective source of income being rental from shop spaces on the resettlement estates, with social welfare provision distributed by the local state. In Xi'an, an intermediary case, there has been little collective organization at the scale of the former administrative village, and as a result there is little income to reinvest, with much of the former collective agricultural land having been gradually sold off to developers, leaving both villagers and migrants vulnerable to sudden and brutal eviction in 2018. Basic welfare benefits are distributed by the local state, but villagers are strongly encouraged to seek employer-funded pensions and insurance (chapter 1).

Despite the administrative fiat that redefined rural villages as urban overnight, the prevailing idea is that only redevelopment can truly transform the villages and rid them of their chaotic (*luan*), insanitary and unsafe characteristics. The urgent need for their obliteration is seen as justifying the violent eviction of villagers, as occurred in River Hamlet. Yet such projects can be successful only with a certain amount of investment in parks, transportation, and schools to make them attractive to future buyers. Public-goods provisioning is highly conditional on the path followed by villages-in-the-city: municipal authorities do not start financing public goods immediately after a village is turned into an urban administrative entity, but only when the redevelopment plans have been launched.

Yet this notion of readiness for demolition and reconstruction, again in spite of the state's demiurgic discourse about turning urban villages into "proper" urban communities, is also conditioned upon the village's rural past and its investment in public goods prior to its administrative urbanization. While River Hamlet and South Gate had little in terms of a legacy of prior village social goods, Pine Mansion, with its long tradition of support from its diaspora, was left to its own devices to finance its public goods until the local state made it a primary target of its redevelopment policies. For the same reason, Pine Mansioners were able to cleverly circumvent the funeral reform by maintaining their cremated ancestors' remains within the limits of their village territory, commoning a public good for the free use of all native villagers. The poorer and much less unitary villagers in River Hamlet were only able to negotiate transport to the new and remote public cemeteries. Pine Mansion is a primary instance of how the state expropriates existing village social goods based on village commons and converts them to urban public goods to create favorable conditions for forthcoming redevelopment projects (chapter 2).

Changes in provisioning paths follow the pace at which urban communities are redeveloped, and redevelopment projects generally put a definite end to many village commons, such as roads and transportation funded by village collectives. The authorities allow urban villages' informal economies to thrive as long as they generate value; but when this value falls below what can be expected in the surrounding city's real-estate boom, as it did in Xi'an, or with the impact of the global financial crisis on export manufacturing, as in Shenzhen, they resort to the wholesale demolition and rebuilding of entire areas. While village infrastructure has been left in the hands of the collectives in urbanized communities for as long as an informal real-estate economy was tolerated, redevelopment projects trigger state intervention in matters of garbage disposal, electricity, sewerage, street lighting, greening, cleaning, and security; that is, the public goods closely associated with the broader Chinese discourse on urbanization as a civilizing process. The provision of these infrastructural goods, mainly by the Chengguan (urban management unit) and the Wangge (grid surveillance unit), performatively shapes the new urban environment as a primary means of creating a civilized urban community (chapter 3).

Past commons are not only used as assets for the generation of economic value: the rural past becomes a valuable resource in itself, an object of consumption for middle-class native villagers turned rentiers and incoming property buyers. In Chengdu's South Gate a mural displayed at the community center depicting the agricultural fields and labor of the rural past attracts both local and international visitors. In Pine Mansion the position of the new apartments in the redevelopment project next to the ancestral temple, to whose renovation the real estate developer contributed, makes them particularly desirable. The temple not only embellishes the neighborhood but is also the main reason behind middle-class Pine Mansioners exchanging their old houses for apartments in that precise location. In both South Gate and Pine Mansion, funds are granted to communities able to capitalize on the affective dimensions of nostalgia for the rural past. The state's livable community projects in urban villages capitalize on their past, reframing it in terms of Confucian values while aiming to convert them into respectable, modern, urban communities populated by law-abiding, self-governing, high-quality (*suzhi*) citizens (chapters 4 and 5).

Public space features centrally in livability projects. However, state-provided urban public space is generally limited in former villages and overlies former rural public space. In this recombinant urbanization (Kipnis 2016), native villagers tend to maintain certain communal activities in former village spaces, monopolizing them and relegating migrants to their margins. This segregation in the use of public space is most marked in River Hamlet and Pine Mansion, but it is also present in South Gate. This is one less visible but crucial marker of migrant and native inhabitants of urban villages' unequal entitlement to the benefits of urbanization (Webster and Zhao 2010).

Native villagers whose land is requisitioned for redevelopment projects maintain a sense of entitlement and can turn prior assets into value-generating capital. Moreover, local authorities consider that natives' expectations of priority rights to senior care, among other benefits, are grounded not only legally in *hukou* policy but also morally, in reciprocity for their past contribution to economic development and city growth. This was most explicit in Pine Mansion, where such a logic of the countergift legitimizes the provision of free care and lunches for elderly local former villagers by a private senior-care social enterprise. In contrast, many migrants find a source of security in their landholdings in their place of origin, considering their poor chance of being granted *hukou* for the village-in-the-city in which they now live. Some claim a right to the city based on their contribution to building it, and others subscribe to the literal "right-to-the-city" points system for earning *hukou* that has become prevalent in China's largest cities (chapter 5). This framework rests on deliberately unequal recognition of the value produced by different categories of citizen.

Neoliberalism as Graduated Provision

Neoliberalism's usefulness as an analytical lens is increasingly questioned, mainly because it is seen as an all-purpose explanation for a wide range of disparate phenomena (Parnell and Robinson 2012;

Ferguson 2015) due to its lack of internal coherence and mutability across locales (Ong 2006, 2007; Brenner, Peck, and Theodore 2010; Peck, Theodore, and Brenner 2012; Peck and Theodore 2019; Maskovsky and Brash 2014). China's neoliberalization continues to be hotly debated (Anagnost 2004; Greenhalgh and Winckler 2005; Ong 2006; Kipnis 2007; Arrighi 2008; Nonini 2008; Chu and So 2010; Wu 2010, 2017; Peck and Zhang 2012; Pieke 2012; Trémon 2015; Zhang and Bray 2017; Duckett 2020). Despite the state's adoption of capitalist market logics embracing capitalist modes of production and its role in accumulation by dispossession (Harvey 2005), it is very clear that its continuing and even increased commitment to providing public services and social welfare runs counter to the Euro-American narrative of neoliberalism entailing the state backtracking from commitment to redistribution. Moreover, the 2008 global financial crisis triggered a turn, if not a return, to a politics of state intervention and redistribution, especially in countries with authoritarian regimes and/or developing states (Parnell and Robinson 2012; Parnell and Walawege 2014; Collier, Mizes, and von Schnitzler 2016).

Rather than bringing us to the conclusion that China is not neoliberal in any sense, as the CCP Central Committee (2013) would have us believe (see introduction), conventional accounts of neoliberalism may need revision. Saving on expenses in China's urban communities (*shequ*) is intended not to reduce the level of public goods provision but rather to deliver public goods at the lowest possible cost. As several scholars recognize, neoliberal theories (including Buchanan's club goods theory) and reforms have aimed at rationalizing rather than putting an end to established forms of social provision (Hartmann 2005; Collier 2011), and this rationalization is still shaped by moral commitment to redistributive principles (James 2015). However, in the case of China, conditionality based on social and moral worth, rather than universal unconditional redistribution, prevails. Points-based access to *hukou* rewards those who have anticipated the future by buying social insurance and houses, and also volunteers (I expand the discussion of conditionality below). It is now recognized that neoliberal policies tend to appeal to grassroots values such as moral tropes of deservingness and merit (Gledhill 2004: 339; Mikuš 2016; Makovicky, Trémon, and Zandonai 2018), legitimizing them by either suggesting or emphasizing their continuity with older histories and social and cultural dynamics (Narotzky and Smith 2006; Muehlebach 2012).

Of course, neoliberalism as an ideology has Euro-American roots. Many scholars and observers agree that it is not the dominant ideology in China and that if there is neoliberalism in China it is articulated with everyday practices of personalism (Nonini 2008) and of other ethical regimes, e.g., Confucianism (Ong 2006: 9; Kipnis 2007). However, the notion that neoliberalism is either an ideology or a hegemonic discourse also needs rethinking, because it prevents our looking at existing empirical situations and locks us into culturalist approaches. The empirical materials used in the debate on China's neoliberalism deal more with issues of ideology, culture, and ethical regimes than with the actual changes to political and economic organization as they happen on the ground. This results in a false debate; as I have argued elsewhere (2015: 82), while it is clearly not the case that neoliberalism has become the dominant way in which people everywhere make sense of their lives, as Harvey wrote in an awkward foray into culturalist terrain (2005: 3), this does not mean capitalist neoliberalization is not a powerful force. The type of governance that is taking form in China is grounded in both socialism and neoliberalism (Sigley 2006; Pieke 2012).

The doubt cast on the analytical value of neoliberalism is largely due to irreconcilable political-economic and governmentality approaches (Barnett 2005; Hilgers 2012) increasing the impression that in addition to its variegated character, discussed above, neoliberalization describes too wide a range of phenomena: the unleashing of market forces, class formation by dispossession, new public management techniques, moral subject shaping, etc. However, the concept remains useful for capturing and criticizing the only apparently contradictory processes whereby the state allows market logics to prevail everywhere, tempering them only when they become socially unbearable, and fosters capitalist accumulation while remaining firmly in place. This makes capitalist neoliberalization perfectly politically compatible with right-wing populism (Hall 1988; Kalb 2012; Peck and Theodore 2019) and socialist authoritarianism (Duckett 2020).

Since the global recession of 2007–2009, China's economic growth has increasingly been sustained by massive investment in urbanization. This has generated huge fiscal debts for local Chinese governments (Xue and Wu 2015; Harvey 2012: 62–68). The maximization of real-estate value as an instrument for capital accumulation translates into a mode of welfare and public goods provision that ties such provision to the generation of value. As a result, despite the party-state's strong commitment to improving and providing equal access to urban public goods, its provisioning is graduated—that is, uneven and conditional.

It is uneven because it continues to de facto discriminate against the poor while supporting the propertied middle class. City infrastructure planning and resource allocation have largely been carried out with little regard for the needs of many residents, because until recently only the de jure (urban-*hukou*-holding) population was considered in budget allocation. This has changed, but urban welfare benefits in the form of retirement pensions and health insurance schemes remain highly unequally delivered due to city governments' lack of funds, slowness in implementing reforms, and the selectiveness of their points systems for extending urban benefits to non-*hukou* holders. As several other recent studies have shown, social security, old-age pensions, free basic education, and a minimum livelihood guarantee scheme (*dibao*), although granted to enlarged beneficiary groups, remain conditional and selective (Heberer 2009; Frazier 2010; Wong 2010; Solinger 2012; Cai 2016; Duckett 2020; Dong and Goodburn 2020; Huang 2020).

Urban public goods provision is graduated—i.e., differentiated—along class lines and according to the stage that an urban community has reached in the authorities' evolutionary thinking, which combines civilizational discourse about the need to rid villages of their rural backwardness with developmentalist thinking in terms of value-generating potential. Provision is adjusted locally according to both policies decided by upper-level authorities and local authorities' vision of not only what remains to be done but also what can potentially be achieved, considering the community inhabitants' "maturity"—their position in the evolutionary scheme of things. As a result, considerable variation can be found in both urbanized communities and their component neighborhoods, although the governing techniques used for selecting and targeting particular people and places are remarkably similar.

Graduated provision openly prioritizes middle-class residents based on a residential clubbing logic that privileges the idea of the self-governing middle class while serving to prevent conflict and temper potential sources of social instability. This is clearly the case in Chengdu, where the socialist tradition of regulating prices has been reinvigorated to fund community-scale wet markets and guarantee affordable food. Meanwhile, migrants are subjected to minute surveillance, but they are also the beneficiaries of charity events and the main targets of projects aimed at building solidarity. In these projects, funded via a competitive project-based system, some (mainly migrants) are encouraged to care for others (mainly natives), resulting in the graduated provision of care. Value extraction and recognition of the value contributed by diverse categories of the population are highly differentiated, both as economic valorization and as political acknowledgment of social worth (Collins 2017).

Provisioning is conditional because of the way in which public goods provision itself is partly tied to market-value-generation goals resulting from an entrepreneurialization of governance, leaving city dwellers to their own devices to provide or institute the commoning of public goods. Villages-in-the-city are seen as passing through a transitional phase. To reach the modernist civilizational goal of urbanization, some are singled out as "model villages" and are subject to intense attention and priority funding, as happened to South Gate in Chengdu and Pine Mansion in Shenzhen. In an effort to eliminate the remains of the rural villages, a homogenous, civilized urban landscape is being actively shaped via infrastructural improvements that reward the citizens and communities that come closest to the civilizational ideal. Infrastructural intervention is also used conditionally as a governing technique, as when sewerage and electricity services are cut off to compel native residents to accept relocation and compensation plans and to drive out unwanted migrants, as in River Hamlet in Xi'an. This conditionality is perhaps best illustrated by the case of Pine Mansion's public primary school, which was a village commons until it was taken over by the state. State funding turned it into a public good, but a conditional one: the school's extension was conditional on the shareholding companies' acceptance of the redevelopment project, and while enrollment is open to *hukou* and non-*hukou* holders, it excludes poor migrant workers from the points-based system for access to public schools.

Conditionality also underlies community-building policies more indirectly. Urbanized villages are primary targets of such policies, which appeal to Chinese citizens' desire to improve their own quality and to their moral imperative to care for others. Recognition of citizens' social worth or quality (*suzhi*) is conditional on their contributing free labor in the form of volunteering for caritative events and projects to improve the urban environment. Paradoxically, municipal governments promote caring work and volunteering precisely as a means of creating a sense of belonging to the city, shaping migrant-subjects' life plans and incentivizing them to apply for urban citizenship while continuing to control who is eligible for it.

While the Chinese authorities endeavor to neutralize class struggle by limiting inequalities in access to public goods, so far they have not succeeded. On the contrary, the inequalities are becoming increasingly caste-like as the more privileged members of society continue to benefit more from public transfers in education, healthcare, and pensions (Wang 2018). Although China's income inequality has declined since 2008, it remains among the highest in the world (Kanbur, Wang, and Zhang 2017; Picketty, Li, and Zuckman 2017;

Jain-Chandra et al. 2018; Solinger 2018). The National New Urbanization Plan (2021–35) aims at deepening the reforms initiated by the 2014 Urbanization Plan; among other goals, it seeks to further rebalance urban growth to benefit county towns and to change the development mode for megacities.[2] The points system for accessing basic urban benefits will be generalized, and the new plan is therefore likely to deepen and extend the graduated provision of public goods in China's fast-growing cities.

Notes

1. For critiques of Dardot and Laval's (among others) project of replacing private ownership rights with rights of use, see Harribey (2015) and Jongh (2021).
2. Notice of the National Development and Reform Commission on issuing the Key Tasks for New Urbanization and Urban-Rural Integration Development in 2021, 8 April 2021. https://finance.sina.com.cn/china/2021-04-13/doc-ikmyaawa9355317.shtml.

REFERENCES

Abramson, Daniel, and Yu Qi. 2011. "'Urban-Rural Integration' in the Earthquake Zone: Sichuan's Post-disaster Reconstruction and the Expansion of the Chengdu Metropole." *Pacific Affairs* 84(3): 495–523.
Acheson, James M. 2006. "Institutional Failure in Resource Management." *Annual Review of Anthropology* 35(1): 117–34.
Ahern, Emily. 1973. *The Cult of the Dead in a Chinese Village*. Stanford, CA: Stanford University Press.
Amin, Ash, and Philip Howell, eds. 2016. *Releasing the Commons: Rethinking the Futures of the Commons*. New York: Routledge.
Anagnost, Ann. 1994. "The Politics of Ritual Displacement." In *Asian Visions of Authority: Religion and the Modern States of East and Southeast Asia*, edited by Charles F. Keyes, Laurel Kendall, and Helen Hardacre, 221–54. Honolulu: University of Hawaii Press.
——. 2004. "The Corporeal Politics of Quality (*Suzhi*)." *Public Culture* 16(2): 189–208.
Anand, Nikhil, Akhil Gupta, and Hannah Appel, eds. 2018. *The Promise of Infrastructure*. Durham, NC: Duke University Press.
Arrighi, Giovanni. 2008. *Adam Smith in Beijing: Lineages of the Twenty-First Century*. London: Verso.
Audin, Judith. 2015. "Governing through the Neighbourhood Community (shequ) in China: An Ethnography of the Participative Bureaucratisation of Residents' Committees in Beijing." *Revue Française de Science Politique* 65(1): 1–26.
——. 2017. "Civic Duty, Moral Responsibility, and Reciprocity: An Ethnographic Study on Resident-Volunteers in the Neighbourhoods of Beijing." *China Perspectives* (3): 47–56.
Bach, Jonathan. 2010. "'They Come in Peasants and Leave Citizens': Urban Villages and the Making of Shenzhen, China." *Cultural Anthropology*. 25(3): 421–58.
Baden, John, and Douglas S. Noonan, eds. 1998. *Managing the Commons*. Bloomington: Indiana University Press.
Bakken, Børge. 2000. *The Exemplary Society: Human Improvement, Social Control and the Dangers of Modernity in China*. Oxford: Oxford University Press.
Barnett, Clive. 2005. "The Consolations of 'Neoliberalism.'" *Geoforum* 36(1): 7–12.
Bear, Laura, and Nayanika Mathur. 2015. "Introduction: Remaking the Public Good; A New Anthropology of Bureaucracy." *Cambridge Journal of Anthropology* 33(1): 18–34.
Billioud, Sébastien, and Joël Thoraval. 2014. *Le Sage et Le Peuple: Le Renouveau Confucéen En Chine*. Paris: CNRS éditions.
Blaser, Mario, and Marisol de la Cadena. 2017. "Introduction Aux Incommuns." *Anthropologica* 59(2): 194–203.

– 223 –

Boland, Anna, and Jiangang Zhu. 2009. "Boundaries and Belongings in Guangzhou: Changing the Nature of Residential Space in Urban China." In *The Politics of Civic Space in Asia: Building Urban Communities*, edited by Amrita Daniere and Mike Douglass, 134–50. New York: Routledge.

Bollier, David. 2002. *Silent Theft: The Private Plunder of Our Common Wealth*. New York: Routledge.

Bondes, Maria. 2019. *Chinese Environmental Contention: Linking Up against Waste Incineration*. Amsterdam: Amsterdam University Press.

Bourdieu, Pierre. 1970. "La Maison Kabyle ou le Monde Renversé." In *Échanges et Communications*, edited by Claude Lévi-Strauss, Jean Pouillon, and Pierre Maranda, 739–58. Berlin: De Gruyter.

———. 1972. *Esquisse d'une théorie de la pratique*. Genève: Droz.

Borch, Christian, and Martin Kornberger. 2015. "Introduction: Urban Commons." In *Urban Commons: Rethinking the City*, edited by Christian Borch and Martin Kornberger. New York: Routledge.

Brandtstädter, Susanne. 2013. "Counterpolitics of Liberation in Contemporary China: Corruption, Law, and Popular Religion." *Ethnos* 78(3): 328–51.

Bray, David. 2005. *Social Space and Governance in Urban China: The Danwei System from Origins to Reform*. Stanford, CA: Stanford University Press.

———. 2006. "Building 'Community': New Strategies of Governance in Urban China." *Economy and Society* 35(4): 530–49.

Brenner, Neil. 2004. *New State Spaces*. Oxford: Oxford University Press.

Brenner, Neil, Jamie Peck, and Nik Theodore. 2010. "Variegated Neoliberalization: Geographies, Modalities, Pathways." *Global Networks* 10(2): 182–222.

Bresnihan, P., and M. Byrne. 2014. "Escape into the City: Everyday Practices of Commoning and the Production of Urban Space in Dublin." *Antipode* 47(1): 1–19.

Bromley, Daniel W., and David Feeny, eds. 1992. *Making the Commons Work: Theory, Practice, and Policy*. San Francisco: ICS Press.

Bruckermann, Charlotte. 2020. *Claiming Homes: Confronting Domicide in Rural China*. New York: Berghahn Books.

Bruun, Ole. 2003. *Fengshui in China: Geomantic Divination between State Orthodoxy and Popular Religion*. Man and Nature in Asia, no. 8. Copenhagen: NIAS Press.

Buchanan, James M. 1965. "An Economic Theory of Clubs." *Economica* 32(125): 1.

———. 1999. *The Demand and Supply of Public Goods*. Collected Works of James M. Buchanan, vol. 5. Indianapolis: Liberty Fund.

Burawoy, Michael. 2009. *The Extended Case Method: Four Countries, Four Decades, Four Great Transformations, and One Theoretical Tradition*. Berkeley: University of California Press.

Cai, Meina. 2016. "Land for Welfare in China." *Land Use Policy* 55 (September): 1–12.

Carrier, James G., and Don Kalb, eds. 2015. *Anthropologies of Class: Power, Practice and Inequality*. Cambridge: Cambridge University Press.

Carrillo, Beatriz, Johanna Hood, and Paul Kadetz, eds. 2017. "Introduction." In *Handbook of Welfare in China*, edited by Beatriz Carrillo, Johanna Hood, and Paul Kadetz, 1–25. Cheltenham: Edward Elgar Publishing.

Cartier, Carolyn. 2001. *Globalizing South China*. RGS-IBG Book Series. Oxford: Blackwell.

———. 2013. "Building Civilised Cities." In The China Story, Yearbook 2013: Civilising China, chapter 5. https://www.thechinastory.org/yearbooks/yearbook-2013/chapter-5-building-civilised-cities/.

Castells, Manuel. 1977. *The Urban Question: A Marxist Approach*. Cambridge, MA: MIT Press.

Chakrabarty, Dipesh. 2002. *Habitations of Modernity: Essays in the Wake of Subaltern Studies*. Chicago: University of Chicago Press.

Chalfin, Brenda. 2014. "Public Things, Excremental Politics, and the Infrastructure of Bare Life in Ghana's City of Tema: Public Things." *American Ethnologist* 41(1): 92–109.

Chan, Kam Wing. 1994 "Urbanization and Rural-Urban Migration in China since 1982: A New Baseline." *Modern China* 20(3): 243–81.
———. 2009. "The Chinese Hukou System at 50." *Eurasian Geography and Economics* 50(2): 197–221.
———. 2012. "Crossing the 50 Percent Population Rubicon: Can China Urbanize to Prosperity?" *Eurasian Geography and Economics* 53(1): 63–86.
———. 2014. "China's Urbanization 2020: A New Blueprint and Direction." *Eurasian Geography and Economics* 55(1): 1–9.
———. 2021. "Internal Migration in China: Integration Migration with Urbanization Policies and Hukou Reform." Knomad Policy Note 16. https://www.knomad.org/publication/internal-migration-china-integrating-migration-urbanization-policies-and-hukou-reform.
Chan, Kam Wing, and Will Buckingham. 2008. "Is China Abolishing the *Hukou* System?" *China Quarterly* 195: 582–606.
Chan, Kam Wing, and Li Zhang. 1999. "The Hukou System and Rural to Urban Migration in China: Processes and Changes." *China Quarterly* 160: 818–55.
Chan, Roger C. K., Y. M. Yao, and Simon X. B. Zhao. 2003. "Self-Help Housing Strategy for Temporary Population in Guangzhou, China." *Habitat International* 27(1): 19–35.
Chatterton, Paul, and Andre Pusey. 2020. "Beyond Capitalist Enclosure, Commodification and Alienation: Postcapitalist Praxis as Commons, Social Production and Useful Doing." *Progress in Human Geography* 44(1): 27–48.
Chen, Chuanbo, and C. Cindy Fan. 2016. "China's Hukou Puzzle: Why Don't Rural Migrants Want Urban Hukou?" *China Review* 16(3): 9–39.
Chen, Lin. 2016. *Evolving Eldercare in Contemporary China: Two Generations, One Decision*. New York: Palgrave Macmillan.
Chen, Weixing. 1998. "The Political Economy of Rural Industrialization in China: Village Conglomerates in Shandong Province." *Modern China* 24(1): 73–96.
Cheng, Edmund W. 2014. "Managing Migrant Contestation: Land Appropriation, Intermediate Agency, and Regulated Space in Shenzhen." *China Perspectives* (2): 27–35.
Cheng, Mengyao, and Chengrong Duan. 2021. "The Changing Trends of Internal Migration and Urbanization in China: New Evidence from the Seventh National Population Census." *China Population and Development Studies* 5: 275–95.
Cheng, Tiejun, and Mark Selden. 1994. "The Origins and Social Consequences of China's *Hukou* System." *China Quarterly* 139: 644–68.
Cheng, Zhiming. 2012. "The Changing and Different Patterns of Urban Redevelopment in China: A Study of Three Inner-City Neighborhoods." *Community Development* 43(4): 430–50.
Cheng, Zhiming, Ingrid Nielsen, and Russell Smyth. 2014. "Access to Social Insurance in Urban China: A Comparative Study of Rural–Urban and Urban–Urban Migrants in Beijing." *Habitat International* 41: 243–52.
Chengdu Planning and Resources Bureau. 2020. "Chengdu Shi Meili Yiju Gongyuan Chengshi Guihua Ji Guihua Jianshe Dao Ze" [Chengdu's Urban Planning and Construction Guidelines for a Beautiful, Livable Park City]. Annual National Planning Conference, 16 March 2021, Chengdu.
Chu, Yin-wah, and Alvin Y. So. 2010. "State Neoliberalism: The Chinese Road to Capitalism." In *Chinese Capitalisms*, edited by Yin-wah Chu, 46–72. London: Palgrave Macmillan.
Chuang, Julia. 2020. *Beneath the China Boom: Labor, Citizenship, and the Making of a Rural Land Market*. Oakland: University of California Press.
Chung, Him. 2009. "The Planning of 'Villages-in-the-City' in Shenzhen, China: The Significance of the New State-Led Approach." *International Planning Studies* 14(3): 253–73.
———. 2010. "Building an Image of Villages-in-the-City: A Clarification of China's Distinct Urban Spaces; Debates and Developments." *International Journal of Urban and Regional Research* 34(2): 421–37.

———. 2013. "Rural Transformation and the Persistence of Rurality in China." *Eurasian Geography and Economics* 54(5–6): 594–610.
Chung, Him, and Jonathan Unger. 2013. "The Guangdong Model of Urbanisation: Collective Village Land and the Making of a New Middle Class." *China Perspectives* (3): 33–41.
Ciriacy-Wantrup, Siegfried von, and Richard Bishop. 1975. "Common Property as a Concept in Natural Resources Policy." *Natural Resources Journal* 15(4): 713.
Clarke, John. 2008. "Living with/in and without Neo-Liberalism." *Focaal* (51): 135–47.
Collier, Stephen J. 2011. *Post-Soviet Social: Neoliberalism, Social Modernity, Biopolitics*. Princeton, NJ: Princeton University Press.
Collier, Stephen J., James Christopher Mizes, and Antina von Schnitzler. 2016. "Preface: Public Infrastructures / Infrastructural Publics." In *Limn*. https://limn.it/articles/preface-public-infrastructures-infrastructural-publics/.
Collins, Jane Lou. 2017. *The Politics of Value: Three Movements to Change How We Think about the Economy*. Chicago: University of Chicago Press.
Colm, Gerhard. 1956. "Comments on Samuelson's Theory of Public Finance." *Review of Economics and Statistics* 38(4): 408–12.
Costes, Laurence. 2010. "Le Droit à la Ville de Henri Lefebvre: Quel Héritage Politique et Scientifique?" *Espaces et sociétés* 140–41(1): 177.
Coutard, Olivier. 2008. "Placing Splintering Urbanism: Introduction." *Geoforum* 39(6): 1815–20.
CSSB (China State Statistical Bureau). 2009. *Zhongguo tongji nianjian* [China statistical yearbook]. Beijing: China Statistical Press.
Dardot, Pierre, and Christian Laval. 2014. *Commun: Essai Sur La Révolution Au XXIe Siècle*. Paris: La Découverte.
Davis, Deborah, ed. 1995. *Urban Spaces in Contemporary China: The Potential for Autonomy and Community in Post-Mao China*. Cambridge and New York: Cambridge University Press Woodrow; Wilson Center Press.
Dean, Mitchell. 2010. *Governmentality: Power and Rule in Modern Society*. Los Angeles: Sage.
Derleth, James, and Daniel R. Koldyk. 2004. "The *Shequ* Experiment: Grassroots Political Reform in Urban China." *Journal of Contemporary China* 13(41): 747–77.
Dewey, John. 1991 [1927]. *The Public and Its Problems*. Athens: Swallow Press.
Dong, Yiming, and Charlotte Goodburn. 2020. "Residence Permits and Points Systems: New Forms of Educational and Social Stratification in Urban China." *Journal of Contemporary China* 29(125): 647–66.
Douglas, Mary. 1989. "Culture and Collective Action." In *The Relevance of Culture*, edited by Morris Freilich, 39–59. New York: Bergin & Garvey.
Du, Juan. 2020. *The Shenzhen Experiment: The Story of China's Instant City*. Cambridge, MA: Harvard University Press.
Duckett, Jane. 2011. *The Chinese State's Retreat from Health: Policy and the Politics of Retrenchment*. Routledge Studies on China in Transition 36. New York: Routledge.
———. 2020. "Neoliberalism, Authoritarian Politics and Social Policy in China." *Development and Change* 51(2): 523–39.
Dunn, Bill. 2017. "Against Neoliberalism as a Concept." *Capital & Class* 41(3): 435–54.
Dutournier, Guillaume, and Zhe Ji. 2009. "Social Experimentation and 'Popular Confucianism': The Case of the Lujiang Cultural Education Centre." *China Perspectives* 4(80): 67–81.
Dynon, N. 2008. "'Four Civilizations' and the Evolution of Post-Mao Chinese Socialist Ideology." *China Journal* 60(1): 83–109.
Edin, Maria. 2003. "State Capacity and Local Agent Control in China: CCP Cadre Management from a Township Perspective." *China Quarterly* 173: 35–52.
Elias, Norbert, and John L. Scotson. 1994. *The Established and the Outsiders: A Sociological Enquiry into Community Problems*. London: Sage.

Ellickson, Bryan. 1973. "A Generalization of the Pure Theory of Public Goods." *American Economic Review* 63(3): 417–32.
Enright, Theresa, and Ugo Rossi. 2018. "Ambivalence of the Urban Commons." In *The Routledge Handbook on Spaces of Urban Politics*, edited by Kevin Ward, Andrew E. G. Jonas, Byron Miller, David Wilson, 35–46. London: Routledge.
Fan, C. Cindy. 2008. *China on the Move: Migration, the State, and the Household*. Routledge Studies in Human Geography 21. New York: Routledge.
Fang, Chuanglin, and Danlin Yu. 2016. "Spatial Pattern of China's New Urbanization." In *China's New Urbanization*, 179-232. Springer Geography. Berlin, Heidelberg: Springer.
Farquhar, J. 2009. "The Park Pass: Peopling and Civilizing a New Old Beijing." *Public Culture* 21(3): 551–76.
Faubion, James D., ed. 2000. *Power: Essential Works of Michel Foucault 1954–1984*. New York: New Press.
Feeny, David, Fikret Berkes, Bonnie J. McCay, and James M. Acheson. 1990. "The Tragedy of the Commons: Twenty-Two Years Later." *Human Ecology* 18(1): 1–19.
Fei, Xiaotong. 1939. *Peasant Life in China*. London: Routledge.
Feng, Zhanlian. 2017. "Filial Piety and Old-Age Support in China: Tradition, Continuity, and Change." In *Handbook on the Family and Marriage in China*, edited by Xiaowei Zang and Lucy Xia Zhao, 266–85. Northampton, MA: Edward Elgar Publishing.
Ferguson, James. 2015. *Give a Man a Fish: Reflections on the New Politics of Distribution*. Durham, NC: Duke University Press.
Feuchtwang, Stephan D. 1974. *An Anthropological Analysis of Chinese Geomancy*. Vientiane: Vithagna.
———. 1998. "What Is a Village?" In *China's Rural Development: Between State and Private Interests*, edited by Frank N. Pieke, Eduard B. Vermeer, and Woei Lien Wong, 46–74. New York: M. E. Sharpe.
Foucault, Michel. 2000. *Essential Works of Foucault (1954–1984)*, edited by James Faubion. Volume 3: *Power*. New York: New Press.
Frazier, Mark W. 2010. *Socialist Insecurity: Pensions and the Politics of Uneven Development in China*. Ithaca, NY: Cornell University Press.
Friedman, Eli. 2018. "Just-in-Time Urbanization? Managing Migration, Citizenship, and Schooling in the Chinese City." *Critical Sociology* 44(3): 503–18.
Gandy, Matthew. 2006. "Planning, Anti-planning and the Infrastructure Crisis Facing Metropolitan Lagos." *Urban Studies* 43(2): 371–96.
Gaubatz, Piper. 2008. "New Public Space in Urban China: Fewer Walls, More Malls in Beijing, Shanghai and Xining." *China Perspectives* 2008(4): 72–83.
Gazier, Bernard, and Jean-Phillipe Touffut. 2006. "Public Goods, Social Enactions." In *Advancing Public Goods*, edited by Jean-Phillipe Touffut, 1–12. Paris: Edward Elgar.
Gibson-Graham, J. K. 2006. *A Postcapitalist Politics*. Minneapolis: University of Minnesota Press.
Gidwani, Vinay, and Amita Baviskar. 2011. "Urban Commons." *Economic and Political Weekly* 46(50): December 10.
Gioielli, Robert. 2011. "'We Must Destroy You to Save You': Highway Construction and the City as a Modern Commons." *Radical History Review* (109): 62–82.
Gledhill, John. 2004. "Neoliberalism." In *A Companion to the Anthropology of Politics*, edited by David Nugent and Joan Vincent, 332–48. Oxford: Blackwell Publishing.
Goldin, Kenneth D. 1977. "Equal Access vs. Selective Access: A Critique of Public Goods Theory." *Public Choice* 29(1): 53–71.
Goodburn, Charlotte. 2009. "Learning from Migrant Education: A Case Study of the Schooling of Rural Migrant Children in Beijing." *International Journal of Educational Development* 29(5): 495–504.

———. 2015. "Migrant Girls in Shenzhen: Gender, Education and the Urbanization of Aspiration." *China Quarterly* 222: 320–38.
Goodman, David S. G. 2004. "The Campaign to 'Open Up the West': National, Provincial-Level and Local Perspectives." *China Quarterly* 178: 317–34.
Graeber, David. 2014. *The Democracy Project: A History, a Crisis, a Movement.* London: Penguin Books.
Graham, Steve, and Simon Marvin. 2001. *Splintering Urbanism: Networked Infrastructures, Technological Mobilities and the Urban Condition.* London: Routledge.
Greenhalgh, Susan, and Edwin A. Winckler. 2005. *Governing China's Population: From Leninist to Neoliberal Biopolitics.* Stanford, CA: Stanford University Press.
Gudeman, Stephen F. 2001. *The Anthropology of Economy: Community, Market, and Culture.* Malden, MA: Blackwell.
Guldin, Gregory Eliyu. 1992. *Urbanising China.* Westport, CT: Greenwood Press.
———. 1997. *Farewell to Peasant China.* New York: Routledge.
Guo, Youliang, Chengguo Zhang, Ya Ping Wang, and Xun Li. 2018. "(De-)Activating the Growth Machine for Redevelopment: The Case of Liede Urban Village in Guangzhou." *Urban Studies* 55(7): 1420–38.
Guo, Zhonghua, and Tuo Liang. 2017. "Differentiating Citizenship in Urban China: A Case Study of Dongguan City." *Citizenship Studies* 21(7): 773–91.
Gustafsson, Bjorn A., and Deng Quheng. 2011. "Di Bao Receipt and Its Importance for Combating Poverty in Urban China." *Poverty & Public Policy* 3(1): 116–47.
Hall, Stuart. 1988. *The Hard Road to Renewal: Thatcherism and the Crisis of the Left.* New York: Verso.
Han, Chao. 2015. "Wangge Renyuan Luoshi Shequ Minsheng Fuwu Gongzuo" [Grid staff implement community livelihood service work]. *Zhongguo Gongchan Dang Xinwen Wang* [Chinese Communist Party news], 14 February 2015.
Han, Yangdi, and Jin Huang. 2019. "Evolution of Social Welfare in Rural China: A Developmental Approach." *International Social Work* 62(1): 390–404.
Hannerz, Ulf. 1980. *Exploring the City: Inquiries toward an Urban Anthropology.* New York: Columbia University Press.
Hao, Pu. 2015. "The Effects of Residential Patterns and Chengzhongcun Housing on Segregation in Shenzhen." *Eurasian Geography and Economics* 56(3): 308–30.
Hardt, Michael, and Antonio Negri. 2009. *Commonwealth.* Cambridge, MA: Belknap Press of Harvard University Press.
Harribey, Jean-Marie. 2015. *Pour Une Conception Matérialiste Des Biens Communs: Les Possibles.* https://france.attac.org/nos-publications/les-possibles/numero-5-hiver-2015/dossier-les-biens-communs/article/pour-une-conception-materialiste-des-biens-communs.
Hartmann, Yvonne. 2005. "In Bed with the Enemy: Some Ideas on the Connections between Neoliberalism and the Welfare State." *Current Sociology* 53(1): 57–73.
Harvey, David. 2005. *A Brief History of Neoliberalism.* Oxford: Oxford University Press.
———. 2009 [1973]. *Social Justice and the City.* Athens: University of Georgia Press.
———. 2011. *The Enigma of Capital and the Crises of Capitalism.* London: Profile Books.
———. 2012. *Rebel Cities: From the Right to the City to the Urban Revolution.* New York: Verso.
———. 2017. *Marx, Capital and the Madness of Economic Reason.* London: Profile Books.
He, Canfei, Yi Zhou, and Zhiji Huang. 2016. "Fiscal Decentralization, Political Centralization, and Land Urbanization in China." *Urban Geography* 37(3): 436–57.
He, Jianxiong, Yu Xiao, Jiatian Bo, and Guang Zhao. 2012. "Baozhangxing Zhufang Jianshe Beijingxia Chengzhongcun Gaizao de Celue Chutan—Yi Xi'an Shajincun Weili" [A preliminary study on the reconstruction strategy of villages-in-the-city against the background of the construction of affordable housing: The case of Shajing Village in Xi'an]. *Chengshiguihua* 2: 34–35.

He, Shenjing. 2015. "Homeowner Associations and Neighborhood Governance in Guangzhou, China." *Eurasian Geography and Economics* 56(3): 260–84.
He, Shenjing, and Fulong Wu. 2005. "Property-Led Redevelopment in Post-reform China: A Case Study of Xintiandi Redevelopment Project in Shanghai." *Journal of Urban Affairs* 27(1): 1–23.
———. 2009. "China's Emerging Neoliberal Urbanism: Perspectives from Urban Redevelopment." *Antipode* 41: 282–304.
He, Shenjing, and Desheng Xue. 2014. "Identity Building and Communal Resistance against Landgrabs in Wukan Village, China." *Current Anthropology* 55(S9): S126–37.
Heberer, Thomas. 2009. "Evolvement of Citizenship in Urban China or Authoritarian Communitarianism? Neighborhood Development, Community Participation, and Autonomy." *Journal of Contemporary China* 18(61): 491–515.
Heberer, Thomas, and Christian Göbel. 2013. *The Politics of Community Building in Urban China*. London: Routledge.
Heilmann, Sebastian. 2008a. "From Local Experiments to National Policy: The Origins of China's Distinctive Policy Process." *The China Journal* 59(January): 1–30.
———. 2008b. "Policy Experimentation in China's Economic Rise." *Studies in Comparative International Development* 43(1): 1–26.
Heilmann, Sebastian, and Elizabeth J. Perry, eds. 2011. *Mao's Invisible Hand: The Political Foundations of Adaptive Governance in China*. Harvard Contemporary China Series 17. Cambridge, MA: Harvard University Press.
Hertz, Ellen. 1998. *The Trading Crowd: An Ethnography of the. Shanghai Stock Market*. Cambridge: Cambridge University Press.
Hess, Charlotte. 2008. "Mapping the New Commons." *SSRN Electronic Journal*.
Hess, Charlotte, and Elinor Ostrom, eds. 2007. *Understanding Knowledge as a Commons: From Theory to Practice*. Cambridge, MA: MIT Press.
Hilgers, Mathieu. 2012. "The Historicity of the Neoliberal State." *Social Anthropology* 20(1): 80–94.
Hodkinson, Stuart. 2012. "The New *Urban* Enclosures." *City* 16(5): 500–518.
Hoffman, Lisa. 2013. "Decentralization as a Mode of Governing the Urban in China: Reforms in Welfare Provisioning and the Rise of Volunteerism." *Pacific Affairs* 86(4): 835–55.
Holston, James. 1989. *The Modernist City: An Anthropological Critique of Brasília*. Chicago: University of Chicago Press.
———. 2019. "Metropolitan Rebellions and the Politics of Commoning the City." *Anthropological Theory* 19(1): 120–42.
Howard, Pat. 1986. "Some Comments on China's Controversial Rural Economic Reforms." *Contemporary Marxism* 12/13: 163–202.
Howell, Jude. 2016. "Adaptation Under Scrutiny: Peering through the Lens of Community Governance in China." *Journal of Social Policy* 45(3): 487–506.
Huang, Philip C. C. 1993. "'Public Sphere'/'Civil Society' in China? The Third Realm between State and Society." *Modern China* 19(2): 216–40.
Huang, Yasheng. 2008. *Capitalism with Chinese Characteristics: Entrepreneurship and the State*. New York: Cambridge University Press.
Hsing, You-tien. 2006. "Land and Territorial Politics in Urban China." *China Quarterly* 187: 575–91.
———. 2008. "Socialist Land Masters." In *Privatizing China: Socialism from Afar*, edited by Li Zhang and Aihwa Ong, 57–70. Ithaca, NY: Cornell University Press.
———. 2012. *The Great Urban Transformation: Politics of Land and Property in China*. Oxford: Oxford University Press.
Huang, Xian. 2020. *Social Protection under Authoritarianism: Health Politics and Policy in China*. New York: Oxford University Press.

Huang, Yeqing. 2014. "The Continuity and Changes of the Hukou System since the 1990s: A Critical Review." In *Urban China in the New Era*, edited by Zhiming Cheng, Mark Wang, and Junhua Chen, 25–43. Berlin, Heidelberg: Springer.

Huron, Amanda. 2017. "Theorising the Urban Commons: New Thoughts, Tensions and Paths Forward." *Urban Studies* 54(4): 1062–69.

———. 2018. *Carving Out the Commons: Tenant Organizing and Housing Cooperatives in Washington, D.C.* Minneapolis: Minnesota University Press.

Jain-Chandra, Sonali, Niny Khor, Rui Mano, Johanna Schauer, Philippe Wingender, and Juzhong Zhuang. 2018. "Inequality in China: Trends, Drivers and Policy Remedies." *IMF Working Papers* 18(127): 1.

James, Deborah. 2015. *Money from Nothing: Indebtedness and Aspiration in South Africa*. Stanford, CA: Stanford University Press.

Jessop, Bob. 1999. "Retooling the Machine: Economic Crisis, State Restructuring, and Urban Politics." In *The Urban Growth Machine: Critical Perspectives Two Decades Later*, edited by Andrew E. G. Jonas and David Wilson, 141–59. Albany: State University of New York Press.

Jia, Junxue, Qingwang Guo, and Jing Zhang. 2014. "Fiscal Decentralization and Local Expenditure Policy in China." *China Economic Review* 28(March): 107–22.

Jiang, Xuemin. 2005. "Zhengque Renshi Yi Gufengongsi Wei Zhudao de Chengzhongcun Jingji" [Correctly understanding the joint-stock companies' leading role in the urban village economy]. *Kaifang Daobao* 3: 56–60.

Jing, Jun. 1996. *The Temple of Memories: History, Power, and Morality in a Chinese Village*. Stanford, CA: Stanford University Press.

Jing, Xiaofen. 2013. "Kongjian Geli Jiqi Dui Wailairenkou Chengshi Rongru de Yingxiang Yanjiu" [Spatial segregation and its impact on immigrants and their assimilation into the city]. Xi'an: Northwest Agriculture and Forestry University.

Jongh, Maurits de. 2021. "Public Goods and the Commons: Opposites or Complements?" *Political Theory* 49(5) 774–800.

Joyce, Patrick. 2003. *The Rule of Freedom: Liberalism and the Modern City*. London: Verso.

Kalb, Don. 2012. "Thinking about Neoliberalism as if the Crisis Was Actually Happening." *Social Anthropology* 20(3): 318–30.

———. 2014. "Mavericks." *Focaal* (69): 113–34.

———. 2017. "Afterword: After the Commons—Commoning!" *Focaal* (79): 67–73.

Kalb, Don, and Massimiliano Mollona, eds. 2018. *Worldwide Mobilizations: Class Struggles and Urban Commoning*. Dislocations, vol. 24. New York: Berghahn Books.

Kanbur, Ravi, Yue Wang, and Xiaobo Zhang. 2017 "The Great Chinese Inequality Turnaround." BOFIT Discussion Paper no. 6. https://ssrn.com/abstract=2962268.

Kaul, Inge. 2006. "Public Goods: A Positive Analysis." In *Advancing Public Goods*, edited by Jean-Phillipe Touffut, 13–39. Paris: Edward Elgar Publishing.

Kaul, Inge, and Ronald U. Mendoza. 2003. "Advancing the Concept of Public Goods." In *Providing Global Public Goods: Managing Globalization*, edited by Inge Kaul, Pedro Conceição, Katell le Goulven, Ronald U. Mendoza, 78–111. Oxford: Oxford University Press.

Kennedy, Loraine. 2017. "State Restructuring and Emerging Patterns of Subnational Policy-Making and Governance in China and India." *Environment and Planning C* 35(1): 6–24.

Kip, Markus, Majken Bieniok, Mary Dellenbaugh, Agnes Katharina Müller, and Martin Schwegmann, eds. 2015. *Urban Commons: Moving beyond State and Market*, 9–25. Berlin: Birkhäuser.

Kipnis, Andrew B. 1996. "The Language of Gifts: Managing Guanxi in a North China Village." *Modern China* 22(3): 285–314.

———. 1997. *Producing Guanxi: Sentiment, Self, and Subculture in a North China Village*. Durham, NC: Duke University Press.

———. 2006. "School Consolidation in Rural China." *Development Bulletin* 70: 123–25.
———. 2007. "Neoliberalism Reified: Suzhi Discourse and Tropes of Neoliberalism in the People's Republic of China." *Journal of the Royal Anthropological Institute* 13(2): 383–400.
———. 2012. "Constructing Commonality: Standardization and Modernization in Chinese Nation-Building." *Journal of Asian Studies* 71(3): 731–55.
———. 2016. *From Village to City: Social Transformation in a Chinese County Seat*. Berkeley: University of California Press.
———. 2021. *The Funeral of Mr. Wang: Life, Death, and Ghosts in Urbanizing China*. Berkeley: University of California Press.
Klein, Naomi. 2001. "Reclaiming the Commons." *New Left Review* 9 (May–June).
Knight, John, and Lina Song. 1999. *The Rural-Urban Divide*. Oxford: Oxford University Press.
Kotkin, Joel. 2010. "The World's Fastest Growing Cities." *Forbes*, 7 October. https://www.forbes.com/2010/10/07/cities-china-chicago-opinions-columnists-joel-kotkin.html.
Kuo, Lily. 2019. "Inside Chengdu: Can China's Megacity Version of the Garden City Work?" *The Guardian*, 2 April 2019.
Kwong, Julia. 2004. "Educating Migrant Children: Negotiations between the State and Civil Society." *China Quarterly* 180: 1073–88.
Laidlaw, James. 2015. "A Slur for All Seasons." In "The Concept of Neo-liberalism Has Become an Obstacle to the Anthropological Understanding of the Twenty-first Century," 2012 debate of the Group for Debates in Anthropological Theory. S. Venkatesan, J. Laidlaw, T. H. Eriksen, K. Martin, and J. Mair. *Journal of the Royal Anthropological Institute*, 21(4): 912–14.
Lan, Pei-chia. 2014. "Segmented Incorporation: The Second Generation of Rural Migrants in Shanghai." *China Quarterly* 217: 243–65.
Lan, Yuyun. 2001. "Urban Villages: The Last Step of the Disappearing of Villages." *Zhongguo Shehui Kexue Yuan Yanjiusheng Yuan Xuebao* [Journal of Chinese Academy for Social Sciences Graduate Center] 6: 100–112.
———. 2005. *Dushi Lide Cunzhuang* [Villages in the city]. Beijing: Sanlian Shudian.
Lang, Graeme, and Bo Miao. 2013. "Food Security for China's Cities." *International Planning Studies* 18(1): 5–20.
Lazar, Sian. 2014. "Citizenship." In *A Companion to Urban Anthropology*, edited by Donald M. Nonini, 65–82. Oxford: Wiley.
Lazzarato, Maurizio. 2009. "Neoliberalism in Action." *Theory Culture & Society* 26: 109–33.
Lee, Shin, and Chris Webster. 2006. "Enclosure of the Urban Commons." *GeoJournal* 66(1/2): 27–42.
Lefebvre, Henri. 1991 [1974]. *The Production of Space*. Translated by D. Nicholson-Smith. Oxford: Blackwell.
———. 1996 [1968]. "The Right to the City." Reprinted in *Writings on Cities*, edited by Eleonore Kofman and Elizabeth Lebas. Cambridge: Blackwell Publishers.
Lewis, Mark Edward. 2006. *The Construction of Space in Early China*. Albany: State University of New York Press.
Ley, D. 1990. "Urban Liveability in Context." *Urban Geography* 11(1) 31–35.
Liang, Zai, and Yiu Por Chen. 2010. "The Educational Consequences of Migration for Children in China." In *Investing in Human Capital for Economic Development in China*, edited by Gordon G Liu, Shufang Zhang, and Zongyi Zhang, 159–79. World Scientific.
Li, Bin, and Chaoqun Liu. 2018. "Emerging Selective Regimes in a Fragmented Authoritarian Environment: The 'Three Old Redevelopment' Policy in Guangzhou, China from 2009 to 2014." *Urban Studies* 55(7): 1400–1419.
Li, Dan. 2019. "Chengdu 2018 Niandu 'Baijia Shifan Shequ,' 'Shijia' Xilie Mingdan Chulu" [Chengdu's 2018 "One Hundred Model Communities" "Top Ten" list released]. *Sichuan News Network*, 30 December. http://scnews.newssc.org/system/20191230/001020594.html.

Li, Hongbin, and Li-An Zhou. 2005. "Political Turnover and Economic Performance: The Incentive Role of Personnel Control in China." *Journal of Public Economics* 89(9–10): 1743–62.

Li, Jenny Xin, and Yuying Tong. 2020. "Coming Together or Remaining Apart? A Closer Examination of the Contexts of Intergroup Contact and Friendship between Urban Residents and Rural-to-Urban Migrants in China." *Journal of Ethnic and Migration Studies* 46(1): 66–86.

Li, Jia, Xian Zhang, Man Ji, and Xiaolin Chuan. 2009. "Xi'An Chengqu Chengshi Senlin Jianshe Xian Zhuang Ji Fazhan Jianyi" [Present situation and proposals of Xi'an urban forest construction]. *Xibei lin xueyuan xuebao* [Journal of Northwest Forestry University] 24(6): 185–90.

Li, Peilin. 2002. "Jubian: Cunluo de Zhongjie" [Changes: The end of villages]. *Zhongguo Shehui Kexue* [Chinese social sciences] 1: 168–79.

———. 2004. *Cunluo de Zhongjie: Yangcheng Cun de Gushi* [The end of villages: The story of Yangcheng Village]. Beijing: Shangwu yinshuguan.

———. 2020. *Urban Village Renovation: The Stories of Yangcheng Village*. Singapore: Springer and China Social Science Press. Translated and augmented edition of Li 2004.

Li, Ruojian. 2006. "Diwei Huode de Jiyu yu Zhangai: Jiyu Wailai Renkou Juji Qude Zhiye Jiegou Fenxi" [Opportunities and obstacles in obtaining status: An analysis of occupational structure based on migrant population areas]. *Zhongguo Renkou Kexue* [Chinese studies in demographics] 5: 69–78.

Lian, Si. ed. 2009. *Yi Zu: Daxue Biyesheng Jujucun Shilu* [Ant tribe: A record of inhabited village of university graduates]. Guilin, Guangxi: Guangxi Normal University Publishing House.

Liang, Zai, and Zhongdong Ma. 2004. "China's Floating Population: New Evidence from the 2000 Census." *Population and Development Review* 30(3): 467–88.

Lim, Kean Fan. 2014a. "Spatial Egalitarianism as a Social 'Counter-movement': On Socioeconomic Reforms in Chongqing." *Economy and Society* 43(3): 455–93.

———. 2014b. "'Socialism with Chinese Characteristics': Uneven Development, Variegated Neoliberalization and the Dialectical Differentiation of State Spatiality." *Progress in Human Geography* 38: 221–47.

———. 2018. "Researching State Rescaling in China: Methodological Reflections." *Area Development and Policy* 3(2): 170–84.

Lin, George C. S. 2007. "Reproducing Spaces of Chinese Urbanisation: New City-Based and Land-Centred Urban Transformation." *Urban Studies* 44(9): 1827–55.

———. 2015. "The Redevelopment of China's Construction Land: Practising Land Property Rights in Cities through Renewals." *China Quarterly* 224: 865–87.

Lin, George C. S., and Fangxin Yi. 2011. "Urbanization of Capital or Capitalization of Urban Land? Land Development and Local Public Finance in Urbanizing China." *Urban Geography* 32(1): 50–79.

Lin, George C. S., Xun Li, Fiona F. Yang, and Fox Z. Y. Hu. 2015. "Strategizing Urbanism in the Era of Neoliberalization: State Power Reshuffling, Land Development and Municipal Finance." *Urban Studies* 52(11): 1962–82.

Lin, Yanliu, Pu Hao, and Stan Geertman. 2015. "A Conceptual Framework on Modes of Governance for the Regeneration of Chinese 'Villages in the City.'" *Urban Studies* 52(10): 1774–90.

Linebaugh, Peter. 2009. *The Magna Carta Manifesto: Liberties and Commons for All*. Berkeley: University of California Press.

Liu, Chengfang, Linxiu Zhang, Renfu Luo, Scott Rozelle, Brian Sharbono, and Yaojiang Shi. 2009. "Development Challenges, Tuition Barriers, and High School Education in China." *Asia Pacific Journal of Education* 29(4): 503–20.

Liu, Na. 2019. "Consequences of Social Mobility on Social Relationships: A Case Study of Successful Rural Migrants in Beijing." *Journal of Chinese Sociology* 6(1): 19.
Liu, Nicole Ning, Carlos Wing-Hung Lo, Xueyong Zhan, and Wei Wang. 2015. "Campaign-Style Enforcement and Regulatory Compliance." *Public Administration Review* 75(1): 85–95.
Liu, Yia-Ling. 2009. "Zhongguo Dushihua Guochengzhong Xinxingde Nongmin Shouzu Jieji: Wenzhou Yu Wuxi Chengzhongcun de Zhuanxinglujing, Jitikangzheng, Yu Fuli Zhengce" [The rise of the peasant rentier class in urbanizing China: The transition path and welfare policy of urban villages in Wenzhou and Wuxi]. *Taiwan Shehuixue* [Taiwan social science] 18: 5–41.
Liu, Youli. 2016. "Tamen de Gongtong Mingzi: Chengdu Wangge Yuan" [Their common name: Chengdu's grid supervisors]. *Chengdu Shangbao* [Chengdu business journal], 22 December. https://e.chengdu.cn/html/2016-12/22/content_583451.htm.
Liu, Yuting, Shenjing He, Fulong Wu, and Chris Webster. 2010. "Urban Villages under China's Rapid Urbanization: Unregulated Assets and Transitional Neighbourhoods." *Habitat International* 34(2): 135–44.
Loftus, Alex. 2015. "Violent Geographical Abstractions." *Environment and Planning D: Society and Space* 33(2): 366–81.
Logan, John R., and Harvey Luskin Molotch. 2007 [1987]. *Urban Fortunes: The Political Economy of Place*. Berkeley: University of California Press.
Loughran, Kevin. 2014. "Parks for Profit: The High Line, Growth Machines, and the Uneven Development of Urban Public Spaces." *City & Community* 13(1): 49–68.
Low, Setha. 2017. "Public Space and the Public Sphere: The Legacy of Neil Smith." *Antipode* 49: 153–70.
Low, Setha M. 2000. *On the Plaza: The Politics of Public Space and Culture*. 1st ed. Austin: University of Texas Press.
Low, Setha M., and Neil Smith. 2006. "The Imperative of Public Space." In *The Politics of Public Space*, ed. Setha M. Low and Neil Smith, 1–16. New York: Routledge.
Ma, Laurence J. C., and Fulong Wu, eds. 2005. *Restructuring the Chinese City: Changing Society, Economy and Space*. New York: Routledge.
Madsen, Richard. 1984. *Morality and Power in a Chinese Village*. Berkeley: University of California Press.
———. 1993. "The Public Sphere, Civil Society and Moral Community: A Research Agenda for Contemporary China Studies." *Modern China* 19(2): 183–98.
Malkin, Jesse, and Aaron Wildavsky. 1991. "Why the Traditional Distinction between Public and Private Goods Should Be Abandoned." *Journal of Theoretical Politics* 3(4): 355–78.
Makeham, John. 2011. "The Revival of Guoxue: Historical Antecedents and Contemporary Aspirations." *China Perspectives* 1: 14–21.
Makovicky, Nicolette, Anne-Christine Trémon, and Sheyla S. Zandonai. 2018. *Slogans. Subjection, Subversion, and the Politics of Neoliberalism*. New York: Routledge.
Maskovsky, Jeff, and Julian Brash. 2014. "Governance: Beyond the Neoliberal City." In *A Companion to Urban Anthropology*, edited by Donald M. Nonini, 255–70. Oxford: Wiley.
Mayer, Margit. 2009. "The 'Right to the City' in the Context of Shifting Mottos of Urban Social Movements." *City* 13(2–3): 362–74.
McArthur, J., and E. Robin. 2019. "Victims of Their Own (Definition of) Success: Urban Discourse and Expert Knowledge Production in the Liveable City." *Urban Studies* 56(9): 1711–28.
McCay, Bonnie J., and James M. Acheson, eds. 1987. *The Question of the Commons: The Culture and Ecology of Communal Resources*. 3rd ed. Tucson: University of Arizona Press.
McGee, T. G., G. C. S. Lin, A. M. Marton, M. Y. L. Wang, and J. Wu. 2007. *China's Urban Space: Development under Market Socialism*. London: Routledge.

McFarlane, Colin, and Jonathan Rutherford. 2008. "Political Infrastructures: Governing and Experiencing the Fabric of the City." *International Journal of Urban and Regional Research* 32(2): 363–74.

McKinsey Global Institute. 2009. "Preparing for China's Urban Billion." https://www.mckinsey.com/featured-insights/urbanization/preparing-for-chinas-urban-billion.

McShane, Ian. 2010. "Trojan Horse or Adaptive Institutions? Some Reflections on Urban Commons in Australia." *Urban Policy and Research* 28(1): 101–16.

Meng, Ling. 2001. "Goujian 'Da Chengdu JIngji Quan' Chutan" [A preliminary investigation into the construction of the "Greater Chengdu Economic Sphere"]. *Guoji Jingji* 1.

Miao, Julie T. 2019. "Planning Particularities: Reinterpreting Urban Planning in China with the Case of Chengdu." *Planning Theory & Practice* 20(4): 512–36.

Miao, Pu. 2011. "Brave New City: Three Problems in Chinese Urban Public Space since the 1980s." *Journal of Urban Design* 16(2): 179–207.

Mikuš, Marel. 2016. "The Justice of Neoliberalism: Moral Ideology and Redistributive Politics of Public-Sector Retrenchment in Serbia." *Social Anthropology* 24: 211–27.

Miller, Kristine F. 2007. *Designs on the Public: The Private Lives of New York's Public Spaces*. Introduction, ix–xxii. Minneapolis: University of Minnesota Press.

Mitchell, Don. 2003. *The Right to the City: Social Justice and the Fight for Public Space*. New York: Guilford Press.

Mittelstaedt, Jean Christopher. 2022. "The Grid Management System in Contemporary China: Grass-roots Governance in Social Surveillance and Service Provision." *China Information* 36(1): 3–22.

Mobrand, Erik. 2009. "Endorsing the Exodus: How Local Leaders Backed Peasant Migrations in 1980s Sichuan." *Journal of Contemporary China* 18(58): 137–56.

Molotch, Harvey. 1976. "The City as a Growth Machine: Toward a Political Economy of Place." *American Journal of Sociology* 82(2): 309–32.

Muehlebach, Andrea. 2012. *The Moral Neoliberal: Welfare and Citizenship in Italy*. Chicago: University of Chicago Press.

Musgrave, Richard A. 1939. "The Voluntary Exchange Theory of Public Economy." *Quarterly Journal of Economics* 53(2): 213.

Musgrave, Richard A., and Peggy B. Musgrave. 1973. *Public Finance in Theory and Practice*. New York: McGraw-Hill.

Nader, Laura. 1997. "Sidney W. Mintz Lecture for 1995: Controlling Processes Tracing the Dynamic Components of Power." *Current Anthropology* 38(5): 711–38.

Narotzky, Susana. 2012. "Provisioning." In *A Handbook of Economic Anthropology*, edited by James G. Carrier, 78–96. Cheltenham: Edward Elgar.

———. 2013. "What Kind of Commons Are the Urban Commons?" *Focaal* (66): 122–24.

National Bureau of Statistics. 2021. Communiqué of the Seventh National Population Census. http://www.stats.gov.cn/tjsj/.

Naughton, Barry. 1988. "The Third Front: Defence Industrialization in the Chinese Interior." *China Quarterly* 115: 351–86.

———. 1995. *Growing out of the Plan: Chinese Economic Reform, 1978–1993*. New York: Cambridge University Press.

Ngeow, Chow Bing. 2011. "Community Party Building in Urban China." *International Journal of China Studies* 2(2): 213–240.

Ngok, King-Lun, and Genghua Huang. 2014. "Policy Paradigm Shift and the Changing Role of the State: The Development of Social Policy in China since 2003." *Social Policy and Society* 13(2): 251–61.

Ngok, King-Lun, and Yapeng Zhu. 2010. "In Search of Harmonious Society in China: A Social Policy Response." In *Social Cohesion in Greater China*, edited by Ka-Ho Mok and Yu Ku, 69–94. Singapore: World Scientific Publishing.

Nguyen, Thao. 2013. "Governing through Shequ/Community: The Shanghai Example." *International Journal of China Studies* 4(2): 213–31.
Nonini, Donald. 2006. "Introduction: The Global Idea of 'the Commons.'" *International Journal of Social and Cultural Practice* 50(3): 164–77.
———. 2008. "Is China Becoming Neoliberal?" *Critique of Anthropology* 28(2): 145–76.
———. 2017. "Theorizing the Urban Housing Commons." *Focaal* (79): 23–38.
Oakes, Tim. 2019. "Happy Town: Cultural Governance and Biopolitical Urbanism in China." *Environment and Planning A: Economy and Space* 51(1): 244–62.
O'Brien, Kevin J. 1994. "Implementing Political Reform in China's Villages." *Australian Journal of Chinese Affairs* 32(July): 33–59.
———. 2001. "Villagers, Elections, and Citizenship in Contemporary China." *Modern China* 27(4): 407–35.
O'Donnell, Mary Ann. 2001. "Becoming Hong Kong, Razing Baoan, Preserving Xin'an: An Ethnographic Account of Urbanization in the Shenzhen Special Economic Zone." *Cultural Studies* 15(3–4): 419–43.
———. 2012. "Redevelopment" *Shenzhen Noted* (blog). https://shenzhennoted.com/tag/redevelopment/.
———. 2017. "Laying Siege to the Villages: The Vernacular Geography of Shenzhen." In *Learning from Shenzhen: China's Post-Mao Experiment from Special Zone to Model City*, edited by Mary Ann O'Donnell, Winnie Won Yin Wong, and Jonathan P. G. Bach, 107–24. Chicago: University of Chicago Press.
O'Donnell, Mary Ann, Winnie Won Yin Wong, and Jonathan P. G. Bach, eds. 2017. *Learning from Shenzhen: China's Post-Mao Experiment from Special Zone to Model City*. Chicago: University of Chicago Press.
Oi, Jean C. 1989. *State and Peasant in Contemporary China: The Political Economy of Village Government*. Berkeley: University of California Press.
Oi, Jean C., and Shukai Zhao. 2007. "Fiscal Crisis in China's Townships: Causes and Consequences." In *Grassroots Political Reform in Contemporary China*, edited by Elizabeth Perry and Merle Goldman, 75–96. Cambridge: Harvard University Press.
Ong, Aihwa. 2004. "The Chinese Axis: Zoning Technologies and Variegated Sovereignty." *Journal of East Asian Studies* 4(1): 69–96.
———. 2006. *Neoliberalism as Exception: Mutations in Citizenship and Sovereignty*. Durham, NC: Duke University Press.
———. 2007. "Neoliberalism as a Mobile Technology." *Transactions of the Institute of British Geographers* 32(1): 3–8.
Ong, Aihwa, and Li Zhang. 2015. *Privatizing China: Socialism from Afar*. Ithaca: Cornell University Press.
Ong, Lynette H. 2014. "State-led Urbanization in China: Skyscrapers, Land Revenue and 'Concentrated Villages.'" *China Quarterly* 217: 162–79.
Ostrom, Elinor. 1997. "Crossing the Great Divide: Coproduction, Synergy, and Development." In *State-Society Synergy: Government and Social Capital in Development*, edited by Peter B. Evans, 187–89. Berkeley: University of California Press.
———. 2010. "Beyond Markets and States: Polycentric Governance of Complex Economic Systems." *American Economic Review* 100: 641–72.
———. 2015. *Governing the Commons: The Evolution of Institutions for Collective Action*. Cambridge: Cambridge University Press.
Ostrom, Elinor, and Vincent Ostrom. 1977. "Public Goods and Public Choices." In *Alternatives for Delivering Public Services: Toward Improved Performance*, edited by Emanuel S. Savas, 7–49. Boulder, CO: Westview Press.
Otter, Christopher. 2004. "Cleansing and Clarifying: Technology and Perception in Nineteenth-Century London." *Journal of British Studies* 43(1): 40–64.

Pacione, M. 1990. "Urban Liveability: A Review." *Urban Geography* 11(1): 1–30.
Pan, Tianshu. 2011. "Place Attachment, Communal Memory, and the Moral Underpinnings of Gentrification in Shanghai." In *Deep China: The Moral Life of the Person; What Anthropology and Psychiatry Tell Us about China Today*, edited by Arthur Kleinman, Yunxiang Yan, Jing Jun, Sing Lee, Everett Zhang, Pan Tianshu, Wu Fei, and Gua Jinhua. 152–77. Berkeley: University of California Press.
Parish, William L., and Martin King Whyte. 1978. *Village and Family in Contemporary China*. Chicago: University of Chicago Press.
Parnell, Susan, and Jennifer Robinson. 2012. "(Re)Theorizing Cities from the Global South: Looking beyond Neoliberalism." *Urban Geography* 33(4): 593–617.
Parnell, Susan, and Ruwani Walawege. 2014. "Sub-Saharan African Urbanisation and Global Environmental Change." In *Africa's Urban Revolution*, edited by Susan Parnell and Edgar Pieterse, 35–59. London: Zed Books.
Parr, Adrian. 2015. "Urban Debt, Neoliberalism and the Politics of the Commons." *Theory, Culture & Society* 32(3): 69–91.
Payette, Alex. 2016. "Local Confucian Revival in China: Ritual Teachings, 'Confucian' Learning and Cultural Resistance in Shandong." *China Report* 52(1): 1–18.
Peck, Jamie, Nik Theodore, and Neil Brenner. 2012. "Neoliberalism Resurgent? Market Rule after the Great Recession." *South Atlantic Quarterly* 111(2): 265–88.
Peck, Jamie, and Nik Theodore. 2019. "Still Neoliberalism?" *South Atlantic Quarterly* 118(2): 245–65.
Peck, Jamie, and Jun Zhang. 2013. "A Variety of Capitalism ... with Chinese Characteristics?" *Journal of Economic Geography* 13(3): 357–96.
Pei, Xiaolin. 2002. "The Contribution of Collective Landownership to China's Economic Transition and Rural Industrialization: A Resource Allocation Model." *Modern China* 28(3): 279–314.
Perry, Elizabeth J. 2013. "Cultural Governance in Contemporary China: 'Re-orienting' Party Propaganda." Harvard-Yenching Institute Working Papers. http://nrs.harvard.edu/urn-3:HUL.InstRepos:11386987.
———. 2019. "Making Communism Work: Sinicizing a Soviet Governance Practice." *Comparative Studies in Society and History* 61(3): 535–62.
Pickerill, Jenny, John Krinsky, Graeme Hayes, Kevin Gillan, and Brian Doherty. 2015. *Occupy! A Global Movement*. 1st ed. New York: Routledge. https://doi.org/10.4324/9781315742502.
Piketty, Thomas, Yang Li, and Gabriel Zuckman. 2017. "Capital Accumulation, Private Property and Rising Inequality in China, 1978–2015." Working Paper. https://wid.world/document/t-piketty-l-yang-and-g-zucman-capital-accumulation-private-property-and-inequality-in-china-1978-2015-2016/.
Pickhardt, Michael. 2006. "Fifty Years after Samuelson's 'The Pure Theory of Public Expenditure': What Are We Left With?" *Journal of the History of Economic Thought* 28(4): 439–60.
Pieke, Frank N. 2012. "The Communist Party and Social Management in China." *China Information* 26(2): 149–65.
Pithouse, Richard. 2014. "An Urban Commons? Notes from South Africa." *Community Development Journal* 49 (suppl 1): 31–43.
Po, Lanchih. 2008. "Redefining Rural Collectives in China: Land Conversion and the Emergence of Rural Shareholding Co-operatives." *Urban Studies* 45(8): 1603–23.
———. 2011. "Property Rights Reforms and Changing Grassroots Governance in China's Urban–Rural Peripheries: The Case of Changping District in Beijing." *Urban Studies* 48(3): 509–28.
———. 2012. "Asymmetrical Integration: Public Finance Deprivation in China's Urbanized Villages." *Environment and Planning A: Economy and Space* 44(12): 2834–51.

Potter, Sulamith Heins, and Jack M. Potter. 1990. *China's Peasants: The Anthropology of a Revolution*. New York: Cambridge University Press.

Pow, Choon-Piew. 2009. "Neoliberalism and the Aestheticization of New Middle-Class Landscapes." *Antipode* 41(2): 371–90.

Puett, Michael. 2008. "Ritual and the Subjunctive." In *Ritual and Its Consequences: An Essay on the Limits of Sincerity*, edited by Andrew Seligman, Robert Weller, B. Simon, and Michael Puett, 17–42. Oxford: Oxford University Press.

Pun, Ngai. 2005. *Made in China: Women Factory Workers in a Global Workplace*. Durham: Duke University Press.

Purcell, Mark. 2002. "Excavating Lefebvre: The Right to the City and Its Urban Politics of the Inhabitant." *GeoJournal* 58(2/3): 99–108.

Qian, Jiwei, and Ake Blomqvist. 2014. *Health Policy Reform in China: A Comparative Perspective*. Singapore: World Scientific.

Qian, Hui, and Cecilia Wong. 2012. "Master Planning under Urban–Rural Integration: The Case of Nanjing, China." *Urban Policy and Research* 30(4): 403–21.

Qian, Zhu, and Hongyan Li. 2017. "Urban Morphology and Local Citizens in China's Historic Neighborhoods: A Case Study of the Stele Forest Neighborhood in Xi'an." *Cities* 71: 97–109.

Rankin, Mary Backus. 1993. "Some Observations on a Chinese Public Sphere." *Modern China* 19(2): 158–82.

Read, Benjamin L. 2000. "Revitalizing the State's Urban 'Nerve Tips.'" *China Quarterly* 163: 812–13.

———. 2008. "Assessing Variation in Civil Society Organizations: China's Homeowner Associations in Comparative Perspective." *Comparative Political Studies* 41(9): 1240–65.

———. 2012. *Roots of the State: Neighborhood Organization and Social Networks in Beijing and Taipei*. Stanford, CA: Stanford University Press.

Rose, Nikolas S. 1999. *Powers of Freedom: Reframing Political Thought*. Cambridge: Cambridge University Press.

Rose, Nikolas, and Peter Miller. 2010. "Political Power beyond the State: Problematics of Government." *The British Journal of Sociology* 61: 271–303.

Samuelson, Paul A. 1954. "The Pure Theory of Public Expenditure." *Review of Economics and Statistics* 36(4): 387.

Samuelson, Paul A., and William D. Nordhaus. 2010. *Economics*. 19th ed. Boston: McGraw-Hill Irwin.

Sangren, Paul Steven. 1987. *History and Magical Power in a Chinese Community*. Stanford, CA: Stanford University Press.

Scott, Allen J., and Michael Storper. 2015. "The Nature of Cities: The Scope and Limits of Urban Theory." *International Journal of Urban and Regional Research* 39(1): 1–15.

Schoon, S. 2014. "Chinese Strategies of Experimental Governance: The Underlying Forces Influencing Urban Restructuring in the Pearl River Delta." *Cities* 41: 194–99.

Selden, Mark, and Laiyin You. 1997. "The Reform of Social Welfare in China." *World Development* 25(10): 1657–68.

Sennett, Richard. 1977. *The Fall of Public Man*. New York: Alfred A. Knopf.

Shen, Jianfa, Kwan-yiu Wong, and Zhiqiang Feng. 2002. "State-Sponsored and Spontaneous Urbanization in the Pearl River Delta of South China, 1980–1998." *Urban Geography* 23(7): 674–94.

Shen, Yang, and Bingqin Li. 2020. "Policy Coordination in the Talent War to Achieve Economic Upgrading: The Case of Four Chinese Cities." *Policy Studies* (1): 1–21.

Shen, Yaxin, Zijie Song, and Hong Zhu. 2019. "Zhongguo Wei Shenme Yao Jinxing 'Cesuo Gaige'?" [Why is China carrying out a "toilet revolution"?]. *People's Daily Online*, 19 September 2019.

Shenzhen Statistics Bureau. 2021. *Shenzhen Statistical Yearbook 2020*. Shenzhen: China Statistics Press.

Shenzhen Municipal Government. 2005. *Futian District Report on Cities among Villages*. Shenzhen: Shenzhen Municipal Government.

Shi, Shih-Jiunn. 2012. "Towards Inclusive Citizenship? Rethinking China's Social Security in the Trend towards Urban–Rural Harmonization." *Journal of Social Policy* 41(4): 789–810.

Shih, Victor, Christopher Adolph, and Mingxing Liu. 2012. "Getting Ahead in the Communist Party: Explaining the Advancement of Central Committee Members in China." *American Political Science Review* 106(1): 166–87.

Shin, Hyun Bang. 2009. "Residential Regeneration and the Entrepreneurial Local State: The Implications of Beijing's Shifting Emphasis on Urban Regeneration Policies." *Urban Studies* 46(13): 2815–39

Shue, Vivienne. 1980. *Peasant China in Transition: The Dynamics of Development toward Socialism, 1949–1956*. Berkeley: University of California Press.

———. 1984. "The Fate of the Commune." *Modern China* 10(3): 259–83.

Sigley, Gary. 2006. "Chinese Governmentalities: Government, Governance and the Socialist Market Economy." *Economy and Society* 35(4): 487–508.

Siu, Helen F. 1989. *Agents and Victims in South China: Accomplices in Rural Revolution*. New Haven, CT: Yale University Press.

———. 2007. "Grounding Displacement: Uncivil Urban Spaces in Postreform South China." *American Ethnologist* 34(2): 329–50.

Skinner, William. 1971. "Chinese Peasants and the Closed Community: An Open and Shut Case." *Comparative Studies in Society and History* 13(3): 270–81.

Sklair, Leslie. 1991. "Problems of Socialist Development: The Significance of Shenzhen Special Economic Zone for China's Open Door Development Strategy." *International Journal of Urban and Regional Research* 15(2): 197–215.

Smart, Alan. 2018. "Ethnographic Perspectives on the Mediation of Informality between People and Plans in Urbanising China." *Urban Studies* 55(7): 1477–83.

Smart, Alan, and Josephine Smart. 2001. "Local Citizenship: Welfare Reform Urban/Rural Status, and Exclusion in China." *Environment and Planning A* 33(10): 1853–69.

Smart, Josephine, and Cuiling Li. 2012. "Resistance to Becoming Urban: Hukou Politics in a Pearl River Delta Community, China." In *The Emergence of a New Urban China: Insiders' Perspectives*, edited by Zai Liang, 61–85. Lanham, MD: Lexington Books.

Smith, Neil. 1996. *The New Urban Frontier: Gentrification and the Revanchist City*. New York: Routledge.

Smith, Nick R. 2014. "Beyond Top-Down/Bottom-Up: Village Transformation on China's Urban Edge." *Cities* 41: 209–20.

Solinger, Dorothy J. 1999. *Contesting Citizenship in Urban China: Peasant Migrants, the State, and the Logic of the Market*. Berkeley: University of California Press.

———. 2006. "The Creation of a New Underclass in China and Its Implications." *Environment and Urbanization* 18(1): 177–93.

———, ed. 2018. *Polarized Cities: Portraits of Rich and Poor in Urban China*. Lanham, MD: Rowman and Littlefield.

Solinger, Dorothy J., and Yiyang Hu. 2012. "Welfare, Wealth and Poverty in Urban China: The 'Dibao' and Its Differential Disbursement." *China Quarterly* 211: 741–64.

Song, Yan, Yves Zenou, and Chengri Ding. 2008. "Let's Not Throw the Baby out with the Bath Water: The Role of Urban Villages in Housing Rural Migrants in China." *Urban Studies* 45: 313–30.

Song, Jing. 2014. "Space to Maneuver: Collective Strategies of Indigenous Villagers in the Urbanizing Region of Northwestern China." *Eurasian Geography and Economics* 55(4): 362–80.

Staeheli, Lynn A., and Don Mitchell. 2008. *The People's Property? Power, Politics, and the Public*. New York: Routledge.
State Council of the People's Republic of China. 2014. *Opinions of the State Council on Furthering the Reform of the Household Registration System* No. 25, 24 July 2014, http://www.gov.cn/zhengce/content/2014-07/30/content_8944.htm.
Stavrides, Stavros. 2014. "Emerging Common Spaces as a Challenge to the City of Crisis." *City* 1(4–5): 546–50.
Steinmüller, Hans. 2013. *Communities of Complicity: Everyday Ethics in Rural China*. New York: Berghahn Books.
Stiglitz, Joseph E. 2000. *Economics of the Public Sector*. 3rd ed. New York: W. W. Norton.
Strauss, Kendra, and Feng Xu. 2018. "At the Intersection of Urban and Care Policy: The Invisibility of Eldercare Workers in the Global City." *Critical Sociology* 44(7–8): 1163–78.
Summers, Tim. 2016. "China's 'New Silk Roads': Sub-national Regions and Networks of Global Political Economy." *Third World Quarterly* 37(9): 1628–43.
Susser, Ida, and Stéphane Tonnelat. 2013. "Transformative Cities." *Focaal* (66): 105–21.
Swider, Sarah. 2015. "Reshaping China's Urban Citizenship: Street Vendors, *Chengguan* and Struggles over the Right to the City." *Critical Sociology* 41(4–5): 701–16.
Swyngedouw, Erik. 2004. *Social Power and the Urbanization of Water: Flows of Power*. Oxford: Oxford University Press.
Tan, Gang. 2005. "Chengzhoncun Jingji Zhuti, Jingji Huodong Ji Zhuyao Tezheng: Shenzhen Shi Futian Quyu Chengzhongcun Diaocha" [Collective economy, collective activities and main characteristics of villages-in-the-city: A study of villages-in-the-city in Futian district, Shenzhen]. *Kaifang Daobao* [Open herald] 3: 51–56.
Tang, Beibei. 2015. "'Not Rural but Not Urban': Community Governance in China's Urban Villages." *China Quarterly* 223: 724–44.
———. 2020. "Grid Governance in China's Urban Middle-Class Neighbourhoods." *China Quarterly* 241 (March): 43–61.
Tang, Wing-Shing, and Him Chung. 2002. "Rural–Urban Transition in China: Illegal Land Use and Construction." *Asia Pacific Viewpoint* 43(1): 43–62.
Tang, Ning, and Fei Sun. 2017. "Shequ Construction and Service Development in Urban China: An Examination of the Shenzhen Model." *Community Development Journal* 52(1): 10–20.
Taylor, Peter, Pengfei Ni, and Kai Liu. 2016. *Global Research of Cities*. Singapore: Springer.
Teo, S. 2014. "Political Tool or Quality Experience? Urban Livability and the Singaporean State's Global City Aspirations." *Urban Geography* 35(6): 916–37.
Thireau, Isabelle. 2013. "Agir ensemble à Dongcun, ou le surgissement caché du politique." In *De proche en proche: Ethnographie des formes d'association en Chine contemporaine*, edited by Isabelle Thireau, 153–94. Bern: Peter Lang.
———. 2020. *Lieux Communs: Une Ethnographie Des Rassemblements Publics En Chine*. Paris: École des hautes études en sciences sociales.
Tian, Li. 2008. "The Chengzhongcun Land Market in China: Boon or Bane? A Perspective on Property Rights." *International Journal of Urban and Regional Research* 32(2): 282–304.
Tomba, Luigi. 2004. "Creating an Urban Middle Class: Social Engineering in Beijing." *The China Journal* 51: 1–26.
———. 2014. *The Government Next Door: Neighborhood Politics in Urban China*. Ithaca, NY: Cornell University Press.
Trémon, Anne-Christine. 2015. "Local Capitalism and Neoliberalization in a Shenzhen Former Lineage Village." *Focaal* (71): 71–85.
———. 2018. "'Start Here': Foundational Slogans in Shenzhen, China." In *Slogans: Subjection, Subversion, and the Politics of Neoliberalism*, edited by Nicolette Makovicky, Anne-Christine Trémon, and Sheyla S. Zandonai, 50–76. London: Routledge.

———. 2020. "Variegated Valuation: Governance and Circuits of Value in Shenzhen." *Focaalblog*. http://www.focaalblog.com/2020/07/20/anne-christine-tremon-variegated-valuation-governance-and-circuits-of-value-in-shenzhen/.

———. 2022. *Diaspora Space-Time: Transformations of a Chinese Emigrant Community*. Ithaca, NY: Cornell University Press.

———. 2023. "Schools as Drivers of Capitalist Accumulation Conditional Socialized Reproduction in Shenzhen." *Dialectical Anthropology*, online: https://link.springer.com/article/10.1007/s10624-022-09682-5.

Tsai, Lily L. 2007. *Accountability without Democracy: Solidary Groups and Public Goods Provision in Rural China*. New York: Cambridge University Press.

Tyner, Adam, and Yuan Ren. 2016. "The *Hukou* System, Rural Institutions, and Migrant Integration in China." *Journal of East Asian Studies* 16(3): 331–48.

United Nations. 2017. "The Right to the City and Cities for All." Habitat III Policy Papers: Policy Paper 1. United Nations Conference on Housing and Sustainable Urban Development, New York.

Unger, Jonathan. 1984. "Remuneration, Ideology, and Personal Interests in a Chinese Village, 1960–1980." *International Journal of Sociology* 14(4): 3–26.

Vogel, Ezra. 1989. *One Step Ahead in China: Guangdong under Reform*. Cambridge: Harvard University Press.

Wang, David Da Wei. 2017. *Urban Villages in the New China*. New York: Palgrave Macmillan.

Wang, Di. 1998. "Street Culture: Public Space and Urban Commoners in Late-Qing Chengdu." *Modern China* 24(1): 34–72.

———. 2008. *The Teahouse: Small Business, Everyday Culture, and Public Politics in Chengdu, 1900–1950*. Stanford, CA: Stanford University Press.

Wang, Fei-Ling. 2005. *Organizing through Division and Exclusion: China's Hukou System*. Stanford, CA: Stanford University Press.

Wang, Feng. 2018. "China's Uphill Battle against Inequality." In *Polarized Cities: Portraits of Rich and Poor in Urban China*, 23–42. Washington, DC: Rowman and Littlefield.

Wang, Fenglong, and Yungang Liu. 2018. "Interpreting Chinese *Hukou* System from a Foucauldian Perspective." *Urban Policy and Research* 36(2): 153–67.

Wang, Jiashun, and Steve Messner. 2012. "Institutional Segmentation and Psychosocial Repellence: Urban Residents' Attitude toward Migrants." In *The Emergence of a New Urban China: Insiders' Perspectives*, edited by Zai Liang, 43–60. Lanham, MD: Lexington Books.

Wang, Jiayuan. 2020. "Revolutionary Potties: China's 'Toilet Revolution,' Five Years On." *Sixth Tone*, 3 August 2020. https://www.sixthtone.com/news/1006003/revolutionary-potties-chinas-toilet-revolution percent2C-five-years-on.

Wang, Lihua. 2016. "Local Adaptation of Central Policies: The Policymaking and Implementation of Compulsory Education for Migrant Children in China." *Asia Pacific Education Review* 17(1): 25–39.

Wang, Tao. 2008. "Xi'an Shi Cheng Zhongcun Gaizao Moshi Ji Duice Tantao" [Inquiry into Xi'an city's model of urban village redevelopment and countermoves]. *Human Geography* 23(4): 46–50.

Wang, Xingzhou. 2015. "Dushi Xiangmin Yu Xiangtu Chuantong de Fuhuo" [Urban villagers and the revitalization of rural traditions]. *Xuehai* 2: 59–66.

Wang, Xingzhou, and Wenhong Zhang. 2008. "Chengshixing: Nongmingong Shiminhua de Xin Fangxiang" [Urbanism: A new direction for the 'citizenization' of migrant workers]. *Shehui Kexue Zhanxian* [Social science front] 12: 173–79.

Wang, Ya Ping, Huimin Du, and Si-Ming Li. 2014. "Migration and the Dynamics of Informal Housing in China." In *Housing Inequality in Chinese Cities*, edited by Youqin Huang and Si-ming Li, 87–102. Routledge Contemporary China Series 115. Abingdon: Routledge.

Wang, Ya Ping, Yanglin Wang, and Jiansheng Wu. 2009. "Urbanization and Informal Development in China: Urban Villages in Shenzhen." *International Journal of Urban and Regional Research* 33(4): 957–73.
Warner, M. 2002. "Publics and Counterpublics." *Public Culture* 14(1): 49–90.
Webster, Chris, and Yanjing Zhao. 2010. "Entitlement to the Benefits of Urbanization: Comparing Migrant and Peri-urban 'Peasants.'" In *Marginalization in Urban China: Comparative Perspectives*, edited by Fulong Wu and Chris Webster, 59–71. London: Palgrave Macmillan.
Whyte, Martin King. 1988. "Death in the People's Republic of China." In *Death Ritual in Late Imperial and Modern China*, edited by Evelyn Rawski and James L. Watson, 289–316. Berkeley: University of California Press.
———. ed. 2010. *One Country, Two Societies: Rural-Urban Inequality in Contemporary China*. Cambridge: Harvard University Press.
Wilczak, Jessica. 2017. "Making the Countryside More like the Countryside? Rural Planning and Metropolitan Visions in Post-quake Chengdu." *Geoforum* 78: 110–18.
Wirth, Louis. 1938. "Urbanism as a Way of Life." *American Journal of Sociology* 44(1): 1–24.
Wolf, Arthur P. 1974. "Gods, Ghosts and Ancestors." In *Religion and Ritual in Chinese Society*, 131–82. Stanford, CA: Stanford University Press.
Wong, Chack-kie, Vai Io Lo, and Kwong-Leung Tang. 2006. *China's Urban Health Care Reform: From State Protection to Individual Responsibility*. Lanham, MD: Lexington Books.
Wong, Christine, 1988. "Interpreting Rural Industrial Growth in the Post-Mao Period." *Modern China* 14(1): 3–30.
———, ed. 1997. *Financing Local Government in the People's Republic of China*. New York: Oxford University Press.
———. 2010. "Paying for the Harmonious Society." *China Economic Quarterly*, 14: 20–25.
———. 2018. "An Update on Fiscal Reform." In *China's 40 Years of Reform and Development: 1978–2018*, edited by Ross Garnaut, Ligang Song, and Cai Fang, 271–90. Canberra: ANU Press.
Wong, Linda. 2004. "Market Reforms, Globalization and Social Justice in China." *Journal of Contemporary China* 13(38): 151–71.
Wong, Linda, and Bernard Poon. 2005. "From Serving Neighbors to Recontrolling Urban Society: The Transformation of China's Community Policy." *China Information* 19(3): 413–42.
Woodman, Sophia, and Zhonghua Guo, eds. 2020. *Practicing Citizenship in Contemporary China*. London: Routledge.
Wright, Teresa. 2010. *Accepting Authoritarianism: State-Society Relations in China's Reform Era*. Stanford, CA: Stanford University Press.
Wu, Fulong. 2002. "China's Changing Urban Governance in the Transition towards a More Market-Oriented Economy." *Urban Studies* 39(7): 1071–93.
———. 2009a. "The State and Marginality: Reflections on *Urban Outcasts* from China's Urban Transition." *International Journal of Urban and Regional Research* 33(3): 841–47.
———. 2009b. "Land Development, Inequality and Urban Villages in China." *International Journal of Urban and Regional Research* 33(4): 885–89.
———. 2010. "How Neoliberal Is China's Reform? The Origins of Change during Transition." *Eurasian Geography and Economics* 51(5): 619–31.
———. 2017. "Planning Centrality, Market Instruments: Governing Chinese Urban Transformation under State Entrepreneurialism." *Urban Studies* 55(7): 1383–99.
———. 2018. "Housing Privatization and the Return of the State: Changing Governance in China." *Urban Geography* 39(8): 1177–94.
Wu, Fulong, Jiang Xu, and Anthony G. Yeh. 2008. *Urban Development in Post-reform China: State, Market, and Space*. London: Routledge.

Wu, Fulong, Fangzhu Zhang, and Chris Webster. 2013. "Informality and the Development and Demolition of Urban Villages in the Chinese Peri-urban Area." *Urban Studies* 50(10): 1919–34.

Wu, Qiyan, Xiaoling Zhang, and Paul Waley. 2016. "Jiaoyufication: When Gentrification Goes to School in the Chinese Inner City." *Urban Studies* 53(16): 3510–26.

Wu, Qiyan, Tim Edensor, and Jianquan Cheng. 2018. "Beyond Space: Spatial (Re)Production and Middle-Class Remaking Driven by Jiaoyufication in Nanjing City, China." *International Journal of Urban and Regional Research* 42(1): 1–19.

Wu Huailian. 1998. *Zhongguo Shehuixue de lilun yu shijian* [Theory and practice of Chinese rural sociology]. Wuhan: Daxue Chubanshe.

Wu, Weiping. 1999. "Reforming China's Institutional Environment for Urban Infrastructure Provision." *Urban Studies* 36(13): 2263–82.

———. 2010. "Urban Infrastructure Financing and Economic Performance in China." *Urban Geography* 31(5): 648–67.

Xiang, Biao. 2005. *Transcending Boundaries: Zhejiangcun; The Story of a Migrant Village in Beijing*. Leiden: Brill.

Xie, Dan, and Chunyao Han. 2014. "Zhu Jianbu Yu Zhengsu 'Da Chai Da Jian': Chai Jiu Jianxin Huanjing Zhenxiang" [The Ministry of Housing and Urban-Rural Development wants to clean up "large-scale demolition and construction": The truth about redevelopment and the environment]. *Nanfang Zhoumo* [Southern weekly], 25 September 2014.

Xie, Zhikui. 2005. "Cuoluo Ruhe Zhongjie: Zhongguo Nongcun Chengshihua de Zhidu Yanjiu" [How to end the villages: A study of the institutions of the rural urbanization in China]. *Chengshi Fazhan Yanjiu* [Urban development studies] 1(5): 22–29.

Xin Liu. 2002. "Urban Anthropology and the 'Urban Question' in China." *Critique of Anthropology* 22(2): 109–32.

Xu, Feng. 2008. "Gated Communities and Migrant Enclaves: The Conundrum for Building 'Harmonious Community/Shequ.'" *Journal of Contemporary China* 17(57): 633–51.

Xu, Jiang, Anthony Yeh, and Fulong Wu. 2009. "Land Commodification: New Land Development and Politics in China since the Late 1990s." *International Journal of Urban and Regional Research* 33(4): 890–913.

Xu, Qingwen. 2007. "Community Participation in Urban China: Identifying Mobilization Factors." *Nonprofit and Voluntary Sector Quarterly* 36(4): 622–42.

Xu, Qingwen, Jianguo Gao, and Miu Chung Yan. 2005. "Community Centers in Urban China: Context, Development, and Limitations." *Journal of Community Practice* 13(3): 73–90.

Xue, Desheng, and Fulong Wu. 2015. "Failing Entrepreneurial Governance: From Economic Crisis to Fiscal Crisis in the City of Dongguan, China." *Cities* 43: 10–17.

Yan, Hairong. 2003. "Spectralization of the Rural: Reinterpreting the Labor Mobility of Rural Young Women in Post-Mao China." *American Ethnologist* 30(4): 578–96.

Yan, Xiaopei, Lihua Wei, and Ruibo Zhou. 2004. "Kuaisu Chengshihua Diqu Chengxiang Guanxi Xietiao Yanjiu: Yi Guangzhoushi Chengzhongcun Gaizao Weili" [Research on the coordination between urban and rural areas in the context of rapid urbanization: A case study of the redevelopment of Guangzhou villages-in-the-city]. *Chengshi Guihua* [Urban planning] 3: 30–38.

Yan, Yunxiang. 1996. *The Flow of Gifts: Reciprocity and Social Networks in a Chinese Village*. Stanford, CA: Stanford University Press.

Yanagisako, Sylvia. 2012. "Immaterial and Industrial Labor: On False Binaries in Hardt and Negri's Trilogy." *Focaal* 64: 6–23.

Yang, Dali. 1990. "Patterns of China's Regional Development Strategy." *China Quarterly* 122: 230–57.

Yang, Ch'ing-k'un. 1959. *A Chinese Village in Early Communist Transition*. Cambridge MA: MIT Press.

Yang, Mayfair Mei-hui. 1994. *Gifts, Favors, and Banquets: The Art of Social Relationships in China*. Ithaca, NY: Cornell University Press.

———. 2004. "Spatial Struggles: Postcolonial Complex, State Disenchantment, and Popular Reappropriation of Space in Rural Southeast China." *Journal of Asian Studies* 63(3): 719–55.

Yang, Tuan. 2016. "Zhongguo Zhangqi Zhaohu de Zhengce Xuanze" [China's long-term elderly care policy choice]. *Zhongguo Shehui Kexue* [Chinese social sciences] 11: 87–110.

Yang, Yongchun Zhang, Deli Meng Qingmin, Yu Wan, and Yuan Li. 2017. "Stratified Evolution of Urban Residential Spatial Structure in China through the Transitional Period: A Case Study of Five Categories of Housings in Chengdu." *Habitat International* 69: 78–93.

Yang, Yuanyuan. 2020. "Guanyu 21 Shiji Chuye Dachaidajian Xingwei de Fansi" [Reflections on large-scale demolition in the early 21st century]. *Jianzhu Jishu Yanjiu* 3(3): 67–68.

Ye, Lin. 2011. "Urban Regeneration in China: Policy, Development, and Issues." *Local Economics* 26(6): 337–47.

Ye, Lin. 2014. "Examining China's Urban Redevelopment: Land Types, Targeted Policies, and Public Participation." In *Maturing Megacities: The Pearl River Delta in Progressive Transformation*, 123–38. New York: Springer.

Ye, Xingqing. 2009. "China's Urban–Rural Integration Policies." *Journal of Current Chinese Affairs* 38(4): 117–43.

Ye, Yumin, and Richard T. LeGates. 2013. *Coordinating Urban and Rural Development in China: Learning from Chengdu*. Cheltenham: Edward Elgar.

Yip, Ngai Ming. 2019. "Housing Activism in Urban China: The Quest for Autonomy in Neighbourhood Governance." *Housing Studies* 34(10): 1635–53.

Yu, Depeng. 2002. *Chengxiang Shehui: Cong Geli Zouxiang Kaifang, Zhongguo Huji Zhidu Yu Hujifa Yanjiu* [Urban-rural society: From segregation to openness, Chinese hukou system and hukou law research]. Jinan: Shandong Renmin Chubanshe.

Yu, Hui. 2009. "Zai Shenhua Gaige Zhong Huajie Banchengshihua Wenti [Solving the Semi-Urbanization Problem in the Deeping Processes of the Reform]." *Kaifang Daobao*, 142: 80–83.

Zhan, Heying Jenny, and Rhonda J. V. Montgomery. 2003. "Gender and Elder Care in China: The Influence of Filial Piety and Structural Constraints." *Gender and Society* 17(2): 209–29.

Zhan, Yang. 2018. "The Urbanisation of Rural Migrants and the Making of Urban Villages in Contemporary China." *Urban Studies* 55(7): 1525–40.

———. 2021. "Beyond Neoliberal Urbanism: Assembling Fluid Gentrification through Informal Housing Upgrading Programs in Shenzhen, China." *Cities*, 112 unpaged.

Zhan, Heying Jenny, Xiaotian Feng, and Baozhen Luo. 2008. "Placing Elderly Parents in Institutions in Urban China: A Reinterpretation of Filial Piety." *Research on Aging* 30(5): 543–71.

Zhang, Chenchen. 2018. "Governing Neoliberal Authoritarian Citizenship: Theorizing *Hukou* and the Changing Mobility Regime in China." *Citizenship Studies* 22(8): 855–81.

Zhang, DaWei, and Miu Chung Yan. 2014. "Community Work Stations: An Incremental Fix of the Community Construction Project in China." *Community Development Journal* 49(1): 143–58.

Zhang, Huafeng. 2016. "Literature Review on Educational Attainment of Migrant Children in China." *Open Journal of Social Sciences* 4(7): 190–206.

Zhang, Lei, Jing Chen, and Rachel M. Tochen. 2016. "Shifts in Governance Modes in Urban Redevelopment: A Case Study of Beijing's Jiuxianqiao Area." *Cities* 53 (April): 61–69.

Zhang, Li. 2006 [2001]. *Strangers in the City: Reconfigurations of Space, Power, and Social Networks within China's Floating Population*. Stanford, CA: Stanford University Press.

———. 2010. *In Search of Paradise: Middle-Class Living in a Chinese Metropolis*. Ithaca, NY: Cornell University Press.

———. 2011. "The Political Economy of Informal Settlements in Post-Socialist China: The Case of Chengzhongcun(s)." *Geoforum* 42(4): 473–83.

———. 2012 "Economic Migration and Urban Citizenship in China: The Role of Points Systems." *Population and Development Review* 38(3): 503–33.

Zhang, Li, and Aihwa Ong, eds. 2008. *Privatizing China: Socialism from Afar*. Ithaca, NY: Cornell University Press.

Zhang, Min, Weiping Wu, and Weijing Zhong. 2018. "Agency and Social Construction of Space under Top-Down Planning: Resettled Rural Residents in China." *Urban Studies* 55(7): 1541–60.

Zhang, Qian Forrest, and Zi Pan. 2013. "The Transformation of Urban Vegetable Retail in China: Wet Markets, Supermarkets, and Informal Markets in Shanghai." *Journal of Contemporary Asia* 43(3): 497–518.

Zhang, Wei, and Mark Bray. 2017. "Micro-Neoliberalism in China: Public-Private Interactions at the Confluence of Mainstream and Shadow Education." *Journal of Education Policy* 32(1): 63–81.

Zhang, Xiaobo, and Ravi Kanbur. 2005. "Spatial Inequality in Education and Health Care in China." *China Economic Review* 16(2): 189–204.

Zhang, Xiaoqing. 2021. *In the Name of Inclusion: The Redevelopment of Urban Villages and Its Implications on Citizenship in China*. Singapore: Springer Nature.

Zhang, Zhaohua, Yuxi Luo, and Derrick Robinson. 2019. "Who Are the Beneficiaries of China's New Rural Pension Scheme? Sons, Daughters, or Parents?" *International Journal of Environmental Research and Public Health* 16(17): 3159.

Zhao, Bo. 2009. "Land Expropriation, Protest, and Impunity in Rural China." *Focaal* (54): 97–105.

Zhao, Guodu, Huihua Zheng, Lihong Wu, and Huiqin Gong. 2003. "Chengzhongcun Shequ Zhili Tizhi Yanjiu: Yi Guangzhou Shi Baiyun Qu Keziling Cun Wei Gean" [Urban village community governance research: Keziling Village, Baiyun District Guangzhou]. *Guojia Xingzheng Xueyuan Xuebao* [Journal of the National School of Administration] 3: 93–97.

Zhao, Li. 2013. "Conceptualizing the Social Economy in China." *Modern Asian Studies* 47(3): 1083–123.

Zhao, Suisheng. 1998. "A State-Led Nationalism: The Patriotic Education Campaign in Post-Tiananmen China." *Communist and Post-Communist Studies* 31(3): 287–302.

Zhe, Xiaoye. 1997. *Cunzhuang de caizao: yi ge 'chaojicunzhuang' de shehui bianqian* [Reconstructing a village: Changes in a "super village"]. Beijing: Zhongguo Shehui Kexue Chubanshe.

Zhe, Xiaoye, and Yingying Chen. 1997. *Chaoji cunzhuang de jiben tezheng ji "zhongjian" xingtai: Shehuixue yanjiu* [Basic characteristics and "middle" form of supervillages]. *Sociological Research* 6: 37–45.

Zhou, Da Ming, and Chong Gao. 2001. *Chengxiang Jiehebu Shequ de Yanjiu: Guangzhou Nanjingcun 50 Nian de Bianqian* [Research on rural-urban fringes: Changes to Guangzhou's Nanjing Village over the past 50 years]. *Shehuixue yanjiu Sociological Research* 4: 99–108.

Zhou, Hua. 2014. *Zongzu Bian Gongsi: Guangzhou Zhangban Cun Cunmin Zuzhi Jiegou de Bainian Yanbian* [Lineages becoming companies: Transition in structures of Zhangban Village in Guangzhou]. Beijing: Contemporary China Publishing House.

Zhou Xin. 2020. "China Turns to 'Street Vendor Economy' to Help Manage Unemployment Crisis," *South China Morning Post*, 5 June.

Zhou, Xueguang. 2012. "Yundongxing zhili jizhi: Zhongguo guojia zhili de zhidu luoji zai sikao" [The mechanism of campaign-style governance: Rethinking the logic of state governance in China]. *Kaifang shidai* 9.

Zhou, Yixing, and Laurence J. C. Ma. 2003. "China's Urbanization Levels: Reconstructing a Baseline from the Fifth Population Census." *China Quarterly* 173: 176–96.

Zhu, Jiangang. 2007. "Space, Power, and the Construction of Community Identity: A Case Study of a Residents' Movement in a Shanghai Neighborhood." *Chinese Sociology & Anthropology* 40(2): 65–90.

Zhu, Jieming. 2004. "Local Developmental State and Order in China's Urban Development during Transition." *International Journal of Urban and Regional Research* 28(2): 424–47.

Zhu, Lin, and Yongshun Cai. 2016. "Institutions and Provision of Public Goods in Rural China: An Empirical Study Based on Villages in Guangdong Province." *China Review* 16(2): 55–83.

Zhu, Tianke, Xigang Zhu, and Jian Jin. 2021. "Grid Governance in China under the COVID-19 Outbreak: Changing Neighborhood Governance." *Sustainability* 13(13): 7089.

Zou, Hua. 2014. *Zongzu Bian Gongsi: Guangzhou Zhangban Cun Cunmin Zuzhi Jiegou de Bai Nian Yanbian* [From lineage to corporation: A century of changing rural organizational structures in Zhangban Village, Guangzhou]. Beijing: Contemporary China Publishing House.

Zuo, Cai (Vera). 2015. "Promoting City Leaders: The Structure of Political Incentives in China." *China Quarterly* 224: 955–84.

INDEX

access, cemeteries, 80–82
activity fees (*huodong fei*), 166–67
adaptive governance, 20
administrative arrangements, 56–66
    Pine Mansion, 57–60
    River Hamlet, 63–66
    South Gate, 61–63
affective community-building, 152–60
agricultural land
    decollectivization, 46–47
    urban renovation, 82–92
ancestral worship, 75–82
    Pine Mansion, 77–80
    River Hamlet, 80–82
anzhi xiaoqu. *See* former farmers
austerity, as a public good, 10
autonomy, 56–66. *See also* administrative arrangements

beautification, 111–23
    Pine Mansion, 115–19
    River Hamlet, 120–23
    South Gate, 111–15
Beneficence Day, 144–47
Benevolence Garden, 52–53
binzang gaige. *See* funeral reform
burial grounds, 75–82. *See also* tomb land

cai shichang. *See* wet markets
cemeteries, 75–82. *See also* tomb land
charitable events, 143–51
    Pine Mansion, 144–47
charity fairs (*yimai*), 145

Chen lineage foundation (*jijinhui*), 78–80
Chengdu
    North Gate, senior care, 157–58
    Park City Plan, 111–15
    South Gate
        administrative arrangements, 61–63
        background, 19, 22–24
        Chengguan offices, 127–29
        collectivist legacies, 49–53
        community gardens, 114–15
        community-building, 150–52, 157–58, 165–68
        demographics, 49–53, 66–68
        development of, 38–41
        gentrification of public space, 193–95
        housing patterns, 49–53
        managed visual disorder, 127–29
        neo-Confucian projects, 165–68
        Park City Plan, 111–15
        parking provisions, 96–98
        points-based *hukou* scheme, 39–40
        property ownership, 198
        public space, 183–85, 193–95
        resettlement, 50–53
        senior care, 157–58
        social disturbance prevention, 133–35
        welfare provisioning, 62–63
        wet market, 94–95
    Urban Master Plan, 183–85

Chengguan offices. *See* Urban Management offices
chengzhongcun (villages-in-the-city). *See* urban villages
chi guoliang. See those who eat state grain
choubei weiyuanhui. See preparatory committee
Chunfen. See spring equinox
civility law, 137
civilized city (*wenming chengshi*) status, 115
  See also infrastructural governance
civilized neighborhoods, 107, 123–9. *See also* infrastructural governance
civilized respects, 79
class
  and club goods/clubbing logics, 16, 103
  and community-building, 139–72
  comportment, 150–51, 194–95
  and education, 98–101, 132, 199–202
  and entitlements, 204–05
  and gentrification, 92–101
  and graduated provisioning, 102–03, 220–21
  and land expropriation, 92
  Maoist legacies, 31–33, 214–17
  and moralized provisioning, 169–71
  and polycentric governance, 93–94
  and property rights, 24, 48–49, 54–55
  and public space usage, 193–95
  and quality, 139–42, 150–51
  and redevelopment, 73, 82–89, 102–03
  and right to the city, 196–205
  and segregated sociality, 185–90
  and tea-serving, 194–95
  and tomb land, 75–82
  and wet markets, 95
  See also household registration system; points-based schemes
club goods and clubbing logics
  and class, 16, 103
  concepts, 11, 16, 30
  education, 98–101, 132, 199–202
  and exclusion, 16, 30, 212–13
  gentrification, 87–88, 91–101, 193–95
  neoliberal frameworks, 15–19, 103, 211–14, 220
  polycentric governance, 93–94
  scales, 16
  See also household registration system; points-based schemes
cognitive capitalism, 12
collectivist era, 31–32
collectivist legacies, 44–56
  Pine Mansion, 45–49
  River Hamlet, 53–56
  South Gate, 49–53
commercial estates (*shangye loupan*), 50
commercial zones, River Hamlet, 83–87
common affluence (*gongtong fuyu*), 31
common-pool resources (CPR), 13–14, 93, 211, 213
commoning, 15–19, 209–14
  and enclosure, 14
  and exclusion, 17, 209–13
  and graduated provisioning, 19–22
  local defenses to, 18
  and rivalry, 213–14
  state encouraged, 18–19
  tomb land, 79–80
commons
  concepts, 11–15
  design principles, 13–14
  enclosure, 14
  neoliberal frameworks, 15–19
  new, 14
  non-rivalry, 175
  tomb land, 75–82
community centers
  Pine Mansion, 58–60, 144–47
  River hamlet, 63–66, 147–49
  South Gate, 61–63, 150–52
  volunteering, 145–47, 150–52
community gardens, 114–15

community nursing homes (*shequ yanglaoyuan*), 157–58
community-building (*shequ jianshe*), 139–72
    community income, 166–67
    moralized provisioning, 169–71
    neo-Confucian projects, 161–69
    party-building, 147–49, 151–52
    Pine Mansion, 144–47, 159–60, 161–65
    quality, 139–42
    River Hamlet, 147–49, 154–57
    senior care, 152–60
    South Gate, 150–52, 157–58, 165–68
    volunteering, 143–51, 157–58
community-building policy (*shequ jianshe*), 17
compensation schemes
    Pine Mansion, 88–92
    River Hamlet, 87–88
competitive funding, neo-Confucian projects, 161–69
comportment, 150–51, 194–95
compulsion, and infrastructural governance, 109–10, 125–27, 135–36
contradictions
    ideological, 3, 20–21, 209, 220–21
    See also graduated provisioning
cooperative development, Pine Mansion, 88–92
cooperative shareholding companies (*gufen hezuo gongsi*), 48–49, 58–60
copycat (*shanzhai*) brands, 84–86
counterfeit goods, 84–86
CPR. *See* common-pool resources
cun. *See* natural villages

dance spaces, River Hamlet, 190–93
dangjian. *See* party-building
danwei. *See* local work units
decollectivization, agricultural land, 46–47
demographics, 45–56, 66–68
    Pine Mansion, 45–49
    population sizes, 2

    River Hamlet, 53–56
    South Gate, 49–53
demolition, River Hamlet, 86–88
design principles, commons, 13–14
development
    and inequality, 2, 19–22
    Pine Mansion, 35–38
    River Hamlet, 41–44
    South Gate, 38–41
    special economic zones, 35–38
    See also redevelopment; resettlement
devolution
    fiscal, 72
    of hukou policy, 34
disconnection, utilities, 125–27
discrimination, 3, 181, 219
    and right to the city, 196–205
    and surveillance, 130–35
    See also exclusion; graduated provisioning; household registration system; inequality; points-based schemes
disorder, managed, 127–29
dispute resolution, Pine Mansion, 134–35
double promotion (*shuang tisheng*), 115

economic development companies (*jingji fazhan gongshi*), 47–49
education access, 98–101, 132, 199–202
enclosure, of commons, 14
equality, ideological contradictions, 3
erasure, ancestral worship, 75–77
evictions
    by utility disconnection, 125–27
    River Hamlet, 81–82, 87–88, 125–27
    tomb land, 81–82
excludable goods, 11, 17
exclusion
    ancestor worship, 80–82
    commoning and clubbing, 16, 30, 212–13
    hukou system, 196–204
    points-based *hukou*, 199–204
    social, 186–90, 199–205

250 | Index

exhumations, 75–77
expropriation of land, 72–92, 102–03
   agricultural, 82–92
   and graduated provisioning, 102–03
   partial, 89
   tomb land, 75–82

factory workers, 46–49, 55–56
feinong. *See* non-peasant status
filial piety (*xiao*), 149, 153
financing
   cemeteries, 77–80, 82
   infrastructural governance, 108
   neo-Confucian projects, 161–69
   public schools, 98–101
   senior care, 154–57, 159–60
   social insurance, 57–58, 60, 62–63, 64
   welfare provisioning, 72–74
fiscal austerity, as a public good, 10
food supply, 94–95
foreign investment, 38–39
former farmers (*anzhi xiaoqu*), 50
Fortune 500 firms, 38–39
fundraising, 145–46
funeral reform (*binzang gaige*), 75–77, 80

garbage collection, Pine Mansion, 117–19
general welfare (*gongyi*), 10, 140, 146–47
gentrification, 92–101
   and compensation schemes, 87–88, 91–92
   parking provisions, 96–98
   public schools, 98–101
   public space, 193–95
   wet markets, 94–95
gonggong shouyi. *See* public income
gongkaixin. *See* letter of protest
gongtong fuyu. *See* common affluence
gongyi. *See* public interest
graduated governance, 19–22
graduated provisioning
   clubbing logics, 16, 91–101, 193–95, 211–14, 220
   concepts, 3–5
   graduated governance, 19–22
   and land expropriation, 102–03
   neoliberalism as, 217–22
   and worthiness, 3, 20–22, 196–205
   See also class; club goods and clubbing logics; exclusion; inequality
graves, 75–82. *See also* tomb land
green spaces
   Pine Mansion, 178–81
   River Hamlet, 182
   South Gate, 183–85
   See also natural services
grid governance (*wangge hua*), 129–36
   migrant surveillance, 130–33
   social disturbance prevention, 133–35
grid management (*wangge hua guanli*), 129–36. *See also* grid governance
gufen hezuo gongsi. *See* cooperative shareholding companies; shareholding cooperative companies

harmonious society, 1
health insurance
   Pine Mansion, 60
   River Hamlet, 63–64
   South Gate, 62–63
heritage spots (*wenwu dian*), 78
high-end populations, 197
historicized approaches, 4, 209
home care (*jujia yanglao*), 153
homestead land (*ziliudi*), 46–47
household registration (*hukou*) system, 2, 20
   access rights, 196–204
   devolution, 34
   introduction under Mao, 31–32
   land use rights, 199
   Pine Mansion, 36, 48–49
   points-based schemes, 32–33, 36, 39–40, 42, 199–204
   quotas, 32, 36
   River Hamlet, 42
   South Gate, 39–40

transfers, 198–201
housing patterns
    Pine Mansion, 45–49
    River Hamlet, 53–56
    South Gate, 49–53
hukou system. *See* household registration system
huodong fei. *See* activity fees

ideology
    contradictions, 3, 20–21, 209, 220–21
    and funeral reform, 75–77
industrial redevelopment, Pine Mansion, 90
inequality
    of development, 2, 19–22
    from reform, 1–3
    graduated provisioning, 3, 19–22, 217–22
    hukou system, 2, 20
    Maoist legacies, 31–33, 214–17
    and surveillance, 129–36
informal economies, 83, 84–87
information collection, 129–36
    migrant surveillance, 130–33
    social disturbance prevention, 133–35
infrastructural governance, 106–38
    beautification campaigns, 111–23
    Chengguan offices, 107, 123–29
    and compulsion, 109–10, 125–27, 135–36
    financing, 108
    garbage collection, 117–19
    grid governance, 129–36
    managed visual disorder, 127–29
    natural services, 111–15, 120–23
    public order, 123–36
    street cleaning, 121–23
    utilities disconnection, 125–27
    visual order, 111–29
    zero tolerance, 124–25
innovation, adaptive governance, 20

jiexin gongyuan. *See* street heart park
jifenzhi. *See* points-based schemes

jijinhui. *See* Chen lineage foundation
jingji fazhan gongshi. *See* economic development companies
jujia yanglao. *See* home care
jumin hukou system. *See* resident registration system
junweihui. *See* residents committees

land expropriation, 72–92, 102–03
    agricultural, 82–92
    and graduated provisioning, 102–03
    partial transfers, 89
    tomb land, 75–82
land leasing fees, 21, 73–74
land use rights
    hukou transfers, 199
    South Gate, 51–52
letter of protest (*gongkaixin*), Pine Mansion schools, 99–100
Lineage Temple, Pine Mansion, 161–65
linpan settlements, 50
littering, 121–23
livable communities (*yiju shequ*), 17, 173–75, 177–85, 217
    Pine Mansion, 178–81
    River Hamlet, 181–83
    South Gate, 183–85
livelihood microprojects (*minwei shishi*), 160
local work units (*danwei*), 7–8
long-spout tea serving, 194–95

mahjong, 49, 157–59, 189
managed disorder, visual, 127–29
Mao, *hukou* system introduction, 31
markets, 94–95
mausoleums, Pine Mansion, 77–80
medical care, 60–64
    Pine Mansion residents, 60
    River Hamlet residents, 63–64
    South Gate residents, 62–63
methods, 22–26
middle-classes
    comportment, 150–51
    elevation of, South Gate, 193–95
    public goods, 92–101

migrants
    Pine Mansion, 47–49
    River Hamlet, 55
    South Gate, 62–63
    surveillance, 130–33
    volunteering, 144–47
migration
    attitudes to, 66–67
    hukou system, 2, 196–205
    Mao, 31
minibuses, 85–86
minwei shishi. See livelihood microprojects
moderately well-off society (*xiaokang shehui*), 3, 31
moral community-building. See community-building
morale, River hamlet, 147–49

National Urbanization Plan, 1–3
native villagers (*yuancunmin*), 48–49
natural services
    Chengdu, 111–15, 183–85
    community gardens, 114–15
    green space, 182, 183–85
    Shenzen, 178–81
    Xi'an, 120–23, 182
natural villages (*cun/ziran cun*), 46, 53
neighborhoods (*wei*), 46
neo-Confucian projects, 161–69
    Pine Mansion, 161–65
    South Gate, 165–68
neoliberalism
    commons and club goods, 15–19, 211–14
    and community-building, 139–42, 171
    debate on whether china is neoliberal, 4, 28, 217–22
    as graduated provisioning, 217–22
    and self-governance, 140–42, 211
    special economic zones, 35–38
    trickle down ideology, 3
    See also project-based funding
new commons, 14
New Rural Pension Scheme (NRPS), 57

non-peasant status (*feinong*), 31
nonexcludability, 15
nongmin. See rural status
nonlocal populations (*wailai renkou*), 134–35
nonrivalry, 15
North Gate, Chengdu, senior care, 157–58
nostalgia, 216–17
NRPS. See New Rural Pension Scheme

Open Up the West campaign (*Xibu Da Kaifa*), 35, 38–39

Park City Plan, Chengdu, 111–15
parking provisions, South Gate, 96–98
partial transfers, land use rights, 89
party-building (*dangjian*), 147–49, 151–52
pensions
    Pine Mansion residents, 60, 159–60
    River Hamlet residents, 64
    schemes, 57
    South Gate residents, 62–63
Pine Mansion, Shenzhen
    administrative arrangements, 57–60
    background, 19, 23–24
    Chengguan offices, 124–25
    collectivist legacies, 45–49
    community-building, 144–47, 159–60, 161–65
    compensation scheme, 88–92
    demographics, 45–49, 66–68
    development of, 35–38
    dispute resolution, 134–35
    garbage collection, 117–19
    housing patterns, 45–49
    industrial redevelopment, 90
    Lineage Temple, 161–65
    mahjong parlors, 189
    migrant surveillance, 130–33
    points-based *hukou* scheme, 36
    points-based system, 144–47, 199–204
    property ownership, 197–98
    public school, 98–101

public space, 178–81, 186–90
public square, 178–81
rectification, 115–19
resettlement, 46–49
segregation, 186–90
senior care, 159–60
shareholding companies, 46–49, 58–60
tomb land, 77–80
volunteering, 144–47
welfare provisioning, 57–60, 159–60
playgrounds, 191–93
points-based schemes (*jifenzhi*), 144–47, 199–204
introduction of, 32–33
Pine Mansion, 36
River Hamlet, 42
South Gate, 39–40
polycentric governance, 93
populations
Pine Mansion, 45–49
River Hamlet, 53–56
sizes, 2
South Gate, 49–53
preparatory committee (*choubei weiyuanhui*), Pine Mansion schools, 100
prevention, social disturbance, 133–35
production teams (*shengchandui*), 44
prohibition of burial (*tuzang*), 77
project-based funding, 161–68
Pine Mansion, 161–65
South Gate, 165–68
property income taxes, 132
property ownership, 47–49, 52, 197–98, 200–03
public, concepts of, 175–76
public goods, 3
and administrative urbanization, 72–105
concepts, 9–11
exclusion, 209–13
from expropriated land, 72–92, 102–03
and gentrification, 92–101
Mao, 31–32

moralized provisioning, 169–71
neo-Confucian projects, 161–68
and redevelopment, 73, 82–92, 102–03
rivalry, 213–14
from tomb land, 75–82
worthiness of access, 3, 196–205
public income (*gonggong shouyi*), 166–67
public interest (*gongyi*), 10, 140, 146–47
public order, 106–10, 123–36
Chengguan offices, 123–29
and compulsion, 125–27, 135–36
migrant surveillance, 130–33
social disturbance prevention, 133–35
public park city (*tianyuan chengshi*), 112
public rusticity, 193–95
public schools, 98–101, 132, 199–202
public space, 173–207, 217
dance spaces, 190–93
gentrification, 193–95
livable communities, 173–75, 177–85
Pine Mansion, 178–81, 186–90
right to the city, 196–205
River Hamlet, 181–83, 190–93
segregation, 186–90
sociality, 174–76, 185–90, 211–13
South Gate, 183–85, 193–95
public squares, 178–81, 182–83, 190–93
public transport, 80–82, 85–86
public-private partnerships, senior care, 160

quality (*suzhi*), 139–42, 150–51
quotas, *hukou* system, 32, 36

recombinant urbanization, 33
rectification (*zhengzhi*), 115–19
redevelopment, 73, 82–92, 102–03
agricultural land, 82–92
aims of, 73–74
commercial zones, 83–87
compensation schemes, 87–92
gentrification, 92–101

legacies of, 214–17
Pine Mansion, 77–80, 88–92, 115–19
River Hamlet, 80–82, 83–88
Three Olds policy, 88–90
tomb land, 75–82
registered urban populations, 2
reinvestment, Pine Mansion, 90
rental certificates, 132
rentier natives, 48–49, 54–55
resettlement
   Pine Mansion, 46–49, 77–80, 88–92
   River Hamlet, 54–55, 80–88
   South Gate, 50–53
   of tombs, 75–82
   and urban renovation, 82–92
resident registration (*jumin hukou*) system, 2
residents committees (*junweihui*), 56, 58–63
   Pine Mansion, 58–60
   South Gate, 61–63
resolution, disputes, 134–35
retired factory workers, 55–56
right to the city, 196–205
   as an oppositional demand, 205
   hukou access, 196–201
ritual, ancestor worship, 75–76, 78–79, 80–81
rivalry, 213–14
   dance space in River Hamlet, 190–93
   hukou system, 199–205
River Hamlet, Xi'an
   administrative arrangements, 63–66
   background, 19, 22–24
   Chengguan offices, 125–27
   collectivist legacies, 53–56
   commercial zones, 83–87
   community-building, 147–49, 154–57
   compensation scheme, 87–88
   dance space, 190–93
   demographics, 53–56, 66–68
   demolition, 86–88
   development of, 41–44
   evictions, 81–82, 87–88, 125–27

   housing patterns, 53–56
   informal economy, 83, 84–87
   playgrounds, 191–93
   points-based *hukou* system, 42
   public space, 181–83, 190–93
   public square, 182–83, 190–93
   resettlement, 54–55
   schooling, 98–99
   senior care, 154–57
   shareholding company, 63–66
   taxation, 86–87
   tomb land, 80–82
   unsafe buildings, 54–55, 83–88
   Urban Landscaping Act, 120–23
   welfare provisioning, 63–64
rural populations, Mao, 31–32
rural status (*nongmin*), 31

sanjiu gaizao. *See* Three Olds Redevelopment policy
schooling, 98–101, 132, 199–202
segregation
   hukou system, 196–205
   Pine Mansion, 186–90
   social exclusion, 186–90, 199–205
self-funding communities, South Gate, 165–67
self-governance (*zizhi*), 140–42
semi-urbanization, 2
senior care, 152–60
   financing, 154–57, 159–60
   North Gate, 157–58
   Pine Mansion, 159–60
   River Hamlet, 154–57
   South Gate, 157–58
   volunteering, 157–58
SEZs. *See* special economic zones
shangye loupan. *See* commercial estates
shanzhai. *See* copycat brands
shareholding companies
   Pine Mansion, 46–49, 58–60
   River Hamlet, 63–66
shareholding cooperative companies (*gufen hezuo gongsi*), 89
shengchandui. *See* production teams
Shenzhen
   civility law, 137

civilized city status, 115–19
Pine Mansion
    administrative zarrangements, 57–60
    background, 19, 23–24
    Chengguan offices, 124–25
    collectivist legacies, 45–49
    community-building, 144–47, 159–60, 161–65
    compensation scheme, 88–92
    demographics, 45–49, 66–68
    development of, 35–38
    dispute resolution, 134–35
    garbage collection, 117–19
    housing patterns, 45–49
    industrial redevelopment, 90
    Lineage Temple, 161–65
    mahjong parlours, 189
    migrant surveillance, 130–33
    points-based *hukou* scheme, 36
    points-based system, 144–47, 199–204
    property ownership, 197–98
    public school, 98–101
    public space, 178–81, 186–90
    public square, 178–81
    rectification, 115–19
    resettlement, 46–49
    segregation, 186–90
    senior care, 159–60
    shareholding companies, 46–49, 58–60
    tomb land, 77–80
    volunteering, 144–47
    welfare provisioning, 57–60, 60, 159–60
  points-based *hukou*, 144–47, 199–204
Shenzhen sudu (Shenzhen speed), 34
shequ. *See* urban communities
shequ jianshe. *See* community-building; community-building policy
shequ yanglaoyuan. *See* community nursing homes
Shije Xiandia Tianyuan Chengshi Guihua. *See* World Modern Garden City Plan

shuang tisheng. *See* double promotion
small businesses, River Hamlet, 83–87
social disturbance, prevention, 133–35
social exclusion, 186–90, 199–205
social insurance
    funding, 57–58
    Pine Mansion residents, 60
    River Hamlet residents, 64
    South Gate residents, 62–63
social media, 147
social workers, volunteering, 145–47
socialism with Chinese characteristics, 3
sociality, 174–76, 185–90, 211–13
socioeconomic inequality
    and development, 2
    from reform, 1–3
    hukou system, 2, 20
    Mao, 31–32
South Gate, Chengdu
    administrative arrangements, 61–63
    background, 19, 22–24
    Chengguan offices, 127–29
    collectivist legacies, 49–53
    community gardens, 114–15
    community-building, 150–52, 157–58, 165–68
    demographics, 49–53, 66–68
    development of, 38–41
    gentrification of public space, 193–95
    housing patterns, 49–53
    managed visual disorder, 127–29
    neo-Confucian projects, 165–68
    Park City Plan, 111–15
    parking provisions, 96–98
    points-based *hukou* scheme, 39–40
    property ownership, 198
    public space, 183–85, 193–95
    resettlement, 50–53
    senior care, 157–58
    social disturbance prevention, 133–35
    welfare provisioning, 62–63
    wet market, 94–95
special economic zones (SEZs), 35–38

spontaneous urbanization, 54–55, 83, 84–85
spring equinox (*Chunfen*), 78–79
staffing
    community centers, 145–52
    senior care centers in Chengdu, 157–58
stakeholder economy, 166–67
status, *hukou* system introduction, 31–32
street cleaning, 121–23
street heart park (*jiexin gongyuan*), 178–79
street vendors, 123–26, 128, 183
Sunshine Lunch (*yangguang wucan*) program, 162
surveillance, 130–35
    migrants, 130–33
    social disturbance prevention, 133–35
suzhi. *See* quality

taxation, River Hamlet, 86–87
taxes, property income, 132
tea-serving, 194–95
temporary urbanization, 2
tenancy contracts, 132
those who eat state grain (*chi guoliang*), 31–32
Three Olds Redevelopment policy (*sanjiu gaizao*), 88
tianyuan chengshi. *See* public park city
Toilet Revolution, 128, 182–83
tomb land, 75–82
    evictions, 81–82
    Pine Mansion, 77–80
    River Hamlet, 80–82
trajectories of urbanization, 33–44
transfers, household registration, 198–201
trickle down ideology, 3
tuzang. *See* prohibition of burial

unsafe buildings, 54–55, 83–88
urban communities (*shequ*), 8
urban growth theories, 90–91
Urban Landscaping Act, Xi'an, 125–27

Urban Management (*Chengguan*) offices, 107, 123–29
    Pine Mansion, 124–25
    River Hamlet, 125–27
    South Gate, 127–29
urban (non-peasant) status (*feinong*), 31
urban populations
    Mao, 31–32
    size of, 2
urban renovation, 73, 82–92, 102–03
    agricultural land, 82–92
    commercial zones, 83–87
    compensation schemes, 87–92
    industrial redevelopment, 90
    Pine Mansion, 77–80, 88–92
    River Hamlet, 80–82, 83–88
    tomb land, 75–82
urban villages (*chengzhongcun*), 4, 5–9
    trajectories of urbanization, 33–44, 68
    See also Pine Mansion; River Hamlet; South Gate
urban-rural integration, 1–2
urbanization, 5–9
    and land expropriation, 82–92
    Mao, 31
    and natural services, 111–15
    public goods provisioning, 72–105
    recombinant, 33
    special economic zones, 35–38
    spontaneous, 54–55, 83
    trajectories, 33–44, 68
        Pine Mansion, 35–38
        River Hamlet, 41–44
        South Gate, 38–41
utilities, disconnection, 125–27

values
    ancestral worship, 75–82
    comportment, 150–51
    filial piety, 149, 153
    quality, 139–42, 150–51
    self-governance, 140–42
    tensions in graduated provision, 3, 20–21, 209
    Xi Jinping, 165, 206

villages-in-the-city (*chengzhongcun*), 4, 5–9
    trajectories of urbanization, 33–44, 68
    See also Pine Mansion; River Hamlet; South Gate
violent abstraction, 76
visual order, 106, 111–29
    beautification, 111–21
    Chengguan offices, 123–29
    garbage collection, 117–19
    managed disorder, 127–29
    Pine Mansion, 115–19, 124–25
    River Hamlet, 120–23, 125–27
    South Gate, 111–15
    street cleaning, 121–23
    zero tolerance, 124–25
volunteering, 143–51
    Pine Mansion, 144–47
    South Gate, 150–52, 157–58

wailai renkou. *See* nonlocal populations
wangge hua. *See* grid governance
wangge hua guanli. *See* grid management
wei. *See* neighborhoods
welfare provisioning, 60–64
    financing, 72–74
    Pine Mansion, 57–60, 159–60
    River Hamlet, 63–64
    South Gate, 62–63
    volunteering, 144–47
wenming chengshi. *See* civilized city status
wenwu dian. *See* heritage spots
wet markets (*cai shichang*), 94–95
Winter Clothes Festival, 80–81
World Modern Garden City Plan (*Shije Xiandia Tianyuan Chengshi Guihua*), 111–15
worthiness, 3, 20–22, 196–205

Xi Jinping
    community-building, 141–42
    livable communities, 17, 173–75, 177–85
    new era, 1

public park cities, 112
Toilet Revolution, 128, 182–83
values, 165, 206
Xi'an
    River Hamlet
    administrative arrangements, 63–66
    background, 19, 22–24
    Chengguan offices, 125–27
    collectivist legacies, 53–56
    commercial zones, 83–87
    community-building, 147–49, 154–57
    compensation scheme, 87–88
    dance space, 190–93
    demographics, 53–56, 66–68
    demolition, 86–88
    development of, 41–44
    evictions, 125–27
    housing patterns, 53–56
    informal economy, 83, 84–87
    playgrounds, 191–93
    points-based *hukou* system, 42
    public space, 181–83, 190–93
    public square, 182–83, 190–93
    resettlement, 54–55
    schooling, 98–99
    senior care, 154–57
    shareholding company, 63–66
    taxation, 86–87
    tomb land, 80–82
    unsafe buildings, 54–55, 83–88
    Urban Landscaping Act, 120–23
    welfare provisioning, 63–64
    Urban Landscaping Act, 125–27
xiao. *See* filial piety
xiaokang shehui. *See* moderately well-off society
Xibu Da Kaifa. *See* Open Up the West campaign

yangguang wucan program. *See* Sunshine Lunch program
yiju shequ. *See* livable communities
yimai. *See* charity fairs
Yimin Vegetable Market Company, 95
yuancunmin. *See* native villagers

zero tolerance policies, visual order, 124–27
zhengzhi. See rectification

ziliudi. See homestead land
ziran cun. See natural villages

www.ingramcontent.com/pod-product-compliance
Lightning Source LLC
Chambersburg PA
CBHW051533020426
42333CB00016B/1903